I0124824

# POST-CONFLICT INSTITUTIONAL DESIGN

# POST-CONFLICT INSTITUTIONAL DESIGN: PEACEBUILDING AND DEMOCRACY IN AFRICA

*Edited by Abu Bakarr Bah*

# ZED

LONDON • NEW YORK • OXFORD • NEW DELHI • SYDNEY

Zed Books
Bloomsbury Publishing Plc
50 Bedford Square, London, WC1B 3DP, UK
1385 Broadway, New York, NY 10018, USA
29 Earlsfort Terrace, Dublin 2, Ireland

BLOOMSBURY and Zed Books are trademarks
of Bloomsbury Publishing Plc

First published in Great Britain 2020
Paperback edition published 2021

Editorial copyright © Abu Bakarr Bah
Copyright in this Collection © Zed Books

Abu Bakarr Bah has asserted his right under the Copyright,
Designs and Patents Act, 1988, to be identified as Editor of this work.

Cover designed by Burgess and Beech
Cover image © David Rose/Panos Pictures

All rights reserved. No part of this publication may be reproduced or
transmitted in any form or by any means, electronic or mechanical,
including photocopying, recording, or any information storage or retrieval
system, without prior permission in writing from the publishers.

Bloomsbury Publishing Plc does not have any control over, or responsibility for,
any third-party websites referred to or in this book. All internet addresses given
in this book were correct at the time of going to press. The author and publisher
regret any inconvenience caused if addresses have changed or sites have
ceased to exist, but can accept no responsibility for any such changes.

A catalogue record for this book is available from the British Library.

A catalog record for this book is available from the Library of Congress.

ISBN: HB: 978-1-7869-9790-6
PB: 978-1-7869-9801-9
ePDF: 978-1-7869-9789-0
eBook: 978-1-7869-9787-6

Typeset in Plantin and Kievit by Swales and Willis Ltd, Exeter, Devon
Index by Molly Reinhoudt

To find out more about our authors and books visit
www.bloomsbury.com and sign up for our newsletters.

To my wife, Rugiatu Bah, and children (Manmadu, Ibrahim, and Aisha) for the love, joy, and enrichment they bring to my work and life.

# CONTENTS

# TABLES

# CONTRIBUTORS

**Abu Bakarr Bah** is Professor of Sociology at Northern Illinois University and Faculty Associate at the Center for Nonprofit and NGO Studies. He is also Editor-in-Chief of *African Conflict & Peacebuilding Review*. He is also African Editor for *Critical Sociology*.

**Michael D. Beevers** is Associate Professor of Environmental Studies at Dickinson College, Carlisle, PA.

**Okaka Opio Dokotum** is Associate Professor of Literature and Film and Deputy Vice-Chancellor (Academic Affairs) at Lira University, Uganda.

**Niklas Hultin** is Assistant Professor of Global Affairs at George Mason University, Fairfax, VA.

**Aditi Malik** is Assistant Professor of Political Science at College of the Holy Cross, Worcester, MA.

**David Mwambari** is an FWO postdoctoral research fellow at the Department of Conflict and Development Studies at Ghent University in Belgium and an adjunct faculty at the African Leadership Centre (ALC) in the Faculty of Social Science and Public Policy at King's College London.

**Iris Nxumalo** is Innovation Manager for Nurturing, an Innovative and Inclusive Society strategy at the DG Murray Trust and a Zanele Mbeki Fellow (2018–2019).

**Fredrick Ogenga** is Associate Professor of Communication and Director of the Centre for Media, Democracy, Peace and Security at Rongo University, Kenya.

# 1 | INTRODUCTION: INSTITUTIONAL DESIGN, PEACEBUILDING, AND DEMOCRACY

*Abu Bakarr Bah*

## Introduction

Since gaining independence from colonial rule, most African countries have been struggling to build democratic and peaceful states. In most cases, these have not yet been achieved. Too often, African countries are plagued by dictatorships or multiparty politics that generate major political violence, and in worst cases civil war. At independence, African countries struggled with the multiparty political systems that emerged at the end of colonial rule. While those multiparty political system may be viewed as democratic systems of governance, in reality they were beset by ethnic and regional political grievances that made meaningful democracy very problematic. As Claude Ake clearly pointed out, democracy never took hold in Africa. In fact, the seeds of one-party dictatorships, coups, and ethnically driven civil wars were planted right after independence.[1] While it would be simplistic to reduce African political conflicts to ethnicity and regionalism, there is a vivid pattern of political conflicts often revolving around ethnic and regional identities. Indeed, even though ethnicity and regionalism are not the only reasons for political violence, as often pointed out in the greed-grievance literature, they are key instruments for mobilization and organizing political violence in the service of elite interests. In this sense, ethnicity and regionalization have always been at the center of political conflicts in Africa.

In West Africa for example, the early democracies were plagued by ethnic violence and quickly degenerated into one-party or military regimes. In Nigeria, the regional and ethnic political competition for power that pitted northerners against southerners, meshed with intermittent conflicts among Hausas, Igbos, and Yoruba, led to a series of coups and the Biafran War.[2] In Sierra Leone too, the supporters of the southern-dominated Sierra Leone Peoples Party (SLPP) and the northern-dominated All Peoples Congress (APC) engaged in major political violence and coups, which culminated in the introduction of one-party rule and the political marginalization of Mende people.[3] Similar problems emerged in Ghana and Liberia.[4] Francophone countries also experienced political violence and ethnic marginalization, which resulted in one-party rule. In particular, Guinea was a notorious case of ethnic polarization and brutal dictatorship.[5] Even relatively well managed Côte d'Ivoire fell victim to the legacies of one-party rule and ethnic marginalization under Félix Houphouët-Boigny.[6]

In Eastern and Central Africa too, the early democracies were beset by political violence in which ethnic and regional groups were pitted against one another. In Kenya for example, ethnic political violence over control of the state and land issues were common especially among major ethnic groups and in the Rift Valley.[7] Similar problems existed in countries such as Uganda and Burundi. In Sudan and Ethiopia, ethnic and regional politics lead to bitter separatist wars. Even after the secessions of South Sudan and Eritrea, the problems still persist in those countries. In all of these countries, multiparty democracy became plagued by violence paving the way for the cynical imposition of de jure or de facto one-party rule, which led to further political violence in the 1990s. In the case of Rwanda, ethnic politics culminated in a genocide.[8]

Even in countries where major political violence is attributed to much broader national struggles, there are instances of identity politics. In the case of South Africa, where race was the central driver of oppression and political violence, significant levels of violence emerged between the Zulu-dominated Inkatha Freedom Party and the African National Congress (ANC), which was heavily supported by Xhosa people.[9] In addition, native people in South Africa have been marginalized by both White rule and Black political movements. In Somalia, clan politics degenerated into political violence in ways that are akin to the conflicts in Liberia and South Sudan.[10] In Zimbabwe, the bitter struggle over White rule and Mugabe's grip on the country masked some of the ethnic political grievances in the country. However, as the Mugabe regime waned, ethnic political grievances became more prominent.[11]

Given the salience of ethnicity and regionalism in African multiparty politics and the persistence of political violence along ethnic lines, this work raises critical questions about the design of political institutions and the challenges of building peaceful democracies. Too often, African political conflicts have been attributed to poor leadership, greed, corruption, dictatorship, and external interference.[12] A key assumption in these kinds of critiques is that democratic rule can resolve most of the problems by holding leaders accountable to the people through the electoral process and the rule of law. This was a key argument that was advanced during the democratic transitions of the 1990s aimed at ending one-party and military regimes in Africa.[13] What was often left out in that debate was the fact that multiparty democracy failed to promote peace during the immediate post-independence period. Driven by neoliberal economic and governance policies, the democratic reforms of the 1990s confounded the principles of democracy with the mechanism of democracy. Too often, simple multiparty electoral systems were seen as sufficient to produce peaceful democracies. Roughly two decades after the second wave of democracy, African countries have again been plagued by multiparty political systems that produce political violence. In Côte d'Ivoire, multiparty politics degenerated into a civil war as ethnic and regional identities were manipulated by the elite. In Kenya, multiparty elections produced major violence in 2008 and continue to be marred by violence and stalemates. Similar problems have emerged in countries such as Togo, Gambia, Sierra Leone, Guinea, and Uganda. A critical issue that still needs to be addressed is whether the mechanism of winner-takes-all neoliberal multiparty democracy contributes to political violence.

## Conflict Drivers: Ethnicity, Governance, and Natural Resources

Studies of conflicts and peacebuilding in Africa have identified a variety of causes of conflict rooted in ethnicity, poor governance, and natural resources. The studies in this book also point to these kinds of causes of conflict across Africa. While it is tempting to focus on any one of these factors as the cause of conflicts in Africa, it may be useful to consider each of them as a critical contributor to violent conflicts in Africa and also to trace their interconnections. Though most studies emphasize one factor over the others, collectively the literature on peace and conflict in Africa has addressed all of them. We take the literature a step further by showing the interconnections among these three factors. Indeed, a deeper reading of the literature on these issues shows interconnections in the way ethnicity, poor governance, natural resources all feed into one another to produce violent political conflicts and in the worst cases civil wars.

Ethnicity, which has long been noted in anthropological and historical studies of Africa, is perhaps the most pervasive factor. However,
the nature of ethnic conflicts and their effects on African states have
evolved along with the states' transformations. In earlier studies of
colonial Africa, ethnicity was simply viewed as an instrument for divide
and rule.[14] Anthropological and historical studies dating back to the
slave trade often refer to tribes and tribal warfare in Africa.[15] Wars
within and between African empires involved people of varying linguistic and cultural identities struggling for territories and political and
social advantages. These tribal conflicts intensified with colonialism as
European powers often aligned with one group to conquer and pacify
other groups that resisted colonial rule. In this earlier period, ethnicity
was framed through localized identities as embodied in the notion of
tribe.[16] Moreover, the causes and effects of ethnic conflicts were always
viewed in relation to colonial intrusions. An important fact of ethnic
conflicts during colonial rule is that they had both internal and external
forms, which were exploited by colonial power. As Peter Ekeh noted in
his critique of the colonial literature:

> Ideological distortions also exist in the characterization of political
> life in pre-colonial Africa. "Tribe against tribe" is the common theme
> in colonial accounts of African struggles. "Inter-tribal," rather than
> "intra-tribal," struggles are given the accent in interpretations of
> African political strife ... By carefully emphasizing "inter-tribal"
> disharmonies in pre-colonial Africa, European colonial administrators
> had two things to gain at once. First, the principle of *divide et impera*
> was effectively employed to create disharmony between groups in the
> colonial situation, a strategy especially apparent in the declining days
> of colonialism in virtually every African nation; second, it gave the
> colonial administrators the image of benevolent interveners, who came
> to Africa because they wanted to establish order.[17]

Ethnicity was reimaged in the African discourse during the immediate postcolonial era within the context of problematic multiparty
democracy and the degeneration of African states into one-party
and military dictatorships.[18] The critical issue was control of the
government. Studies point to ethnic marginalization and grievances
surrounding elections. In Nigeria for example, studies point to the
regional and ethnic divides that resulted in the Biafran War and most
of the ongoing political violence.[19] Similar issues emerged in other

African countries where multiparty democracy degenerated into ethnically driven dictatorship or violent ethnic conflicts, such as in Uganda, Rwanda, Burundi, Kenya, and Sierra Leone.[20] Stefan Lindemann identified three conceptual categories in the literature on coups and the decline of democracy in Africa: ethnic plurality, ethnic dominance, and ethnic matching.[21] Each of these shows the relation between the ethnic constellation of state power and the likelihood of violent overthrow of the government. As Lindemann notes, "The link between ethnicity and African military coups is a long-standing theme in the literature. The main reason for this is that ethnic cleavages are generally known to provide leaders with a particularly effective basis for organising collective action."[22]

One of the interesting debates on the politicization of ethnicity is whether ethnicity is linked to class issues in African politics. Lindemann sees the link between ethnic grievances and coups as further strengthened when ethnic grievances "coincide with political and economic inequalities."[23] In his study of Nigerian politics, Larry Diamond also points to the intersection of ethnicity and economic interest. As he notes, ethnicity is also "a class phenomenon, in that dominant social classes may deliberately stimulate and manipulate ethnic consciousness and conflict to mask their class action and advance their class interest."[24] It is interesting to note that the African debate about ethnicity and class is more centered on elite manipulation of the masses rather the existence of a broad-based class structure that generates an authentic class identity. Class is largely an elaboration of the ethnic economic grievances and their political instrumentalization in the elite struggle for power. In some ways, this elite manipulation of ethnicity is akin to colonial divide-and-rule instrumentalization of ethnicity. Notwithstanding the hidden elite agendas, ethnicity has been one of the key elements in violent conflicts across Africa.

While the discourse on ethnicity and class does not necessarily lead to a clear delineation between the two or a robust notion of class, it does point to an important issue of poor governance which also fuels conflicts in Africa. Interestingly, as the discourse of African politics began to shift from ethnicity to elite class interests, so too did the issue of poor governance become more prominent. The issue of poor governance came to the forefront of African politics during the 1990s with the pro-democracy movements.[25] I should note that poor governance goes beyond economic mismanagement of state resources. I refer to poor governance in its political, economic, and social forms, which makes it inherently connected to the problems identified in the ethnicity literature. Politically speaking, poor governance is a form of authoritarian rule that undermines and inhibits democracy. Economically, poor governance takes the form of corruption and the misappropriation of state resources for personal gain. Socially, poor governance is manifested in the deterioration of basic social services (e.g. education, health, clean water) and declining economic and social wellbeing. Ultimately, poor governance leads to state decay. As Abu Bah argues:

> State decay is a process of deterioration of the civil and political liberties and the material wellbeing of the citizenry. State decay originates in the political arena and manifests itself in the economic and social conditions of the state. This process of deterioration leads to the political, economic, and social grievances fueling political violence and the inability of the state to fulfill its basic political, economic, and social responsibilities.[26]

Most of the early studies of postcolonial politics in Africa have noted the emergency of personal rule and prebendal politics during the 1970s and the 1980s, which foreshadow the contemporary notion of poor governance. A key argument in that body of literature points to the interconnections between authoritarian rule and corruption, which set the conditions for political violence. As Robert Jackson framed the issue:

> African politics are most often a personal or factional struggle to control the national government or to influence it: a struggle that is restrained by private and tacit agreements, prudential concerns, and personal ties and dependencies rather than by public rules and institutions. The consequences of such policies have usually been increased political instability and occasionally the deterioration of the game of politics into a "fight" among personal and factional contenders for power. But, speaking generally, the result has not been the political disorder that Hobbes and some other theorists would lead us to expect. The contemporary African political experience suggests, rather, that a relatively stable public life is attainable in the large-scale territorial states that are neither institutionalized "civil societies" nor anti-political totalitarian regimes. In many African countries that presently lack effective political institutions, a measure of political order has been attained without the complete suspension of politics.

But it is usually, an order resting on personal–political arrangements, which are more subject to repudiation and therefore to disruption than are legitimate institutions.[27]

Richard Joseph went even further in his study of Nigerian politics to characterize politics and office holding as simply overt corruption for the benefit of the elite and their factional group. As Joseph stated, prebendal politics

> refer to the patterns of political behaviour which rest on the justifying principle that such offices should be competed for and then utilized for the personal benefit of office holders as well as their reference or support group. The official public purpose of the office often becomes a secondary concern, however much that purpose might have been originally cited in its creation or during the periodic competition to fill it.[28]

Patrick Chabal and Jean-Pascal Daloz also point to a similar issue of corruption tied to elites and factional interests and its damaging effects on the state through the deterioration of institutions.[29]

The studies on personal rule, prebendal politics, patrimonialism, and other forms of corruption and oppression in governance all point to two important facts about poor governance – in both its economic and political forms. First is the inherent connection between ethnicity and poor governance. The studies consistently show that corruption and oppression are enacted and enabled through the exploitation of ethnic and regional divisions. In some ways, this generation of poor governance literature dovetails with the studies of ethnicity. However, ethnicity in this case is focused more on elite interests and tactics rather than collective ethnic grievances. The second fact is that poor governance created conditions for long-term instability and political violence, even though the regimes seemed stable. This fact became more evident in the later generation of studies dealing with the civil wars and political violence that erupted in the 1990s. The link between poor governance and the Hobbesian state of disorder became clearly visible in countries such as Sierra Leone, Liberia, Côte d'Ivoire, Burundi, and Rwanda, which experienced brutal civil wars. In all these countries ethnicity and corruption blended into the kind of dire poor governance that resulted in civil war.[30]

The other issue that has featured prominently in the later generation of scholarship on peace and conflict in Africa is the natural resources argument, notably the greed and grievances and the resource curse hypotheses.[31] The critical issues in this literature are the grievances resulting from claims to natural resources, especially among pastoral and farming communities, the unequal distribution of revenues from mineral resources, and the use of revenues from natural resources to wage wars. As with the poor governance literature, the natural resources literature also dovetails with ethnicity. In some ways, the natural resources arguments can be viewed as extensions of the poor governance and ethnicity arguments. Both ethnicity and poor governance are connected to resource distribution. Ethnicity is particularly connected to conflicts over rights to land in localized conflicts among pastoralists and farmers, while poor governance is strongly connected to the exploitation of mineral resources.

One strand of the natural resources literature deals with localized conflicts tied to access to farming and grazing land and water resources. In Kenya, for example, there have been numerous natural resources conflicts in the Rift Valley area and other parts of the country.[32] In Uganda too, there are numerous conflicts over ownership of and access to land.[33] Another set of works deals with the unequal distribution of revenue from minerals and the adverse impact of mineral exploitation on the lives of local communities. Studies of the delta regions of Nigeria, for example, often point to the connections between oil production and violent struggles for environmental, economic, and social justice in the region.[34] The most recent variant of the natural resources literature is the political economy of war argument, which focuses on the link between natural resources exploitation and civil wars. A key point is that civil wars are perpetuated by warlords and criminal networks who materially benefit from war. Some of the most notorious examples are Sierra Leone, Liberia, and the Democratic Republic of the Congo, where illicit mining and timber exploitation have been used to fund brutal civil wars.[35]

The chapters in this book tap into all three causes of conflicts across Africa. Collectively, the book shows the interconnections among ethnicity, poor governance, and natural resources in African conflicts. In the case studies addressed in this book, ethnicity often stands out and dovetails with the other causes of conflict. This is not surprising given the fact that ethnic cleavages have always been exploited by political elites in Africa in ways that breed authoritarian rule and corruption. Too often ethnicity becomes a source of conflict, though not because ordinary people do not constructively interact across ethnic lines or develop harmonious inter-ethnic relations. Rather ethnicity becomes a source of conflict because it is used by the power elite as an instrument for poor governance and regime survival.

## Peacebuilding and Institutional Design

The link between institutional design and the consolidation of peace and democracy is an important, but understudied, academic and policy issue. As Catherine Boone rightly notes, these issues "have implications for how we understand African state-building, for formulating and justifying strategies for institutional reform, and for envisioning Africa's economic future."[36] Too often, democratization and peacebuilding are disconnected in the literature, even though they address related problems. Moreover, both the democracy and the peacebuilding studies tend to leave out the issue of institutional design even though it is critical for the consolidation of peace and democracy. Interestingly, studies of democracy and conflicts in Africa evoke two interrelated overarching questions: (1) what are the underlying causes of violent conflicts? (2) How can African countries design institutions that create conditions for peace and democracy?

The democracy literature reduces these two overarching questions largely to a question of how to successfully transition from dictatorship to democracy. Within this approach, the main cause of Africa's political problems is seen to be the absence of liberal democracy.[37] As African countries moved toward democracy, the question shifted toward structural impediments to the consolidation of democracy.[38] However, institutional design remains the weakest aspect of studies on African democracy. Studies of democratic regimes in Europe and Latin America have addressed the problem of how to design a democracy: electoral system, federalism, presidential versus parliamentary system, etc.[39] However, there are very few comparable studies of institutional design for African countries. As Boone points out, much of the work on African reforms focuses on exogenous forces.[40] Efforts to study institutional design in Africa are limited to works on federalism and minority rights in South Africa and Nigeria.[41] Boone tried to extend the issue of institutional design to Senegal, Côte d'Ivoire, and Ghana by addressing the interconnections among "power, political capacity, and state institutions in rural Africa."[42] However, her work remains trapped in an agrarian view of African states and their geographically uneven internal pace of development. Boone's work on institutional design at the rural level is important, but does not deal with the more pressing issue of the design of the state as a whole.

Similar gaps between peacebuilding and institutional design exist in the literature. Security studies view African civil wars through their causes and forms or the mechanics of peacekeeping. Wars are attributed to ethnicity and oppressive and corrupt rule – as most evident in the *greed versus grievance* thesis.[43] Other studies continue to focus on the brutal nature of the wars and peacekeeping.[44] Africa security studies, too, fail to explore the links between institutional design and the structural conditions for peace. Instead, structural factors are framed within the political economy of war discourse.[45]

The more specialized studies on transitional justice and postwar reconstruction address the broader issues of human development and peacebuilding. However, they are more concerned with human rights and postwar human development than addressing structural challenges to democracy and the institutional design options. Transitional justice studies typically focus on war crimes.[46] To its credit, the postwar reconstruction literature has addressed institutional reforms, especially in the security sector.[47] A key part of postwar reconstruction studies rests on analysis of the peace-dividend associated with generous international development assistance and the promotion of good governance and human development.[48] However, institutional reforms in the postwar reconstruction literature are limited to questions of implementation and enhancing the effectiveness of extant institutions. The studies focus on good governance and human development without addressing the core question of institutional choices and design.

Another strand of the security studies literature deals with the regional and pan-African mechanisms for peacebuilding and democracy promotion. It should be noted that while regional and pan-African mechanisms are aimed at influencing the political and security conditions of African states, they are not ready-made mechanisms that can be adopted by African countries. Rather, they set the terms of international interventions in troubled African countries and the principles to reinforce democracy and good governance, with the aim of ameliorating the conditions that lead to violent political conflicts. The core mechanisms are the African Peace and Security Architecture (APSA), the African Charter on Democracy, Elections, and Governance (ACDEG), and the New Partnership for African Development (NEPAD).[49] APSA sets the mechanism for addressing the core humanitarian and security issues necessitated by civil wars. Key among these are peace mediation by the Panel of Eminent Persons and peacekeeping through the African Standby Force. The issues of multiparty democracy and constitutional change of government are addressed through ACDEG, while "NEPAD focuses on enhancing management, procurement processes, accountability and creating transparent government policies."[50] All of these mechanisms are anchored in the African Union (AU) doctrine of non-indifference to security and humanitarian problems in the continent. A central tenet of all of these mechanisms is that addressing authoritarian rule and corruption are key to promoting peace in Africa.

One key issue that often comes out in the literature on African mechanisms for good governance and security is whether those mechanisms are driven by neoliberal political and economic policies embedded in Western agendas. While some studies are critical of the neoliberal elements in the pan-African mechanism, others see them as largely strategic policies aimed at asserting African agency and thwarting Western domination in African political and security matters.[51] This literature on African security and governance mechanisms is useful for understanding the dynamic of change across Africa, especially Africa's relations with Western powers. However, it does not offer much in terms of the institutional reforms African countries undertake to deal with the underlying causes of conflict.

The missing link in the above literature is a historically grounded study of the relations between institutional design and the consolidation of peace and democracy. By examining the post-conflict institutional reforms in several African countries, this book will not only shed light on the common causes of violent conflicts but more importantly on how institutional design can affect the conditions for peace and democracy in Africa. To thoroughly address this linkage, the book, through its various chapters, focuses on conceptual and practical questions of designing inclusive state institutions and the way institutions are perceived by the citizenry. In particular, it addresses the issues of political autonomy and the management and control of natural resources, which are often key sources of grievances and demands for political autonomy. Moreover, it examines the symbolic and everyday meanings of institutional reforms and the overarching questions of institutional choices.

## Themes and Scope

The chapters in this edited book address a variety of institutional design issues that are critical for peace and democracy in Africa. In particular, they examine reform efforts in Sierra Leone, Liberia, Kenya, Uganda, South Africa, and Africa more broadly. Two main themes emerge from the chapters, which provide unique perspectives into the interconnections between institutional design and the promotion of peace and democracy in the continent. The first theme is about identities and their representation within state institutions, while the second theme is about institutional mechanisms for the equitable and proper management of and access to state resources.

### Identity, Postwar Narratives, and Memory Institutions

Identity has been a salient issue in both violent political conflicts and in multiparty electoral politics. Notably, ethnicity, religions, and regionalism have been central drivers of identity. As Benn Eifert and colleagues note, the salience of ethnic identities in African politics is attributed to hardwired traditional loyalties and to their functionality in mobilizing people for elite interests.[52] Ethnic identities dovetail with regional and religious identities in part due to the geographical clustering of populations.[53] Mahmoud Mamdani also notes the colonial context of ethnic and regional identity construction and instrumentalization, which shapes African state-building experiences.[54] More recently, gender- and sex-based identities are becoming prominent issues in African politics. Women's issues have moved from the socio-economic inequalities and development realm into the arenas of politics and civil war.[55] Women are no longer simply victims of discrimination and war, but active participants in peacebuilding and the struggle for good governance.[56] In South Africa in particular, the manifestation of lesbian identity is a liberatory practice to affirm civil rights and assert political recognition in the context of South Africa's long history of liberation struggle.[57] All of these forms of identity and their infusion into politics and violent conflict point to the importance of identity.

While much has been written about identity grievances and ethnic and regional mobilization in political conflicts, the foundational questions of identity and autonomy are often missing in sociological and anthropological studies of peacebuilding and governance in Africa. Similarly, the way ethnic political identities are represented and contested in the everyday experiences of people is often lost within the depictions of violence, causes of conflicts, or barriers to democracy. Three of the chapters in this book address these critical identity issues. Niklas Hultin provides a panoramic overview and critique of collective identities and political demands for autonomy and the legal and anthropological frameworks for understanding identity politics and conflicts in Africa. Okaka Opio Dokotum also addresses the issue of ethnic identity and political reform in Uganda at the ground level through a rich analysis of music videos and artistic representation of political grievances and violence through regional and ethnic lenses. David Mwambari and Iris Nxumalo weave the macro and the micro through an in-depth study of the memorialization of political violence in South Africa. A critical issue in their study is the way native people, women, and sexuality are represented within the memory institutions and the broader implication for issues of group rights, political recognition, and participation in South Africa. Collectively, the chapters reveal the anthropological aspect of identity politics and institutional reforms by examining both the symbolic nature of institutions and the taken-for-granted everyday experiences of the masses.

Institutional reforms aimed at addressing identity grievances beg a basic question: Do groups have a right to autonomy? As Hultin notes in his chapter:

> Much of the scholarly discussion of the institutional design of deeply divided, fragile, and/or post-conflict societies focuses on the desirability (or not) of an arrangement that gives a measure of self-government – i.e. autonomy – to specific ethnic groups and how such arrangements can be optimized. The question of whether there is a right to autonomy is a different one, however, and it is an important one for a couple of different reasons. One reason is practical and instrumental – if there is a right established by law, there presumably is a corresponding remedy (whether such a remedy is effective is a different discussion). In other words, if a given group's right to autonomy has been violated, said group – or an organization acting on its behalf – can challenge this violation in a court or equivalent body. A second reason is the signaling effect of legalization – that is, if a principle is encoded in a treaty as a right, it suggests a normative commitment to the realization of that right by parties to that treaty.

Hultin addresses this question of group right to autonomy by carefully weaving legal debates with anthropological insights of indigenous people's incorporation into states and agitations for native rights through the human rights legal systems and rich critiques of the extant liberal peacebuilding model of state creation and international interventions.

The central pillar of Hultin's analysis is the jurisprudence of the African human rights system as embodied in the African Commission on Human and Peoples' Rights (ACHPR), the African Court on Human and Peoples' Rights (ACtHPR), and article 20 of the Charter of the African Union. While much of the study on African peace and conflict has been dominated by civil wars, Hultin's work reminds us of the rich legal struggles through which ethnic and regional political grievances have been addressed in African conflicts and the possibilities for creative institutional solutions. Some of these include the Katanga in Congo (i.e. Zaire), Ogoni in Nigeria, Western Sahara separatists, the Dioulas in Côte d'Ivoire, the people of Cabinda in Angola, the people of Darfur in Sudan, and the Endorois and Ogiek in Kenya. In all of these cases, the issues of identity and ethnic discrimination are central to the conflict and the potential institutional arrangements that could resolve the grievances. One notable feature of the African legal system is the reluctance to legally reinforce the notion of minority or indigeneity, which is in sharp contrast to the European system of recognizing national minorities. Instead, African jurisprudence emphasizes a broad array of human rights which any people can claim. By so doing, any group can claim to be unique people and thereby demand their political rights and exert their identity. However, Hultin cautions:

> There is nothing in the African Commission's jurisprudence that stipulates that territorial autonomy is the required way to address peoples' rights violations. It is, however, a *permissible* way to address these violations. A somewhat more affirmative conclusion can be drawn for cultural autonomy. While, as of yet, there does not appear to be a requirement that a country grants a population cultural autonomy, it does seem that the African Court's findings in the Ogiek's case would go some way in that direction in that it is difficult to envision a non-cultural autonomy approach to cultural rights as defined in the decision.

In essence, while African states and the AU legal systems generally accept cultural autonomy as a way to address ethnic and regional grievances, they do not necessarily accept political autonomy as a way to resolve group political grievances. This brings us back to the core issues of this book: (1) What are the underlying causes of violent conflicts?

(2) How can African countries design institutions that create conditions for peace and democracy?

Clearly, the effort to get recognition as a people is borne out of belief that members of that ethnic or regional group are discriminated against by the state. Indeed claims to land ownership, fair share of revenues from natural resources, or proper representation in government have been at the center of all the cases that have been brought to the ACHPR and ACtHPR. Moreover, such grievances are at the heart of many civil wars in Africa. Ideally, such grievances should be resolved through creative institutional arrangements. However, for such institutional arrangements to be developed there needs to be more explicit and honest recognition of groups, as a peoples, and their collective identity in African states. While the reluctance to embrace the notion of minority, especially in ways that can lead to territorial autonomy, is directly tied to the colonial roots and balkanization of Africa and the fear of formalizing tribalism; in reality evading ethnic and minority identities simply inhibits the development of appropriate national power-sharing and institutional models that structurally address group grievances.[58] As Hultin notes, the conundrum for African states is that "while there is no robust right to autonomy as such, the African human rights system is increasingly embracing the idea that some ethnic groups may be entitled to some form of self-government." Hultin points to two findings, which are highly informative of the potentials and challenges of promoting peace and democracy through institutional reforms in the multiethnic states of Africa. As he notes:

[T]wo general conclusions can be drawn from this thumbnail sketch of the right to autonomy in international law: Firstly, in a general sense, autonomy is a permitted (but not required) arrangement consistent with the right to self-determination. Secondly, a presumptive right to autonomy in Africa must include three elements: firstly, there must be a recognition of groupness and, relatedly, some way to claim such groupness over the objections of the affected state … Secondly, the group must be viewed as of the right "kind" to have this right … Thirdly, there must be a recognition that such groups can demand self-government in either a specific territory or in a specific social domain and, once again, this demand must be able to overcome state objections. As we will see, the African human rights system is not yet fully recognizing these three elements though it is trending in that direction.

In sum, the existence of ethnic identities coupled with their politicization and the legal room for rights and self-governance make it even more urgent for African countries to seriously rethink state institutions and group access to power and resources. Unfortunately, African states and the African human rights system are too wedded to the Westphalian notion of state sovereignty and the inherited models of Western democracies. Perhaps, demands for group rights can be addressed through a variety of institutional arrangements that provide for formal modes of power-sharing, including decentralization, quotas for key national offices, parliamentary rules that emphasize super majorities, and even self-rule. While such arrangements may not satisfy all the ethnic political grievances, collectively they may reduce their volume and intensity to the point where nonviolent and democratic options can be adequate options for addressing grievances.

In Dokotum's analysis of political violence, democracy, and peacebuilding in Uganda, the central question is about how groups experience oppression, express their grievances, challenge their oppression, and view the peacebuilding process and its related institutional reforms. In this work, peacebuilding and postwar institutional reforms aimed at promoting democracy are an everyday experience that is characterized by group disappointment about the way their political grievances are addressed in the postwar setting. Dokotum captures this experience by examining how artistic political works, notably music videos, represent the war experiences, political grievances, and disappointments of the Acholi people of northern Uganda. As Dokotum points out in his chapter,

> Poets not only mirror the present, but through their art provide the social, political and cultural barometer that registers shifts in the social and cultural fabric of society and predict the future. They participate in critiquing and improving democratic and cultural power structures.

By bringing this artistic approach to democracy and peacebuilding, Dokotum provides a rare angle on our understanding of democracy, peacebuilding, and institutional reforms. Too often, studies of institutional reforms do not echo the voices of the people who are affected by those reforms. In Uganda, we saw that "music videos are also platforms for resistance to injustice and human rights abuses, and a forum for asserting human dignity," and have become an "important avenue for witnessing and dialoguing on the history of Uganda, and realizing psychological and emotional healing." In essence, Acholi music became "the aesthetic forum for celebrating Ugandan history while highlighting the traumatic fault lines, provoking national debate, celebrating the victims of individual, state-inspired, rebel-induced and other complex forms of violence" which problematizes Acholi perception of the Ugandan state. By so doing, the work not only provides a rich ethnographical lens onto the fusion of arts, war, and politics, but more importantly how institutional reforms are viewed and inserted into the collective political memory of ethnic and regional groups. In this way, institutional reforms move from the purely technical issues of institutional design to the symbolic meanings of political reforms, perceptions of their fairness, and the satisfaction of group grievances. As Dokotum summed it up, the chapter shows

> how selected music videos from Uganda interface with democratic
> institutions to promote peace, justice, and human dignity in the
> postwar era; how the traumatic experiences are revisited, exposed,
> analyzed, managed, contested, and even transformed into a celebration
> of human dignity in light of democracy and human rights. These
> videos tackle the right to protection of lives and property, the right to
> education, freedom of the press, and freedom of assembly.

All of this analysis is fused with a rich historical account of ethnic political marginalization, civil war, and the postwar peacebuilding programs and reforms in Uganda.

Methodologically, most of the chapter is a content analysis of selected music videos and the ethnic political symbolisms associated with the songs and the artists. Key among those are Lucky Bosmic Otim, X-NO P feat Small Luo, Master Loketto Lee, and Robert Kyagalunyi Ssentamu aka Bobi Wines. Lucky Bosmic Otim's songs analyzed in the chapter include "Peace Return" and "Wang Ceng Oter" ["Let the Sun Set with It"]. For X-NO P feat Small Luo, his main music video is "Peace Anthem." Three of the music videos – "Peace Talks in Juba," "Bigombe," and "We Don't Mind We Don't Care" – are by Master Loketto Lee. The other key music video, "Situka" ["Rise Up"], is by Robert Kyagalunyi Ssentamu aka Bobi Wines. Through these music videos, Dokotum's chapter examines four critical reform issues that are central to peace and democracy in Uganda and the rest of Africa.

These are: (1) war violence and crimes, (2) peace mediation and transitional justice, (3) democratic politics and elections, and (4) postwar reconstruction to improve economic and social conditions.

Any discourse of institutional design aimed at peace and democracy in Uganda must first recognize the bitter violence associated with the war and lack of justice for the victims. Otim's "Peace Return" captures the violence and shows how the Acholi people suffered from both the government and the Lord's Resistance Army (LRA). As Dokotum writes, "The song goes on to lament that even the government soldiers who die at the front line fighting the LRA are recruits from Acholi, compounding the tragedy of the sub-region." In both Loketto's "We Care Now" and Serugo's "We Don't Care," the plight of the people living in Internally Displaced People's camps are addressed, which again adds to the collective victimization image that often shapes ethnic political violence.

With respect to the peace mediation and transitional justice, the music videos focus on the failed Juba Peace Talks that ran from July to September 2006. Frustration with the talks and risks of failure are apparent in the direct appeals, through music, to combatants to lay down their weapons and embrace peace. For the artists, the Juba Peace Talks were the right moment for the government and LRA rebels to sign a lasting peace agreement and end the protracted war and the atrocities committed by both sides which led to massive violations of human rights. As Dokotum notes, "The videos aim at mobilizing popular support from the fan base of the artists and politicians to support the peace processes." A critical issue in peace mediation is justice for the war victims. Ugandan artists have called for forgiveness and reconciliation, while also wanting justice. Lucky Bosmic Otim's "Wang Ceng Oter" ["Let the Sun Set with It," literally, "Let the Sun's Face Take It"] in particular seeks swift justice for victims of the LRA insurgency. Reconciliation and justice are both significant elements of peacebuilding and the restoration of the rule of law as evident in numerous transitional justice mechanisms and war crimes trials in Uganda and other African countries. Postwar institutional reforms in Africa must find the right balance between reconciliation and delivering symbolic justice as a way to heal memories of collective victimization. More importantly, reforms need to address the broader justice sector and rule of law so as to make democracy more meaningful. As Dokotum points out, "The failure of the judiciary in Uganda to prosecute LRA war criminals is the rationale for Otim's song calling on God to judge the perpetrators. It also indicts the Uganda government for its failures to pay reparations to victims."

The artists also engaged the democratic process and the economic and social problems by critiquing electoral politics, distancing themselves from politics, or directly engaging with politics, and supporting peaceful protests. The artists critique or praise politicians depending on whether they align with the government or with opposition parties. Other artists produce oppositional songs simply to point out the social and political dysfunctions of Uganda. As Dokotum notes in one example, "Bobi Wine has refused to throw his lot in with any political party openly in order to act as a mirror reflecting and critiquing democratic processes in Uganda, especially presidential elections – the cornerstone of free and fair political participation." Other artists enter into politics while critiquing the political system. Kyagulanyi, for example, ran for parliament as an independent candidate in Kyadondo East constituency, which he won. As Dokotum notes, "He represents the artist who is disarticulated from all party power centers, government or opposition, choosing rather to be an Independent politician, artist, and commentator who is free to audit democratic processes in Uganda and to critique its institutions." His political participation dovetails with his music. In his post-2016 election song "Situka" ["Rise Up"], he challenged politicians to enact a dual political reform, first of themselves and second of the electoral process and institutions of democracy. As Dokotum observes,

> While the song "Situka" tends to be apolitical and calls for personal reform of attitudes towards national development beyond party politics, the video is loaded with images of raw state power and its deconstruction through peaceful protests as well as metaphors of violent resistance.

The varying critiques of the political process all seem to exhibit a subtle yet consistent dissatisfaction with the economic and social conditions of Uganda. An important component of peacebuilding and democracy is the postwar reconstruction efforts to promote economic and social wellbeing. Economic neglect and atrocity tourism are important themes of the economic marginalization that emerged in the artistic critique of postwar reconstruction in Uganda. As with the issue of justice, there is a clear sense that the Acholi people are left out. Economic neglect of northern Uganda by the government and international actors is a central theme in Loketto Lee's song video, "We Don't Mind, We Don't Care" and its sequel, "Now We Care." While most of the works on democracy and postwar reconstruction are focused on elite agency and structural issues, Dokotum's chapter on Uganda reminds us that "The role of the artist in peace-building ... is evident. It helps in postwar reconstruction as well as strengthening democratic structures." The chapter underscores the everyday experiences and collective imageries of political, economic, and social marginalization, which impede peace and democracy. The critical lesson for African countries is how to factor these everyday ethnic and regional grievances into the institutions of postwar multi-party politics and reconstruction.

The issue of identity in African conflicts and democracy-building cuts across both macro and micro issues. David Mwambari and Iris Nxumalo's chapter on memory institutions in South Africa provides a powerful micro–macro link in the way we approach identity issues in the efforts to build peace. At the heat of their chapter is the way women and queer and native people have been presented in monuments and institutions that memorialize the victims of apartheid and the strug-gle for equality and basic rights for all people. The chapter provides a broad discussion of the memorialization, notably through the truth and reconciliation process, and a more focused discourse of key monu-ments and institutions of memorialization that are central to the way women and queer and native people are left out and their effort to ensure that they are appropriately memorialized. As they note, their

> chapter explores the politics of memory and reconciliation in
> South Africa by centralizing acts of remembering and forgetting
> as they relate to the use of memory institutions for peacebuilding
> and justice in South Africa. Although these memory institutions are
> designed to be repositories of collective memory, ... [the] chapter
> argues that processes of remembering also exhibit acts of forgetting
> that institutionalize the silencing and erasure of particular
> historical narratives.

While numerous studies have examined the politics of memoriali-zation, the chapter takes the issue further by examining the ways in which memorialization relates to the broader postwar peacebuilding and democratization effort. As they argue,

[I]nstitutional forgetting and social amnesia undermine the post-conflict institution-building. By illuminating the ways in which the memory project "achieves status by erasing more complex histories," we seek to demonstrate the bearing that this has on the quest for building sustainable (and positive) peace in South Africa.

For Mwambari and Nxumalo, any efforts to silence certain identities, namely women and queer and native people, in the reconciliation and peacebuilding process "has the potential to generate new grievances and cripple attempts to redress the multiple violences of South Africa's slave, colonial, and apartheid histories through memory institutions." By infusing memorialization with institutional design issues, the chapter points to a significant finding, which should be a lesson for democracy and peacebuilding in Africa. Notwithstanding South Africa's ongoing effort to preserve democracy and maintain peace, Mwambari and Nxumalo found that "South Africa has based its reconciliation policies of the past two decades on promoting state-led exercises to promote memory as central to national reconciliation while suppressing certain alternative narratives." Again, the critical questions in this book are: (1) What are the underlying causes of violent conflicts? (2) How can African countries design institutions that create conditions for peace and democracy? Indeed, none of the marginalized identities (women, queer, and natives) are likely to start a civil war in South Africa in the foreseeable future. However, the issues of peace and democracy go well beyond the absence of violence. A critical element of peacebuilding and democracy is addressing structural violence. The practical question that emerges from the chapter is: How can postwar memory institutions be made more equitable and representative of the diverse identities and thereby enhance peace and democracy?

To demonstrate the memorialization marginalization and the struggles for appropriate representation, the chapter examines the broader memorialization institutions, such as the Truth and Reconciliation Commission (TRC), and the specific efforts to assert proper memorialization of women and queer and native people. South Africa has been acclaimed for its novel model of transitional justice. The TRC in South Africa was to deliver a restorative justice mechanism that would allow people to tell their stories, confess, and earn forgiveness. However, the TRC became too centered on individuals and political elite reconciliation at the expense of group identities. As Mwambari and Nxumalo note,

The TRC's engagement with collective memory-making through testimonies and confessions was viewed as a powerful form of alternative historiography that brought to light what was silenced and obscured by the modus operandi of the apartheid state, and included those voices and narratives that were previously excluded from the canons of knowledge.

Ironically, "this operationalization neglected the structural, legal, and institutional components of apartheid, which consequently shuffled out the everyday violence of apartheid and excluded most women from contributing to the memory-making mechanism of the TRC." In some ways, the process got caught up in the tricky balance between substantial memorialization and social amnesia, which was done at the expense of women and queer and native people.

In addition to the core TRC process, the chapter examines several cases of memorialization. Key among these are: (a) the Apartheid Museum in Gold Reef City (Johannesburg), (b) the Robben Island Museum (RIM), (c) the District Six Museum, and (d) community memorials and monuments. A key feature of the Apartheid Museum is its temporary exhibitions. Some of the notable exhibitions featured education segregation, the Freedom Charter, the constitution, women, and the lives of Steve Biko and Ahmed Timol. While most of the exhibits are male-dominated, it is import to recognize that the *Journeys of Faith: Navigating Sexual Orientation and Gender Diversity* exhibition created "a space where individuals could explore the reconciliation of their gender and sexual identities with their religious and spiritual beliefs, through their life stories and testimonies." In a similar way, RIM suppressed the history of women since they were not imprisoned in Robben Island. However, women, too, suffered as they were imprisoned in places such as Boksburg, Nylstroom, and Kroonstad. While RIM is the epicenter of the prison memorialization, women's prison experiences are memorialized through the Women's Jail at Constitutional Hill in Johannesburg. As a people's museum established by former residents of the area, District Six Museum has a much broader gender stroke in part because of its quotidian nature. Community memorials and monuments were aimed at commemorating acts of apartheid violence in specific communities and rebuilding trust among community members. Some of the most notable are the Thokoza Monument and Thembisa Monuments commemorating the violence between ANC and Inkatha Freedom Party supporters.

There are also others aimed at highlighting state violence such as the Sharpeville Massacre Memorial and the Duncan Village Massacre Memorial. Community memorials are largely funded by local and/or provincial governments, which may hinder the representation of women and queer and native people.

The issue of identity is directly addressed through specific cases that underscore the struggles of women and queer and native people for representation. The first case is that of Sara Baartman, who "was an enslaved Khoi woman sent to London and Paris to be paraded, abused, displayed in museums and subsequently taken away from public view." After a lot of lobbying by Nelson Mandela and the South African government, her body was returned from Paris to South Africa in 2002. Baartman's return was an important part of the memorialization of the slavery and colonial history of South Africa. After a long delay, the Sarah Baartman Centre of Remembrance was opened in 2008. Baartman's memorialization speaks not only to the South African variant of slavery and colonialism, but also the suffering of native people, notably the Khoi and San people. More importantly, Baartman's memorialization "demonstrate[s] the gendered and racialized ways in which the memory project is utilized for nation-building in South Africa."

Perhaps, the most visible memorialization of women and recognition of gender is through the National Monument to the Women of South Africa, which is located in Union Building in Pretoria. While there are a few other women's monuments, the National Monument to the Women of South Africa was the first national-level memorialization of women. The establishment of a privately and publicly funded women's monument represents a significant assertion of women's stories and experiences into a largely male-dominated narrative and institutions. As Mwambari's and Nxumalo note,

> The bidding, deliberation, and design of the monument reflected feminist interventions on memorialization that sought to resist the grandeur and monumentality of patriarchal expressions of power and importance by imbibing a different set of notions and standards, sometimes anchored in understatement and humility.

The issue of gender also dovetails with sexuality. Despite the salient role of the LGBT community in the struggle against apartheid, much of the state-level memorialization has left out queer activism and thereby created a new terrain for queer activism and claims to recognition. As Mwambari and Nxumalo point out,

> The erasure of Black queer histories is the most sustained form of silence and institutional forgetting that pertains to historical narratives and the use of memory institutions to redress colonialism, slavery, and apartheid histories in South Africa today. Despite the gains secured through LGBT activism that not only advanced the anti-apartheid struggle, but also advocated for legal reform and redress through recognition, equal treatment, and protection under the law in post-apartheid South Africa, there is no state-driven initiative to memorialize the contributions of the LGBT community to South Africa's history.

### Accessing and Controlling Resources and Institutions of Power

As noted earlier, the other key theme of the chapters in the book is the institutional arrangements for accessing and controlling resources and power. The issue of resources and political power leads us back to the core questions of the book: (1) What are the underlying causes of violent conflicts? (2) How can African countries design institutions that create conditions for peace and democracy? While the greed-grievance and democracy literatures have extensively addressed how natural resources, governance, and corruption lead to and fuel civil wars in Africa, there is very little on the postwar institutional reforms aimed at providing mechanisms for the proper management of resources and more equitable access to power. The question of postwar institutional reform is addressed in three of the chapters in the book, which move the debate from merely understanding the causes and nature of civil wars to examining the novel institutional mechanisms through which wars may be averted. Michael Beevers' chapter examines the postwar reforms in the management of natural resources in Sierra Leone and Liberia. The central issue in the chapter is how the proper management of natural resources contributes to peacebuilding. Aditi Malik takes on the issue of political power by examining the effects of devolution on electoral violence in Kenya. The critical issue for Malik is whether the devolution reforms that were implemented in Kenya in the wake of the 2008 post-election violence have led to a reduction in ethnic-based political violence during elections. The chapter by Abu Bah and Fredrick Ogenga provides a broader overview of key institutional design challenges typical in Africa and insights into possible design options to reduce ethnically motivated political violence.

Beever's chapter is a notable effort in extending the natural resources literature in peace and conflict studies from the causes of war and mechanics of peace mediation to the critical institutional design issues that are central to durable peace and democracy. As Beevers notes in his chapter,

> Peacebuilding was initially a short-term project concerned with negotiating peace agreements, monitoring ceasefires, provisioning humanitarian aid, providing electoral assistance, and overseeing the disarmament of combatants, although this did not appear adequate to pave the way for a durable peace. In response, a broadened concept of peacebuilding shifted to incorporate a range of issues including traditional development goals of poverty alleviation and economic growth, violations of human rights, transparent and accountable governance, promotion of democracy, rule of law, religion, ethnicity, and resources and environmental issues.

The chapter focuses on postwar natural resources governance in Liberia and Sierra Leone. In Liberia, Beevers examines the rules and mechanism for the proper management of timber, while in Sierra Leone he examines the diamond mining sector. A key finding in both countries is that the reforms left out the fundamental problem of access to land. As he notes,

> The larger point is that in both Liberia and Sierra Leone grievances and struggle over natural resources were largely about land and a failure to benefit directly from their vast natural resources. What is problematic for natural resources governance, which remains focused on governing natural resources for state revenue and economic growth, is that international actors may not address land-related issues that concern and affect much of the population. In fact, there is a real threat that extraction of minerals and timber could exacerbate already existing tensions with regard to land.

Despite the failure to address land access issues, Beevers points to notable efforts in both Liberia and Sierra Leone to revive the export of raw materials and better manage the extraction process. In Liberia, the most immediate postwar challenge was simply getting international sanctions lifted and generating revue. Naturally, the timber sector was Liberia's primary means of economic revival. Liberia's blueprint for timber was to get UN sanctions lifted, pass reforms, and attract investment through fast-track processes.

In Liberia, the reform was spearheaded by president Ellen Johnson Sirleaf and the Liberian Forest Concession Review Committee. A key part of the initial institutional reform was the establishment of the Governance and Economic Management Assistance Program (GEMAP), which sought the help of international experts. Executive Order 1, issued by Sirleaf in early 2006, canceled all forest concessions and placed a moratorium on commercial timber harvests. The core reform was the passage of the National Forestry Reform Law (NFRL), which sought to assert the government's authority over forests. Under the law, "the government not only holds in trust all forestlands for the Liberian people, but is the sole authority over all matters concerning their use." The law revolved around the "three Cs" concept of forest management, notably efficient commercial use, community participation, and conservation of natural resources. The law was ambitious and perhaps overestimated the revenues that would be received by the state. An interesting unanticipated phenomenon resulting from the reform was the widespread use of Private Use Permits (PUP), which effectively became a loophole for evading many of the state regulations in the extraction and export of timber. As Beevers observed,

> Between 2010 and 2012, approximately 70 PUPs were issued covering roughly 40 percent of the country's forest lands, and comprising three-quarters of its timber exports. PUPs allowed private landowners to sell timber to companies. While PUPs required social agreements and environmental assessments, unlike conventional timber contracts on "public lands," no payments to the government or local communities were required. In addition, there was no open bidding process or plan for sustainable management.

Even more troubling was that PUPs became corrupted as government officials were issuing PUPs without regard to the proper process and too often for bribes. As Beever further notes, "most PUPs were actually bogus. Most, if not all, were signed with little or no community involvement and there was no compensation for local communities. The PUPs portended serious consequences for the overharvesting of Liberia's forests." In 2013, President Sirleaf halted the granting of PUPs.

In Sierra Leone, the reforms centered on diamond mining, which was a major factor in the civil war. The government passed a number of laws and undertook to implement the Kimberly Process Certification Scheme (KPCS). The laws include the Diamond Trading Act, the Alluvial Diamond Mining Amendments to the Mines and Minerals Act of 2009, Mines and Minerals Regulations, and the Diamond Cutting and Policy Act. All of these were aimed at removing sanctions on Sierra Leone diamonds and more importantly ensuring that diamond revenues go the state, which would normally use it to revive the economy and alleviate poverty. As Beevers notes, "The KPCS was intended to disincentivize the illicit smuggling that had occurred before and during the war by improving transparency, and increasing the export of diamonds through official government channels."

At the micro level, several reform programs were introduced to improve conditions for diamond miners. The Integrated Diamond Management Program sought to secure higher prices for miners by establishing cooperatives aimed at bypassing the big diamond dealers. Even though around fifty cooperatives were established, the program collapsed under the weight of corruption. Another major micro reform program was the Diamond Area Community Development Fund (DACDF). DACDF focused on communities in the diamond mining areas in order to reduce smuggling and bring resources to the communities. Such communities were to be allocated 0.75 percent of the government's 3 percent export tax share of diamond revenues.

Aditi Malik's chapter on decentralization in Kenya provides a lucid analysis of the impact of post-conflict institutional reforms on political violence. While the few available works on institutional design tend to be broad comparisons geared toward theoretical argument, Malik's work is an empirical analysis of an actual case of institutional reform. More importantly, she connects the devolution reforms to political violence. As she notes, the chapter "assesses the effects that devolution has had on patterns of election-related conflict in Kenya. In doing so, it considers the relationship between post-conflict institutional design on the one hand and electoral violence – at both the national and sub-national levels – on the other." In the wake of the 2007/8 post-election violence, Kenya focused on institutional reforms aimed at mitigating ethnic political conflicts. A focal point of the chapter is the effect of the devolution mandated in the 2010 Constitution, which created forty-seven new counties and shifted major resources and power from the central government to the counties. Under Article 16 of the 2010 Constitution, the Commission of Revenue Allocation (CRA) determines the way national revenue is shared between the national government and the county governments, as well as the share of each county government. So far, counties have been receiving over 15 percent of the revenue. As Malik notes:

> [F]or the last few years, county governments have received over 200 billion Shillings per annum, which is well over the 15 percent allocation that they were initially promised. In 2015–2016, for instance, Kenya's forty-seven counties received 259 billion Shillings (approximately 2.44 billion dollars) in unconditional grants, which exceeded 30 percent of the national revenue for that fiscal year.

As indicated in article 174 of the 2010 Constitution, devolution essentially entailed enabling communities to self-manage their development agenda. By allowing counties to determine and manage their development projects, Kenyans hoped to gain a more democratic and accountable exercise of power and reduction in conflicts among groups, notably at the national level. As Malik's paper shows, devolution has largely been implemented. Moreover, devolution has significantly increased the stakes in county politics because of the huge resources that county governments control. By examining the actual impacts of devolution on ethnic political violence, the chapter provides critical insights into the central questions in this book, namely: (1) What are the underlying causes of violent conflicts? (2) How can African countries design institutions that create conditions for peace and democracy?

While studies of devolution tend either to see it as a good way to reduce conflict or simply dismiss it as ineffective, Malik's study provides a critical nuance.[59] Her unique contribution emanates from important observations about election violence in Kenya since 2010. As she notes, "Compared to 2007–2008 as well as the elections of the 1990s, Kenya's 2013 presidential election concluded relatively peacefully. At the same time, however, to say that the 2013 elections were entirely peaceful would be a gross exaggeration." On the face of it, devolution has led to more violence in local elections. However, it is clear from her work that devolution has potentially reduced the political violence at the national level. As she rightly observes,

> Taken together, the research demonstrates that under Kenya's new constitutional dispensation, devolution has been a partial success: while it has shifted the locus of electoral competition from the national to the local level and has thereby reduced the high stakes historically associated with presidential elections, the county system has also created sub-national contests around which election violence is likely to occur in the future. These findings raise important questions about when constitutional re-engineering can reduce election-time conflict and when such reforms can actually generate new incentives for instrumentalizing violence.

More importantly, Malik's finding points to an important lesson, which Kenya may utilize to further reduce ethnic political violence. One potential step for Kenya would be to also decentralize the counties so that communities at the ward level have more representation and control over resources. Clearly, if devolution has reduced national ethnic political violence, it is also likely to be useful in reducing county-level ethnic political violence. In essence, the ethnic political struggles to access and control resources are a common problem at the national and county level. Devolution, which has been a solution at the national level, can provide similar remedies at the county level.

To assess the impact of devolution on political violence, Malik's chapter examines the 2013 local elections in three counties, namely: Tana River, Marsabit, and Isiolo. Like the rest of Kenya, each of these counties is multiethnic, which makes the issue of ethnic political access to the county-level executive and legislature akin to the ethnic political problems at the national level. Devolution led not only to the disbursement of huge amounts of development funds from the central government to the counties, but also to high-stakes elections as ethnic groups intensely compete for access to those funds through political office-holding. Through archival and in-depth interview data, Malik's "study identifies a range of causal pathways through which devolution contributed to electoral clashes in these places."

In the coastal county of Tana River, the electoral violence was mainly between the pastoral Orma and farming Pokomo, which left over 150 people dead and many more wounded. The Pokomo constitute roughly 40 percent of the population, while the Orma make up approximately 28 percent. Both groups vigorously competed for political power, especially the highly powerful position of governor. As such, they tried to form an alliance with the Wardei community. The Orma and Wardei have some important cultural similarities, including language and Islamic religion. While there have been long-standing discontents among these groups, devolution significantly increased the importance of county elections. As Malik notes:

> [D]evolution in Tana River first and foremost created conditions that favored the organization of violence by rendering the long-standing fault-line between the region's agricultural and pastoral communities electorally salient. With these crucial conditions in place, and with the aim of preventing the Pokomo from casting their votes, conflict was ignited by pastoral (largely Orma) politicians who drew on narratives and fears of marginalization to mobilize the Orma and Wardei against the Pokomo.

In end, the Orma and Wardei succeeded in ousting the Pokomo and gaining political power, including the position of governor.

Similar issues of county-level ethnic political violence occurred in Marsabit during the 2013 elections. The main protagonists in the conflicts were the Gabra, who aligned with the Rendille and Burji to form the ReGaBu ethnic coalition, and the historically dominant Borana. As Malik points out:

> [F]or a considerable period of time, local patterns of power-holding in Marsabit were quite stable, and favored the Borana. Although several other communities were arguably disadvantaged by these conditions, election-related conflict in the region was fairly rare … because, prior to the 2013 elections, political power was concentrated in the presidency, and none of the communities in Marsabit (including the Borana) had much to gain from the Kikuyu and Kalenjin presidents who controlled the national purse-strings.

Clearly, devolution altered that by making the counties very important holders of state resources. In fact, Marsabit was allocated 3.6 billion Shillings in 2013–2014. Although the election results were mixed, ReGaBu got the governorship and thereby ousted the Borana. Over a hundred people were killed after the election results were announced.

The final case examined in Malik's chapter is that of Isiolo, inhabited by various communalities, including the Borana, Samburu, Turkana, Somalis, and Meru. However, most of the political violence has been between the Somalis on the one hand and the Borana and Samburu on the other. Isiolo is divided into north and south. However, the Borana have had a major political advantage as they are the largest group in both the north and the south. Historically, they have also held most of the major political offices. Overall, the Borana managed to gain a narrow victory. However, the 2013 election was bitterly contested along ethnic lines largely as a result of the added stakes to county government brought by devolution. As Malik notes:

> [T]he availability of these funds rendered pre-existing ethnic divisions electorally relevant and manipulable in many parts of the country. In Tana River, for example, a long-standing divide between the pastoral Orma and agricultural Pokomo took on new electoral meaning in the run-up to the elections, and local politicians used this divide to organize violence in a bid to capture prized county-level positions. Similarly, in Isiolo, devolution and the associated promise of accessing devolved fiscal resources amplified divisions between different pastoral groups.

In the final chapter, Bah and Ogenga take on the issue of institutional design providing a panoramic analysis and critique of prior models of governance in Africa. The central question is whether creative institutional design can actually lead to more peaceful and democratic states in Africa. Although the chapter stops short of providing a blueprint of institution, it does raise several historical cases to challenge African countries into thinking out of the box and embracing ethnicity as a factor for inclusion instead of merely denying the diabolical impact of ethnicity in African politics. In essence, the chapter revolves around the idea of consociationalism, though it does not provide a blueprint.

The argument for institutional design by way of embracing ethnicity and consociationalism emerges from the basic observation that orthodox multiparty democracy in African countries is often associated with ethnic political violence. As such, the argument for creative institutional design comes with a subtle critique of the neoliberal model of democracy that has been problematically pervasive in African countries. As Bah and Ogenga frame it:

[D]emocracy in Africa is challenged by growing disconnections between the notion of representations embedded in the doctrine of democracy and the electoral rules and processes that often produced winner-takes-all electoral outcomes. At its roots, democracy is about equal representation of the people in the institutions of the state. Such representation has often been understood in terms of individual citizens. Under the individualistic notion of representation, one-person-one-vote is an adequate way to ensure democratic representation. However, this is only true to the extent that voting is based largely on individual interests and considerations. While many voters do make (rational) individual decisions on whom to vote for, it is equally true that voting is heavily influenced by identity and group interests. In many African countries, ethnic identity has been central to the way people vote, which is evident in the regional and ethnic voting patterns in many African countries. Ethnic and other forms of identity interests and voting patterns raise a fundamental question about democratic representation, namely: Who is to be represented in the institutions of the state? What happens when individualistic representation does not produce group (e.g. ethnic) representation? This is the conundrum of regular multiparty democracy in Africa. These kinds of problems have led to violent conflicts in countries such as Nigeria, Liberia, Kenya, Côte d'Ivoire, Guinea, Central African Republic, South Sudan and Ethiopia.

The chapter provides a conceptual frame of institutional design by linking it to the extant discourses and historical cases of democracy and peacebuilding. As Bah and Ogenga state:

Institutional design refers to the deliberate and creative choice of political arrangements to foster a peaceful and democratic system of governance. Such choices are made through selective, informed, strategic, and well-intentioned adoption of existing rules and procedures for democratic governance that have worked in other countries. Also, such choices must entail appropriate customization to adequately meet the historical, social, economic, and cultural realities of each African country. By institutional design, we do not mean a total recopying of the procedures and practices of other countries to be instantly transplanted in African countries. Institutional design is actually the opposite of blind and wholesale copying of Western political institutions or those of any other country for that matter.

This notion of institutional design is developed out of a critique of prior models of governance, political representation, and institution-building.

The chapter first examines the immediate postcolonial era during which African countries adopted the political systems of the former colonial powers, notably the British multiparty parliamentary system and French republicanism. These were classic cases of neoliberal democracy, which failed largely due to their inability to ensure proper ethnic political representation. The second historical phase was African one-party and military regimes. The one-party system was viewed as the solution to the ethnic animosities that became the hallmark of multiparty elections. However, one-party systems were grossly inadequate in large part because they were rooted in problems of class inequality instead of ethnic marginalization. In the end, one-party systems simply became vehicles for ethnic marginalization in most African countries. The third phase was the multiparty democratic transition of the 1990s. Bah and Ogenga view this transition as a missed opportunity for creative institutional design to mitigate the negative impacts of ethnicity on African politics. For them, the national conferences that took place during that time should have been golden opportunities to design creative consociational arrangements that would promote ethnic political representation and thereby reduce violent political conflicts in Africa. The final phase relates to the African Union rules on democracy and constitutional rule. In particular, they examined AU rules prohibiting coups and the unconstitutional change of presidential term limits.

In addition to the historical phases that shape the nature of political institutions in Africa, Bah and Ogenga also examine the cases of Nigeria and Côte d'Ivoire. While each of these countries has had civil war and major forms of political violence along ethnic and regional lines, what is also remarkable are the kinds of institutional arrangements that were developed to end the wars and mitigate ethnic political violence. In the case of Nigeria, they see the federal system and the creation of new states and local government areas as creative ways of enhancing ethnic political representation. However, they also recognize that these institutional arrangements have not always been maintained in good faith or buttressed with proper political leadership. In the case of Côte d'Ivoire, the chapter sees the Ouagadougou Peace Accord as a fairly good example of consociationalism. Indeed, the Ouagadougou Peace Accord ended the ethnic-cum-regional war.

As Bah and Ogenga note, however, Côte d'Ivoire missed the opportunity to integrate the consociational principles of the peace agreement into the Ivoirian Constitution. Not surprisingly, Côte d'Ivoire slipped back into ethnic political violence as soon as it went back to orthodox multiparty elections.

Ultimately, the chapter not only critiques neoliberal models of multiparty politics, but also makes a strong case for consociational politics aimed at enhancing ethnic political representation and thereby reducing violent political conflicts. For Bah and Ogenga, "African countries must creatively design their institutions of governance so that they remain democratic and refrain from creating grievances rooted in marginalization." They also recognize the importance of political leadership. Bah and Ogenga seem to allude to a symbiosis of good political leadership and institutional design. As they sum up,

> Indeed, institutions alone would not be enough – we need good leadership. However, good leadership alone is not enough either. Good institutions are needed because even the best of leaders can get old, sick, and eventually pass away. Good institutions can reduce political chaos, even when you have occasional poor leadership.

## Conclusion

In the end, the core questions posed in this book about the underlying causes of violent conflicts and institutional design to create conditions for peace and democracy are aimed at provoking African scholars, practitioners, and leaders to thinking out of the box. The book, including the various cases addressed, is not a blueprint for institutional design. Rather, the cases should stimulate further debate about the diabolical effects of identity politics and marginalization on peace and democracy, and more importantly serve as lessons and inspirations for creatively redesigning political institutions in ways that recognize ethnicity and regionalism and the importance of consociational and inclusive institutional arrangements for peaceful democracy.

This book is not a mere critique of extant studies of peacebuilding and democracy. Instead, it is an effort to move the debates and actions forward by pointing to the intrinsic connections between democracy, peace, and postwar reconstructions. All of this is framed in terms of institutional design in post-conflict settings. A key part of the link is institutional reforms aimed at devising creative institutions that address the ethnic and regional marginalization problems that lead to war in the first place. The chapters add to our knowledge of the issues by engaging the anthropological and artistic aspects of identity politics in African countries. The three chapters by Hultin, Dakotum, and Mwambari and Nxumalo all bring unique ways of addressing the interconnections between identity, politics, and violence in Africa. These chapters not only address the causes of violent political conflicts, but also show us some of the ways in which identity issues are addressed in the postwar reconstruction process. The other three chapters, by Beevers, Malik, and Bah and Ogenga, take on the practical question of how to redesign institutions so that they reduce the chances of violent political conflicts. Each of the cases in those chapters examine specific kinds of institutional reform. The contributions of these chapters to the broader debate about institutional design is not that they provide a blueprint. Rather, their contributions are in showing that postwar institutional reforms have to be creative and actually challenge and even move away from some of the beaten-path orthodoxies of neoliberal democracy and state-building.

## Notes

1  Ake, *Democracy and Development in Africa*; Ake, *Feasibility of Democracy in Africa*.

2  Bah, *Breakdown and Reconstitution*; Suberu, *Federalism and Ethnic Conflict in Nigeria*; Otite, *Ethnic Pluralism, Ethnicity, and Ethnic Conflicts in Nigeria*.

3  Bah, "State Decay and Civil War"; Abdullah, "Bush Path to Destruction"; Gberie, *A Dirty War in West Africa*.

4  Ellis, *The Mask of Anarchy*; Ahorsu, "A Poststructuralist Approach to the Dagbon Chieftaincy Crisis in Northern Ghana"; Smock and Smock, *The Politics of Pluralism*.

5  Bangura, "Young People and the Search for Inclusion and Political Participation in Guinea"; Kaba, "Guinean Politics."

6  Bah, "Democracy and Civil War"; Toungara, "Ethnicity and Political Crisis in Côte d'Ivoire."

7  Kenya, National Cohesion and Integration Act, 2008; Ndegwa, *Two Faces of Civil Society*; Bratton and Kimenyi, "Voting in Kenya."

8  Elischer, *Political Parties in Africa: Ethnicity and Party Formation*.

9  Adam, "The Politics of Ethnic Identity"; Giliomee, "Democratization in South Africa."

10  Mohamed, "State and Clan Violence in Somalia."

11  Mpofu, "Social Media and the Politics of Ethnicity in Zimbabwe"; Muzondidya and Ndlovu-Gatsheni, "Echoing Silences."

12  Collier and Hoeffler, "Greed and Grievance in Civil War"; Bayart, *The*

*State in Africa*; Ross, "How Do Natural Resources Influence Civil War?"; Jackson and Rosberg, *Personal Rule in Black Africa*.

13  Bratton and Van de Walle, *Democratic Experiments in Africa*; Bratton and Mattes, "Support for Democracy in Africa"; Bah, "Changing World Order and the Future of Democracy in Sub-Saharan Africa"; Bah, "People-Centered Liberalism."

14  Mamdani, *Citizen and Subject*; Davidson, *The Black Man's Burden*; Coleman, *Nigeria*; Montana, *The Abolition of Slavery in Ottoman Tunisia*; Law, "Ethnicity and the Slave Trade"; Diop, *Precolonial Black Africa*.

15  Ajayi and Smith, *Yoruba Warfare in the Nineteenth Century*; Falola, *The Political Economy of a Pre-colonial African State*.

16  Stannus, "Notes on Some Tribes of British Central Africa"; Wright, "What Do You Mean There Were No Tribes in Africa?"

17  Ekeh, "Colonialism and the Two Publics in Africa," 98.

18  Zolberg, "The Structure of Political Conflict in the New States of Tropical Africa"; Zolberg, "The Military Decade in Africa"; McGowan, "Coups and Conflict in West Africa, 1955–2004"; Wells, "The Coup d'Etat in Theory and Practice"; Morrison and Stevenson, "Cultural Pluralism, Modernization, and Conflict."

19  Kirk-Greene, *The Genesis of the Nigerian Civil War and the Theory of Fear*; Mustapha, "The National Question and Radical Politics in Nigeria"; Bah, *Breakdown and Reconstitution*; Adebanwi, *Yorùbá Elites and Ethnic Politics in Nigeria*; Obadare, *Pentecostal Republic*.

20  Lindemann, "The Ethnic Politics of Coup Avoidance"; Uvin, "Ethnicity and Power in Burundi and Rwanda"; Kandeh, "Politicization of Ethnic Identities in Sierra Leone"; Bah, "State Decay and Civil War"; Ajulu, "Politicised Ethnicity, Competitive Politics and Conflict in Kenya."

21  Lindemann, "The Ethnic Politics of Coup Avoidance."

22  Ibid., 6.

23  Ibid., 6.

24  Diamond, *Class, Ethnicity, and Democracy in Nigeria*, 8.

25  Bratton and Van de Walle, *Democratic Experiments in Africa*; Chabal and Daloz, *Africa Works*; Bah, "Changing World Order and the Future of Democracy in Sub-Saharan Africa."

26  Bah, "State Decay," 72.

27  Jackson and Rosberg, *Personal Rule in Black Africa*, 1.

28  Joseph, *Democracy and Prebendal Politics in Nigeria*, 8.

29  Chabal and Daloz, *Africa Works*.

30  Bah, "State Decay and Civil War"; Bah, "Democracy and Civil War"; Reno, *Corruption and State Politics in Sierra Leone*; Mamdani, *When Victims Become Killers*; Lemarchand, *Burundi*.

31  Collier and Hoeffler, "On Economic Causes of Civil War"; Ross, "The Political Economy of the Resource Curse"; Obi, "Oil as the 'Curse' of Conflict in Africa"; Le Billon, *Fuelling War*.

32  Green, "Ethnicity and the Politics of Land Tenure Reform in Central Uganda"; Anderson and Lochery, "Violence and Exodus in Kenya's Rift Valley, 2008."

33  Green, "Ethnicity and the Politics of Land Tenure Reform in Central Uganda."

34  Babatunde, "Environmental Insecurity and Poverty in the Niger Delta"; Obi, "Oil Extraction, Dispossession, Resistance, and Conflict in Nigeria's Oil-rich Niger Delta."

35  Lake, "Ending Impunity for Sexual and Gender-Based Crimes"; Gberie, *A Dirty War in West Africa*; Hirsch, *Sierra Leone*; Reno, "The Business of War in

Liberia"; Nest et al., *The Democratic Republic of Congo*.

36  Boone, *Political Topographies of the African State*, 1.

37  Bratton and Van de Walle, "Neopatrimonial Regimes and Political Transitions in Africa"; Van de Walle, "Africa's Range of Regimes"; Randall and Svåsand, "Political Parties and Democratic Consolidation in Africa"; Resnick and Van de Walle, *Democratic Trajectories in Africa*.

38  Bratton and Mattes, "Support for Democracy in Africa"; Ball, *Beyond Structural Adjustment*.

39  Lijphart, *Democracy in Plural Societies*; Linz and Stepan, *Problems of Democratic Transition and Consolidation*; Elster et al., *Institutional Design in Post-Communist Societies*; McFaul, "Institutional Design, Uncertainty, and Path Dependency during Transitions"; Reynolds, *The Architecture of Democracy*.

40  Boone, *Political Topographies of the African State*.

41  Diamond, *Class, Ethnicity, and Democracy in Nigeria*; Horowitz, *A Democratic South Africa?*; Suberu, *Federalism and Ethnic Conflict in Nigeria*; Sisk, *Democratization in South Africa*; Bah, *Breakdown and Reconstitution*.

42  Boone, *Political Topographies of the African State*, 1.

43  Bah, "State Decay and Civil War"; Bah, "State Decay"; Collier and Hoeffler, "Greed and Grievance in Civil War"; Jackson and Rosberg, *Personal Rule in Black Africa*; Reno, *Corruption and State Politics in Sierra Leone*; Chabal and Daloz, *Africa Works*.

44  Autesserre, *The Trouble with the Congo*; Bah, "The Contours of New Humanitarianism"; Bah, "Civil Non-State Actors in Peacekeeping and Peacebuilding in West Africa"; Straus, *The Order of Genocide*; Adebajo, *Building Peace in West Africa*; Ellis, *The Mask of Anarchy*.

45  Zack-Williams, "Sierra Leone"; Ross, "How Do Natural Resources Influence Civil War?"

46  Wilson, *The Politics of Truth and Reconciliation in South Africa*; Shaw, "Memory Frictions"; Linton, "Cambodia, East Timor and Sierra Leone"; Jalloh, "Special Court for Sierra Leone"; Corey and Joireman, "Retributive Justice."

47  Ebo, "The Challenges and Lessons of Security Sector Reform in Post-Conflict Sierra Leone"; Bah, "People-Centered Liberalism"; Gbla, "Security Sector Reform under International Tutelage in Sierra Leone"; Sawyer, "A Case for (Restructuring) Chiefdom Governance in Post-Conflict Sierra Leone."

48  Schümer, *New Humanitarianism*; Bah, "People-Centered Liberalism"; Hoffman, "The Civilian Target in Sierra Leone and Liberia"; Duffield, *Global Governance and the New Wars*; Bah, "The Contours of New Humanitarianism."

49  Bah, "People-Centered Liberalism"; Bah, "African Agency in New Humanitarianism and Responsible Governance"; Obi, "The African Union and the Prevention of Democratic Reversal in Africa"; Darkwa and Attuquayefio, "Analysis of Norm Diffusion in the African Union and the Economic Community of West African States."

50  Bah, "People-Centered Liberalism," 994.

51  Obi, "The African Union and the Prevention of Democratic Reversal in Africa"; Bah, "People-Centered Liberalism"; Akuffo, "The Politics of Interregional Cooperation"; Edozie, "Pan-African Security and Pax Africana."

52  Eifert et al., "Political Competition and Ethnic Identification in Africa."

53  Le Billon, "Identity, Space and the Political Economy of Conflict in Central Africa"; Nnoli, "Ethnic Conflicts and Democratization in Africa"; Bah, *Breakdown and Reconstitution*.

54  Mamdani, *Citizen and Subject.*
55  Zerai and Sanya, *Safe Water,
Sanitation, and Early Childhood
Malnutrition in East Africa*; Mama,
"Challenging Subjects"; Mama, "Feminism
or Femocracy?"
56  Meintjes et al., *The Aftermath*;
Bah, "Civil Non-State Actors in

Peacekeeping and Peacebuilding in West
Africa."
57  Kotze and Bowman, "Coming-Out
Confessions."
58  Mamdani, *Citizen and Subject*;
Davidson, *The Black Man's Burden.*
59  Brancati, *Peace by Design*;
Brancati, "Decentralization."

## References

Abdullah, Ibrahim. "Bush Path to
    Destruction: The Origin and
    Character of the Revolutionary
    United Front/Sierra Leone." *The
    Journal of Modern African Studies* 36,
    no. 2 (1998): 203–235.

Adam, Heribert. "The Politics of Ethnic
    Identity: Comparing South Africa."
    *Ethnic and Racial Studies* 18, no. 3
    (1995): 457–475.

Adebajo, Adekeye. *Building Peace in West
    Africa: Liberia, Sierra Leone, and
    Guinea-Bissau.* Boulder, CO: Lynne
    Rienner, 2002.

Adebanwi, Wale. *Yorùbá Elites and Ethnic
    Politics in Nigeria: Ọbáfẹmi Awólowo
    and Corporate Agency.* Cambridge:
    Cambridge University Press, 2014.

Ahorsu, Ken. "A Poststructuralist
    Approach to the Dagbon Chieftaincy
    Crisis in Northern Ghana." *African
    Conflict and Peacebuilding Review* 4,
    no. 1 (2014): 95–119.

Ajayi, J.F. Ade, and Robert Smith. *Yoruba
    Warfare in the Nineteenth Century.*
    Ibadan: Ibadan University Press, 1971.

Ajulu, Rok. "Politicised Ethnicity,
    Competitive Politics and Conflict
    in Kenya: A Historical Perspective."
    *African Studies* 61, no. 2 (2002):
    251–268.

Ake, Claude. *Feasibility of Democracy
    in Africa.* Dakar: Council for the
    Development of Social Science
    Research in Africa, 2000.

Ake, Claude. *Democracy and
    Development in Africa.* Washington,

DC: Brookings Institution Press,
    2001.

Akuffo, Edward Ansah. "The Politics
    of Interregional Cooperation: The
    Impact of NATO's Intervention
    in Libya on Its Relations with the
    African Union." *African Conflict and
    Peacebuilding Review* 4, no. 2 (2014):
    108–128.

Anderson, David, and Emma Lochery.
    "Violence and Exodus in Kenya's
    Rift Valley, 2008: Predictable and
    Preventable?" *Journal of Eastern
    African Studies* 2, no. 2 (2008):
    328–343.

Autesserre, Séverine. *The Trouble
    with the Congo: Local Violence
    and the Failure of International
    Peacebuilding.* New York: Cambridge
    University Press, 2010.

Babatunde, Abosede Omowumi.
    "Environmental Insecurity and
    Poverty in the Niger Delta: A
    Case of Ilaje." *African Conflict and
    Peacebuilding Review* 7, no. 2 (2017):
    36–59.

Bah, Abu Bakarr. "Changing World Order
    and the Future of Democracy in
    Sub-Saharan Africa." *Proteus* 21, no. 1
    (2004): 3–12.

Bah, Abu Bakarr. *Breakdown and
    Reconstitution: Democracy, the
    Nation-State, and Ethnicity in
    Nigeria.* Lanham, MD: Lexington
    Books, 2005.

Bah, Abu Bakarr. "Democracy and Civil
    War: Citizenship and Peacemaking in

Côte d'Ivoire." *African Affairs* 109, no. 437 (2010): 597–615.

Bah, Abu Bakarr. "State Decay and Civil War: A Discourse on Power in Sierra Leone." *Critical Sociology* 37, no. 2 (2011): 199–216.

Bah, Abu Bakarr. "State Decay: A Conceptual Frame of Failing and Failed States in West Africa." *International Journal of Politics, Culture, and Society* 25, no. 1–3 (2012): 71–89.

Bah, Abu Bakarr. "Civil Non-State Actors in Peacekeeping and Peacebuilding in West Africa." *Journal of International Peacekeeping* 17, no. 3–4 (2013): 313–336.

Bah, Abu Bakarr. "The Contours of New Humanitarianism: War and Peacebuilding in Sierra Leone." *Africa Today* 60 (2013): 3–26.

Bah, Abu Bakarr. "African Agency in New Humanitarianism and Responsible Governance," pp. 148–169, in *International Security and Peacebuilding: Africa, the Middle East, and Europe*, edited by Abu Bakarr Bah. Bloomington, IN: Indiana University Press, 2017.

Bah, Abu Bakarr. "People-Centered Liberalism: An Alternative Approach to International State-Building in Sierra Leone and Liberia." *Critical Sociology* 43, no. 7–8 (2017): 989–1007.

Ball, Nicole, and Vijaya Ramachandran, eds. *Beyond Structural Adjustment: The Institutional Context of African Development*. New York: Palgrave Macmillan, 2006.

Bangura, Ibrahim. "Young People and the Search for Inclusion and Political Participation in Guinea." *African Conflict and Peacebuilding Review* 8, no. 1 (2018): 54–72.

Bayart, Jean-François. *The State in Africa: The Politics of the Belly*. New York: Polity Press, 2009.

Boone, Catherine. *Political Topographies of the African State: Territorial Authority and Institutional Choice*. New York: Cambridge University Press, 2003.

Brancati, Dawn. "Decentralization: Fueling the Fire or Dampening the Flames of Ethnic Conflict and Secessionism?" *International Organization* 60, no. 3 (2006): 651–685.

Brancati, Dawn. *Peace by Design: Managing Intrastate Conflict through Decentralization*. New York: Oxford University Press, 2009.

Bratton, Michael, and Mwangi S. Kimenyi, "Voting in Kenya: Putting Ethnicity in Perspective." *Journal of Eastern African Studies* 2, no. 2 (2008): 272–289.

Bratton, Michael, and Robert Mattes. "Support for Democracy in Africa: Intrinsic or Instrumental?" *British Journal of Political Science* 31 (2001): 447–474.

Bratton, Michael, and Nicolas Van de Walle. "Neopatrimonial Regimes and Political Transitions in Africa." *World Politics* 46, no. 4 (1994): 453–489.

Bratton, Michael, and Nicholas Van de Walle. *Democratic Experiments in Africa: Regime Transitions in Comparative Perspective*. New York: Cambridge University Press, 1997.

Chabal, Patrick, and Jean-Pascal Daloz. *Africa Works: Disorder as Political Instrument*. Bloomington, IN: Indiana University Press, 1999.

Coleman, James Smoot. *Nigeria: Background to Nationalism*. Berkeley, CA: University of California Press, 1960.

Collier, Paul, and Anke Hoeffler. "On Economic Causes of Civil War." *Oxford Economic Papers* 50, no. 4 (1998): 563–573.

Collier, Paul, and Anke Hoeffler. "Greed and Grievance in Civil War." *Oxford*

*Economic Papers* 56, no. 4 (2004): 563–595.

Corey, Allison, and Sandra F. Joireman. "Retributive Justice: The Gacaca Courts in Rwanda." *African Affairs* 103, no. 410 (2004): 73–89.

Darkwa, Linda, and Philip Attuquayefio. "Analysis of Norm Diffusion in the African Union and the Economic Community of West African States." *African Conflict and Peacebuilding Review* 4, no. 2 (2014): 11–37.

Davidson, Basil. *The Black Man's Burden: Africa and the Curse of the Nation-State.* Oxford: James Currey, 1992.

Diamond, Larry Jay. *Class, Ethnicity, and Democracy in Nigeria: The Failure of the First Republic.* Syracuse, NY: Syracuse University Press, 1988.

Diop, Cheikh Anta. *Precolonial Black Africa.* Chicago, IL: Chicago Review Press, 1988.

Duffield, Mark. *Global Governance and the New Wars: The Merging of Development and Security.* London: Zed Books, 2001.

Ebo, Adedeji. "The Challenges and Lessons of Security Sector Reform in Post-Conflict Sierra Leone: Analysis." *Conflict, Security & Development* 6, no.4 (2006): 481–501.

Edozie, Rita Kiki. "Pan-African Security and Pax Africana: Navigating Global Hierarchies." *African Conflict and Peacebuilding Review* 4, no. 2 (2014): 38–59.

Eifert, Benn, Edward Miguel, and Daniel N. Posner. "Political Competition and Ethnic Identification in Africa." *American Journal of Political Science* 54, no. 2 (2010): 494–510.

Ekeh, Peter P. "Colonialism and the Two Publics in Africa: A Theoretical Statement." *Comparative Studies in Society and History* 17, no. 1 (1975): 91–112.

Elischer, Sebastian. *Political Parties in Africa: Ethnicity and Party Formation.* New York: Cambridge University Press, 2013.

Ellis, Stephen. *The Mask of Anarchy: The Destruction of Liberia and the Religious Dimension of an African Civil War.* New York: NYU Press, 2007.

Elster, Jon, Claus Offe, and Ulrich K. Preuss. *Institutional Design in Post-Communist Societies: Rebuilding the Ship at Sea.* New York: Cambridge University Press, 1998.

Falola, Toyin. *The Political Economy of a Pre-colonial African State: Ibadan, 1830–1900.* Ifẹ, Nigeria: University of Ifẹ Press, 1984.

Gberie, Lansana. *A Dirty War in West Africa: The RUF and the Destruction of Sierra Leone.* Indianapolis, IN: Indiana University Press, 2005.

Gbla, Osman. "Security Sector Reform under International Tutelage in Sierra Leone." *International Peacekeeping* 13, no. 1 (2006): 78–93.

Giliomee, Hermann. "Democratization in South Africa." *Political Science Quarterly* 110, no. 1 (1995): 83–104.

Green, Elliott D. "Ethnicity and the Politics of Land Tenure Reform in Central Uganda." *Commonwealth & Comparative Politics* 44, no. 3 (2006): 370–388.

Hirsch, John L. *Sierra Leone: Diamonds and the Struggle for Democracy.* Boulder, CO: Lynne Rienner, 2001.

Hoffman, Danny. "The Civilian Target in Sierra Leone and Liberia: Political Power, Military Strategy, and Humanitarian Intervention." *African Affairs* 103, no. 411 (2004): 211–226.

Horowitz, Donald L. *A Democratic South Africa? Constitutional Engineering in a Divided Society.* Berkeley, CA: University of California Press, 1991.

Jackson, Robert H., and Carl Gustav Rosberg. *Personal Rule in Black Africa: Prince, Autocrat, Prophet, Tyrant.* Berkeley, CA: University of California Press, 1982.

Jalloh, Charles Chernor. "Special Court for Sierra Leone: Achieving Justice?" *Michigan Journal of International Law* 32, no. 3 (2011): 395–460.

Joseph, Richard A. *Democracy and Prebendal Politics in Nigeria.* New York: Cambridge University Press, 2014.

Kaba, Lansine. "Guinean Politics: A Critical Historical Overview." *The Journal of Modern African Studies* 15, no. 1 (1977): 25–45.

Kandeh, Jimmy D. "Politicization of Ethnic Identities in Sierra Leone." *African Studies Review* 35, no. 1 (1992): 81–99.

Kenya. National Cohesion and Integration Act, 2008. National Cohesion and Integration Commission.

Kirk-Greene, Anthony Hamilton Millard. *The Genesis of the Nigerian Civil War and the Theory of Fear.* Uppsala: Nordiska Afrikainstitutet, 1975.

Kotze, Ella, and Brett Bowman. "Coming-Out Confessions: Negotiating the Burden of Lesbian Identity Politics in South Africa." *Journal of Homosexuality* 65, no. 1 (2018): 1–18.

Lake, Milli. "Ending Impunity for Sexual and Gender-Based Crimes: The International Criminal Court and Complementarity in the Democratic Republic of Congo." *African Conflict and Peacebuilding Review* 4, no. 1 (2014): 1–32.

Law, Robin. "Ethnicity and the Slave Trade: 'Lucumi' and 'Nago' as Ethnonyms in West Africa." *History in Africa* 24 (1997): 205–219.

Le Billon, Philippe. *Fuelling War: Natural Resources and Armed Conflicts.* London: Routledge, 2013.

Le Billon, Philippe. "Identity, Space and the Political Economy of Conflict in Central Africa," pp. 248–276, in *The Geopolitics of Resource Wars*, edited by Philippe Le Billon. London: Routledge, 2017.

Lemarchand, René. *Burundi: Ethnic Conflict and Genocide.* New York: Cambridge University Press, 1996.

Lijphart, Arend. *Democracy in Plural Societies: A Comparative Exploration.* New Haven, CT: Yale University Press, 1977.

Lindemann, Stefan. "The Ethnic Politics of Coup Avoidance: Evidence from Zambia and Uganda." *Africa Spectrum* 46, no. 2 (2011): 3–41.

Linton, Suzannah. "Cambodia, East Timor and Sierra Leone: Experiments in International Justice." *Criminal Law Forum* 12 (2001): 185–246.

Linz, Juan J., and Alfred Stepan. *Problems of Democratic Transition and Consolidation: Southern Europe, South America, and Post-Communist Europe.* Baltimore, MD: Johns Hopkins University Press, 1996.

Mama, Amina. "Feminism or Femocracy? State Feminism and Democratization in Nigeria." *Africa Development* 20, no. 1 (1995): 37–58.

Mama, Amina. "Challenging Subjects: Gender and Power in African Contexts." *African Sociological Review* 5, no. 2 (2001): 63–73.

Mamdani, Mahmood. *When Victims Become Killers: Colonialism, Nativism, and the Genocide in Rwanda.* Princeton, NJ: Princeton University Press, 2014.

Mamdani, Mahmood. *Citizen and Subject: Contemporary Africa and the Legacy of Late Colonialism.* Princeton, NJ: Princeton University Press, 2018.

McFaul, Michael. "Institutional Design, Uncertainty, and Path Dependency during Transitions: Cases from Russia." *Constitutional Political Economy* 10, no. 1 (1999): 27–52.

McGowan, Patrick J. "Coups and Conflict in West Africa, 1955–2004: Part II, Empirical Findings." *Armed Forces & Society* 32, no. 2 (2006): 234–253.

Meintjes, Sheila, Meredeth Turshen, and Anu Pillay. *The Aftermath: Women in Post-Conflict Transformation.* London: Zed Books, 2001.

Mohamed, Haji Ingiriis. "State and Clan Violence in Somalia." *African Conflict and Peacebuilding Review* 8, no. 1 (2018): 73–96.

Montana, Ismael M. *The Abolition of Slavery in Ottoman Tunisia.* Gainesville, FL: University Press of Florida, 2013.

Morrison, Donald G., and Hugh M. Stevenson. "Cultural Pluralism, Modernization, and Conflict: An Empirical Analysis of Sources of Political Instability in African Nations." *Canadian Journal of Political Science/Revue canadienne de science politique* 5, no. 1 (1972): 82–103.

Mpofu, Shepherd. "Social Media and the Politics of Ethnicity in Zimbabwe." *Ecquid Novi: African Journalism Studies* 34, no. 1 (2013): 115–122.

Mustapha, Abdul Raufu. "The National Question and Radical Politics in Nigeria." *Review of African Political Economy* 13, no. 37 (1986): 81–96.

Muzondidya, James, and Sabelo Ndlovu-Gatsheni. "Echoing Silences: Ethnicity in Post-Colonial Zimbabwe, 1980–2007." *African Journal on Conflict Resolution* 7, no. 2 (2007): 275–297.

Ndegwa, Stephen N. *Two Faces of Civil Society.* West Hartford, CT: Kumarian Press, 1996.

Nest, Michael Wallace, Francois Grignon, and Emizet F. Kisangani. *The Democratic Republic of Congo: Economic Dimensions of War and Peace.* Boulder, CO: Lynne Rienner, 2006.

Nnoli, Okwudiba. "Ethnic Conflicts and Democratization in Africa." *Nigerian Journal of Social Sciences* 4, no. 1 (2007): 1–23.

Obadare, Ebenezer. *Pentecostal Republic: Religion and the Struggle for State Power in Nigeria.* London: Zed Books, 2018.

Obi, Cyril. "Oil as the 'Curse' of Conflict in Africa: Peering through the Smoke and Mirrors." *Review of African Political Economy* 37 no. 126 (2010): 483–495.

Obi, Cyril. "Oil Extraction, Dispossession, Resistance, and Conflict in Nigeria's Oil-rich Niger Delta." *Canadian Journal of Development Studies* 30, no. 1–2 (2010): 219–236.

Obi, Cyril. "The African Union and the Prevention of Democratic Reversal in Africa: Navigating the Gaps." *African Conflict and Peacebuilding Review* 4, no. 2 (2014): 60–85.

Otite, Onigu. *Ethnic Pluralism, Ethnicity, and Ethnic Conflicts in Nigeria.* Ibadan: Shaneson C. I., 2000.

Randall, Vicky, and Lars Svåsand. "Political Parties and Democratic Consolidation in Africa." *Democratization* 9, no. 3 (2002): 30–52.

Reno, William. *Corruption and State Politics in Sierra Leone.* New York: Cambridge University Press, 1995.

Reno, William. "The Business of War in Liberia." *Current History* 95, no. 601 (1996): 211–215.

Resnick, Danielle, and Nicolas Van de Walle, eds. *Democratic Trajectories in Africa: Unravelling the Impact of Foreign Aid.* New York: Oxford University Press, 2013.

Reynolds, Andrew. *The Architecture of Democracy: Constitutional Design, Conflict Management, and Democracy.* New York: Oxford University Press, 2002.

Ross, Michael. "The Political Economy of the Resource Curse." *World Politics* 51, no. 2 (1999): 297–322.

Ross, Michael. "How Do Natural Resources Influence Civil War?

Evidence from Thirteen Cases." *International Organization* 58, no. 1 (2004): 35–68.

Sawyer, Edward. "A Case for (Restructuring) Chiefdom Governance in Post-Conflict Sierra Leone." *African Affairs* 107, no. 428 (2008): 387–403.

Schümer, Tanja. *New Humanitarianism: Britain and Sierra Leone, 1997–2003.* New York: Palgrave Macmillan, 2008.

Shaw, Rosalind. "Memory Frictions: Localizing the Truth and Reconciliation Commission in Sierra Leone." *International Journal of Transitional Justice* 1, no. 2 (2007): 183–207.

Sisk, Timothy D. *Democratization in South Africa: The Elusive Social Contract.* Princeton, NJ: Princeton University Press, 1995.

Smock, David R., and Audrey C. Smock. *The Politics of Pluralism: A Comparative Study of Lebanon and Ghana.* New York: Elsevier, 1975.

Stannus, Hugh S. "Notes on Some Tribes of British Central Africa." *The Journal of the Royal Anthropological Institute of Great Britain and Ireland* 40 (1910): 285–335.

Straus, Scott. *The Order of Genocide: Race, Power, and War in Rwanda.* Ithaca, NY: Cornell University Press, 2013.

Suberu, Rotimi. *Federalism and Ethnic Conflict in Nigeria.* Washington, DC: US Institute of Peace Press, 2001.

Toungara, Jeanne Maddox. "Ethnicity and Political Crisis in Côte d'Ivoire." *Journal of Democracy* 12, no. 3 (2001): 63–72.

Uvin, Peter. "Ethnicity and Power in Burundi and Rwanda: Different Paths to Mass Violence." *Comparative Politics* (1999): 253–271.

Van de Walle, Nicolas. "Africa's Range of Regimes." *Journal of Democracy* 13, no. 2 (2002): 66–80.

Wells, Alan. "The Coup d'Etat in Theory and Practice: Independent Black Africa in the 1960s." *American Journal of Sociology* 79, no. 4 (1974): 871–887.

Wilson, Richard. *The Politics of Truth and Reconciliation in South Africa: Legitimizing the Post-Apartheid State.* New York: Cambridge University Press, 2001.

Wright, Donald R. "What Do You Mean There Were No Tribes in Africa?: Thoughts on Boundaries – and Related Matters – in Precolonial Africa." *History in Africa* 26 (1999): 409–426.

Zack-Williams, Alfred B. "Sierra Leone: The Political Economy of Civil War, 1991–98." *Third World Quarterly* 20 (1999): 143–162.

Zerai, Assata, and Brenda N. Sanya, eds. *Safe Water, Sanitation, and Early Childhood Malnutrition in East Africa: An Africana Feminist Analysis of the Lives of Women in Kenya, Tanzania, and Uganda.* Lanham, MD: Lexington Books, 2018.

Zolberg, Aristide R. "The Structure of Political Conflict in the New States of Tropical Africa." *American Political Science Review* 62, no. 1 (1968): 70–87.

Zolberg, Aristide R. "The Military Decade in Africa." *World Politics* 25, no. 2 (1973): 309–331.

## 2 | THE AFRICAN HUMAN RIGHTS SYSTEM AND THE RIGHT TO AUTONOMY

*Niklas Hultin*

### Introduction

This chapter examines the right to autonomy in Africa. Much of the scholarly discussion of the institutional design of deeply divided, fragile, and/or post-conflict societies focuses on the desirability (or not) of an arrangement that gives a measure of self-government – i.e. autonomy – to specific ethnic groups and how such arrangements can be optimized.[1] The question of whether there is a right to autonomy is a different one, however, and it is an important one for a couple of different reasons. One reason is practical and instrumental – if there is a right established by law, there presumably is a corresponding remedy (whether such a remedy is effective is a different discussion). In other words, if a given group's right to autonomy has been violated, said group – or an organization acting on its behalf – can challenge this violation in a court or equivalent body. A second reason is the signaling effect of legalization – that is, if a principle is encoded in a treaty as a right, it suggests a normative commitment to the realization of that right by parties to that treaty. Even if human rights standards are often decried as ineffectual and honored mostly in their breach, they nonetheless are important signals to domestic state and non-state actors and thereby contribute to the wider socialization of human rights norms.[2] The question of whether there is a right to autonomy in Africa is consequently not only a question of conflict resolution but also a question of conflict prevention.[3] Insofar as a conflict is potentially provoked by ethnic marginalization and discrimination, a successful claim to autonomy may defuse the situation – and, inversely, in such a scenario, a government's denial of autonomy may constitute a human rights violation, further evidence of marginalization, and the exacerbation of the underlying conflict dynamics.

Accordingly, this chapter examines the jurisprudence of the African human rights system, consisting of the African Commission on Human and Peoples' Rights (ACHPR) and the African Court on Human and Peoples' Rights (ACtHPR). As part of the African Union (AU) and the only international human rights tribunals covering virtually all of Africa, including North Africa and the smaller island states, these organizations are the closest thing to an African voice on this matter. Note, however, that the focus on these two organizations is not to suggest that there are no other institutions potentially important to a right to autonomy in Africa. Not only are assorted United Nations (UN) treaties and bodies relevant to the question at hand, but other organs of the AU and various sub-regional organizations (such as the Economic Community of West African States, or ECOWAS) are also becoming increasingly important as human rights actors (see next section). But, up to this point, sub-regional organizations have not made any substantial statements on the right to autonomy or related matters, nor, it should be noted, are their activities applicable beyond a subset of African countries. Furthermore, whether the activities of UN entities give rise to a right of autonomy is a much broader question given the lack of geographic circumscription. While, of course, UN standards do matter to African countries – as will be discussed below – this chapter will limit itself to the African system and therein address whether or not there is a distinctively African contribution to the matter.

One other disclaimer is necessary: this chapter is agnostic on the point of whether a right to autonomy ought to exist. Some critics of territorial autonomy arrangements have argued that it entraps conflict resolution in an impoverished commitment to the "liberal peace" and the juridification of autonomy as a right only exacerbates this entrapment. Marchetti and Tocci, for example, criticize the EU's efforts to resolve the Israel–Palestine conflict as preoccupied with the establishment of Palestinian self-government to the detriment of a commitment to human rights and humanitarian law.[4] This line of criticism echoes both the skepticism, shown by scholars such as Bah and Duffield, among others, toward an interventionist liberal order as well as critiques of multiculturalism and tolerance as intrinsic and incontrovertible goods.[5] Other scholars have pointed to the not inconsiderable practical difficulties of autonomy regimes. For example, autonomy regimes may make regional transactions more difficult and thereby undermine any potential gains for the autonomous group concerned. Moreover, many African ethnic groups are too dispersed geographically to make an ethnically homogenous territorial unit feasible.[6] Autonomy regimes may also lead to discrimination against members of other ethno-religious groups, counteract worthwhile goals of the national government (such as environmental standards or women's rights), and, in extreme cases, entice other countries to intervene to address the situation of their co-ethnies.[7] There is thus reason to be skeptical of the desirability of a blanket, sweeping, right to autonomy.

The chapter proceeds as follows: in the section immediately following this introduction, the African human rights system is introduced within the context of the AU, its other relevant organs (such as the African Peace and Security Architecture), and Africa's sub-regional organizations. This discussion is admittedly brief; its purpose is not to address these latter organizations comprehensively, but rather to highlight how the African human rights system differs from them. In the next section, the concept of autonomy, as it has been discussed by legal scholars, is briefly reviewed, together with the closely linked notion of "self-determination" in international law. Next, the focus is specifically on the African Charter of Human and Peoples' Rights – not only the foundational document of the African human rights system but a treaty very much central to any discussion of peoples' rights. In the following section, the ACHPR's key decisions, in terms of implications for a right to autonomy, will be reviewed. The final section will discuss the only African Court case relevant to the right to autonomy – a case that is widely perceived as a landmark in African human rights jurisprudence and the only sustained discussion of indigenous peoples' rights in the African human rights system. The chapter will conclude that while there is no robust right to autonomy as such, the African human rights system is increasingly embracing the idea that some ethnic groups may be entitled to some form of self-government. The implications of this development are, as we will see, potentially significant but they also open up a new set of questions regarding what groups are covered or not by this embryonic right.

## The African Human Rights System, the AU, and Sub-Regional Organizations

Historically, human rights were of only marginal interest to the Organization for African Unity (OAU), with the exception of the status of refugees, the independence struggles against the remaining colonial governments (in Guinea-Bissau, for example), and the apartheid regime in South Africa (and the white regime in Zimbabwe).[8]

The OAU did establish the ACHPR in 1986, with the coming into force of the African Charter on Human and Peoples' Rights. The ACHPR's beginning was not particularly auspicious as it was widely considered toothless, though, starting in the 1990s, it has made several important contributions to human rights jurisprudence and its decisions carry more and more weight.[9] In 2004, the AU established the ACtHPR to complement and strengthen the African Commission and, as will also be discussed below, it has made a particular contribution to the area of indigenous peoples' rights in Africa.

Beyond these core organizations of the African human rights system, the AU has other constitutive elements potentially relevant to human rights. With the transformation of the OAU into the AU, and the establishment of the New Partnership for Africa's Economic Development (NEPAD), the number of continental institutions that at least on paper focus to some extent on human rights has increased significantly. The AU Constitutive Act affirms its right to intervene in member states in case of war crimes, genocide, and crimes against humanity – though while this is noteworthy in terms of the overall history of liberal interventionism in the human rights world, it does not authorize AU intervention except for in very limited circumstances.[10] The African Peace and Security Architecture (APSA) is the main component of the AU charged with peace and security on the continent and, as such, it in a limited sense complements the African Commission and Court. APSA is not an organization as such but really an umbrella term encompassing several AU institutions, including the Peace and Security Council, the Panel of the Wise, the African Standby Force, the Continental Early Warning System (CEWS), the Peace Fund, and the African Capacity for Immediate Response to Crises. It also covers the sub-regional organizations, referred to as regional economic communities, such as ECOWAS, the Southern African Development Community (SADC), and the Economic Community of Central African States (ECCAS).[11]

It is important to note that the African human rights system and APSA are in practice and conceptually distinct. APSA is aimed at resolving and preventing specific conflicts and not to elaborate justiciable standards. Aspects of APSA that one might expect to be relevant to a discussion of autonomy have a mixed record. For example, insofar as conflicts are caused by ethnic marginalization, one would expect equality, access, and discrimination to be major facets of CEWS, but this is not fully the case.[12] Some research also suggests that APSA is heavily indebted to the OAU/AU legacy of sovereignty and intergovernmental politics, and therein is less well-equipped to address human rights, humanitarian, and post-national challenges.[13] The African Union-hosted African Peer Review Mechanism (APRM), which is intended to assess governance, political stability, and fairness in its member states, with an eye toward effective and equitable development, is similarly hampered by methodological shortcomings that prevent careful scrutiny of the root causes of conflicts.[14] Parts of its ineffectiveness also stem from the fact that many of its members would very much not like to subject themselves to the scrutiny intrinsic to the APRM and due to the absence of effective oversight and follow-up.[15] It is thus no surprise that both the AU and NEPAD have been criticized for missing an opportunity to strengthen human rights on the continent.[16] And while the AU endorsed its Structural Conflict Prevention Framework in 2015, which emphasizes structural factors behind conflicts and their constraints on conflict prevention and resolution, how to address claims of sub-national groups is not a major facet.[17]

Africa's sub-regional organizations have hitherto had little to do with autonomy. ECOWAS is the sub-regional organization that has been most involved in human rights-related matters, not just in terms of military operations in the Mano River region in the 1990s and, most recently, its mission in the Gambia (starting in 2017 and ongoing as of this writing).[18] The ECOWAS Community Court of Justice, though technically not a human rights court, has issued decisions on human rights matters. A notable example is the decision in *Hadijatou Mani Koroua v. Niger*, when it found that Niger had failed to live up to its human rights commitments due to its failure to protect the applicant from slavery.[19] The ECOWAS Court has yet to hear a case pertinent to autonomy, however. The other sub-regional organizations have been even less relevant to the topic at hand. While both IGAD (Intergovernmental Authority on Development) and SADC have played important conflict resolution and peacebuilding roles in the Horn and in Southern Africa, respectively, they have not been effective standard-setters for institutional design in divided societies. In fact, in 2011 the heads of state of SADC dissolved the SADC Tribunal after the latter had found Zimbabwe's land seizure program to be a human rights violation.[20]

A reasonable assessment is thus that, at the present time, the only regional or sub-regional institution that has gestured in the direction of establishing a potential right to autonomy is the African human rights system. Of course, this is in part due to the nature of human rights law – by its very definition it is standard setting in a way that a policy-focused organization need not be. There is also no specific reason to think that ECOWAS or another organization will not be more important to autonomy-related issues in the future. However, given present-day circumstances and that the goal of this chapter is to ascertain whether there is an incipient right to autonomy in Africa, the African Commission and Court on Human and Peoples' Rights is where the investigation needs to focus.

## Autonomy and Self-Determination

In brief, the concept of autonomy refers to the idea that a group recognized as distinct, typically along ethnic or religious lines, should have a measure of self-government in its affairs but not to a point where it could leave (or secede from) the greater polity of which it is part. More succinctly, Hurst Hannum refers to autonomy as the "right to be different and to be left alone."[21] Autonomy as a concept is usually subdivided into a number of different varieties. Although the vocabulary differs among authors – for instance, Hannum distinguishes between political and personal autonomy, while Kymlicka refers to territorial and non-territorial forms of autonomy, and Ghai contrasts "corporate" and "territorial" autonomy – there nonetheless is broad agreement that there is a difference between autonomy invested in a particular geographical territory and autonomy invested in a particular social group.[22] Territorial autonomy is when a given territory is granted self-government (falling short of independence). This self-government can be broad or limited to a specific issue such as education. Whatever its scope, it would theoretically apply to everyone in that territorial unit, regardless of an individual's ethnic, religious, or other background. Typically, such an arrangement would be enshrined in the country's constitution. A distinction can further be made between an arrangement whereby every constituent territory of a state has the same kind and degree of autonomy (i.e. a federal system), and an arrangement where a subset of constituent entities has powers of self-governing not given to otherwise equivalent units in the polity. While discussions of autonomy typically focus on the latter arrangement, the former, strictly speaking, is a form of autonomy as well.[23] In most cases of territorial autonomy, the territory is an island or somehow geographically separated from the rest of the policy, though that is not always the case.[24]

The second type of autonomy is cultural autonomy, which stipulates that a given group should be given self-government in specific domains of activity, irrespective of territory. A country could, say, give a religious minority self-government in matters of marriage and inheritance. This is common practice in many African countries with significant Muslim populations, such as Nigeria, where a legacy of European colonialism is the, as An-Na'im puts it, "codification of Shari'a principles" in specific domains of life (inheritance and family law) and, as a consequence, the separation of Islam from "official political authority."[25] It should be noted that cultural autonomy is distinct from non-discrimination. The latter simply requires a state (or perhaps a private party) not to discriminate (on the basis of religion, ethnicity, etc.), while the former requires a state to accept that some activities of a given group are essentially off-limits to state intervention and regulation. Historically and conceptually, non-discrimination rests on the individualism of classic liberalism whereas autonomy (cultural or territorial) is indebted to liberal pluralism. The latter holds that the protection and promotion of (some forms of) ethno-religious diversity is in itself a public good.[26] To classic liberalism, this position is a fraught one as it potentially exacerbates ethno-religious tension by accentuating (and preserving) differences – indeed, the relative silence on minority rights (beyond non-discrimination) in the international human rights community until very recently is in no small part attributable to this skepticism.[27] At any rate, with these two broad categories of autonomy, it is possible to envision multiple, overlapping, and nesting arrangements. For instance, it is conceptually possible for a group to have cultural autonomy within a territorial autonomy arrangement.

Although autonomy emerged as a central theme in the human rights literature in the 1990s, the idea has a deeper history. Legal scholars such as Thomas Musgrave, for example, have discussed it as something of an offshoot of the right to self-determination in international law.[28] The antecedents of contemporary autonomy discussions can thus be found in efforts such as WWI-era discussions of self-determination and minority rights. While a detailed discussion of the right to self-determination is beyond the scope of this chapter, a brief overview is necessary. Simplifying somewhat, conceptually and historically, self-determination comes in two different forms – one internal, referring to system of government, and one external, referring to territory.[29] These two views have different origins, the former in the nationalism of Eastern Europe as well as the anti-colonial struggles of the twentieth century, and the latter in notions of popular sovereignty and democracy emphasized in the United States and Western Europe.

The internal notion of self-determination appears in the UN Charter as well as the Atlantic Charter in the form of "self-government." Subsequent developments in the UN system enshrined this notion of self-government in the context of trusteeship. The UN's Committee on Information from Non-Self-Governing Territories defined "internal self-government" in terms of an indigenous government of some sort, effective public participation in government (without a foreign government's interference) and a "[d]egree of autonomy in respect of economic, social and cultural affairs."[30] In 1959, another General Assembly committee reevaluated self-government, and asserted the following two conditions: free association with a state, including "the freedom to modify the status of that Territory through the expression of their will by democratic means and through constitutional processes," and the "right to determine its internal constitution without outside interference."[31] This is also the meaning of self-determination as enshrined in the International Covenant on Civil and Political Rights and the International Covenant on Economic, Social and Cultural Rights. Autonomy is very much consistent with public participation and self-government – i.e. internal self-determination – but public participation and self-government does not, it seems, require autonomy. The right to internal self-determination only permits autonomy; it does not require a government to grant a specific form of internal self-determination to a group, i.e. to let the group "declare what type of protection it seeks."[32]

The external variety of self-determination was forcefully developed in a couple of landmark General Assembly resolutions. The Declaration on the Granting of Independence to Colonial Countries and Peoples, passed by the General Assembly in December of 1960, established that the unit of external self-determination is not a people, but a colonial territory.[33] Paragraph 6 of that declaration unambiguously states that "[a]ny attempt aimed at the partial or total disruption of the national unity and the territorial integrity of a country is incompatible with the purposes and principles of the Charter of the United Nations."[34] The principle of external self-determination in colonial cases was subsequently confirmed by the International Court of Justice in the Namibia Case, the Western Sahara Case as well as in the East Timor Case (*Portugal v. Australia*). In the Western Sahara Case, the Court re-affirmed the importance of internal self-determination, suggesting that "the application of the right of self-determination requires a free and genuine expression of the will of the people."[35] The subsequent Declaration on Principles of International Law concerning Friendly Relations and Co-operation among States in accordance with the Charter of the United Nations extended self-determination beyond the colonial context by making clear that subjugation occurs in any context of alien domination (e.g. military invasion). In effect, this declaration linked together both the internal and external forms of self-determination. As summed up by Special Rapporteur Asbjørn Eide: if a "[g]overnment does not allow all segments and all peoples to participate, the question of the right to self-determination of the different components becomes more pertinent."[36] This understanding of self-determination gained additional purchase with the violence in former Yugoslavia in the 1990s as well as through the Vienna Declaration on Human Rights.[37]

A second set of issues with a hypothetical right to autonomy, which it would inherit, so to speak, from the right to self-determination is the "groupness" of the putative subject of autonomy, stemming from the recognition that individual rights as envisioned by classical liberalism are insufficient to address the grievances and concerns of groups. That is, there has to be a collective viewed as sufficiently discrete and different from the rest of the country (or larger unit) to merit what in essence is special treatment. International law gives us several different labels to capture such "groupness": "people," "minority" (or "national minority"), and "indigenous people." Each of these terms have different implications for the right to autonomy and needs to be discussed. Murray and Wheatley, for example, suggest that "indigenous people" can "make claims for territorial self-government" while "minorities" (or "national minorities") "make claims for cultural security" (which could be interpreted as linked to cultural autonomy).[38]

In international law, "people" is typically associated with the already discussed right to self-determination. "People" here is not synonymous with ethnic group but rather refers to a narrower set of populations. According to Cassese's analysis of the International Covenant on Civil and Political Rights, these are: "(1) entire populations living in independent and sovereign states, (2) entire populations of territories that have yet to attain independence, and (3) populations living under foreign military occupation."[39] The word "entire" is significant as it does not countenance the possibility that a segment of a territory's population could be classified as a "people." An ethnic group, say, could thus not be a "people" unless it is coterminous with the population of an already existing state or meet either of the other two criteria – a determination of which is largely a political question rather than a legal one, as evidenced by the number of cases of groups that have failed to secure widespread acceptance of its self-determination claims (e.g. the inhabitants of the Casamançe, Senegal, or the Kurds of Turkey, Iraq, and Syria). Bracketing off situations of colonial domination or military occupation, self-determination is transformed into a prescription for the domestic political arrangement – in essence, Cassese's first variety of a people's right to self-determination means freedom from an authoritarian government. It is also clear, Cassese argues, that ethnic minorities are not covered by the right to self-determination, suggesting, somewhat counterintuitively, that a minority is not a "people."

Indeed, that a "minority" is something other than a "people" is widely recognized in international law. The post-WWI minority treaties regime that sought to protect the rights of European minorities was premised precisely on this idea that, since minorities are not "peoples," they should not be entitled to self-determination (again, where a group falls on the "minority"/"people" divide is more of a political than a legal question). The term "national minority" is used, principally in the European context, to differentiate minority groups that exhibit a lot of the characteristics of a "people" from minorities defined solely by religion or ethnicity ("ethnic minority" and "religious minority" are thus used differently than "national minority," though the dividing lines are not entirely clear).[40] A minority's right to not be discriminated against is widely recognized in international law; Article 2 of the African Charter on Human and Peoples' Rights, for example, states that the enumerated rights must be enjoyed equally by all without distinction based on ethnicity, religion, etc. But note that the African Charter does not use the term minority as such and there is no African document specifically on "minorities" – in contrast to the European human rights system where the Framework Convention for the Protection of National Minorities sets out, not without controversy, a series of political and cultural rights. It also, like virtually all human rights treaties, includes an explicit prohibition on secession and other violations of the territorial integrity of signatory states. This lack of a specific mention of minorities in the African Charter – which then also means the lack of an explicit contrast between "peoples" and "minorities" – muddies the analytical waters somewhat and suggests the possibility that "minorities," in the African context, may in fact be "peoples."

The distinction between people and minority is furthermore important because a determination of peoplehood can be interpreted as a challenge to the state concerned, especially insofar as the former may suggest a right to self-determination and the latter is conceptually and symbolically tied to ethnicity.[41] The language of minority status does not challenge this tie in a fundamental way as a minority is by definition something other than a people. That is, a recognition of a group as a minority does not in and of itself challenge the state of which it is a part (except in terms of invalidating any claims to homogeneity) as it signals a measure of acceptance of a difference not irredeemably at odds with national membership. In contrast, the recognition of a group as a people implies something beyond mere minority status, perhaps a sort of nation-in-waiting status. The classification of a group as a people, however, is only to a limited extent a legal one and is largely a political and a "branding" one.[42] The concerned state, for its part and assuming it objects to letting the given ethnic group or territory go, has an interest in making sure that such claims to peoplehood are not considered valid by the international community and that the ethnic group is in fact a minority.

The term "indigenous peoples" is both narrower (in scope) and broader (in terms of legal rights accruing to this kind of subject) than minority. Much work has been done at the UN level to codify indigenous people's rights, culminating in the (non-binding) United Nations Declaration on the Rights of Indigenous Peoples. It incorporates in its Article 4 the right to autonomy as part of indigenous peoples' right to self-determination. In the vote to adopt this declaration, no African country voted against it (only Australia, Canada, New Zealand, and the USA did) but the continent's response was not unambiguously in favor of this document as Burundi, Kenya, and Nigeria abstained and many African countries were absent.[43] The resolution also does not define the term indigenous. Indeed, in the African context, governments have been reluctant to embrace the concept of indigeneity for a few different reasons. One is that the definition of the term indigenous is often used to refer to a country's population that existed prior to colonization, which would make just about all Africans indigenous (and if every African is indigenous, carving out a special set of rights for a subset of the population does not make a lot of sense). Another reason is the worry that the terminology of indigeneity, with its connotation of autochthony and "being first," might encourage ethnic tension or "tribalism."[44] Nonetheless, the term indigenous has gradually become a key part of the African human rights landscape, largely due to the work of the ACHPR and the activism of specific African groups such as the Maasai as well as "northern" NGOs. The understanding of indigeneity that has thus developed prioritizes geographical isolation, marginalization, subsistence strategy, and self-identification over a history of colonial occupation as such.[45] Note that this is not a strict definition and, as we will see, the African Commission has wrestled with the applicability of the indigenous peoples label to specific groups. From this point of view, any African group that has a distinct mode of life (especially insofar as this mode is tied to the land), compared to that of other groups in the same country and with a history of marginalization may, in a sense, be eligible for indigenous status.

In sum, two general conclusions can be drawn from this thumbnail sketch of the right to autonomy in international law: Firstly, in a general sense, autonomy is a permitted (but not required) arrangement consistent with the right to self-determination. Secondly, a presumptive right to autonomy in Africa must include three elements: firstly, there must be a recognition of groupness and, relatedly, some way to claim such groupness over the objections of the affected state (that is, a state cannot claim that group X really isn't a group). Secondly, the group must be viewed as of the right "kind" to have this right – if the African human rights system establishes that "people" have a right to autonomy but is very restrictive in the applicability of that term, the right might, in practicality, be meaningless. Thirdly, there must be a recognition that such groups can demand self-government in either a specific territory or in a specific social domain and, once again, this demand must be able to overcome state objections. As we will see, the African human rights system is not yet fully recognizing these three elements though it is trending in that direction.

## The African Commission, Self-Determination, and the Meaning of "Peoples"

The ACHPR permits individuals and NGOs to bring complaints of violations of the Banjul Charter by state parties (which includes all countries in Africa except for Morocco – although with Morocco re-joining the AU in 2017, this might change in the near future). The ACHPR also conducts fact-finding missions, reviews periodic reports, and engages in other promotional and protective activities. The ACtHPR was established by the AU as a more robust supplement to the ACHPR, addressing, among other things, the weak enforcement powers of the ACHPR.[46] For example, the ACtHPR has discretionary jurisdiction over alleged violations of all human rights treaties ratified by a state party, not only the African Charter.[47] By default, however, the ACtHPR does not allow individuals and NGOs to submit claims. For that to be allowed, the state concerned must have declared the competency of the court to hear such claims. As of May 2017, about a quarter of the thirty African states who have ratified the Protocol to the African Charter on Human and Peoples' Rights on the Establishment of an African Court on Human and Peoples' Rights have issued such a declaration.[48]

From its inception, the African human rights system was intended to encode an understanding of human rights somewhat different from human rights as embodied in the UN system and the European human rights system. This strived-for difference is manifested, on paper at least, in a few different ways. The African Charter and related documents, such as the African Charter on the Rights and Welfare of the Child (ACRWC), make multiple references to African values, civilization, and traditions. Legal scholars have also pointed to features such as the emphasis on amicable resolution as the embodiment of if not an "African" approach to human rights at least a different approach to human rights.[49] For present purposes, the key difference between the Banjul Charter and other treaties is the inclusion of a range of "peoples' rights." These rights are to be found in Articles 19 through 24 of the Banjul Charter. They are often discussed as collective rights, solidarity rights, or as third generation rights (assuming that civil and political rights are the first generation and socio-economic rights the second generation). Article 19 asserts the equality of all people; Article 20 asserts that "all people shall have the right to existence"; Article 21 asserts that people have right to their natural resources; Article 22 asserts that peoples have the right to their own cultural development and a right to development; Article 23 asserts that all peoples have the right to "national and international peace and security"; and Article 24 asserts that all people have a right to a "satisfactory environment." In addition to these provisions, the African Charter also contains a series of individual civil and political rights – the prohibition of discrimination (Article 2), the assertion of equality before the law (Article 3), freedom of religion (Article 8), and so on – that may have an indirect impact on the right to autonomy (see discussion below).

But what does the ACHPR mean by "people"? As we have seen, how this term, and related ones, are operationalized is absolutely fundamental to the question of a right to autonomy. Unfortunately, this operationalization is not entirely clear as the Charter deliberately does not define "people," nor does it, taken on its own, mention minorities nor indigenous peoples. Richard Kiwanuka, one of the earliest scholars examining this issue, showed that "people" can mean different things depending on which specific Article is being referenced – "people" can refer to groups in a country yet to achieve independence (with the implication that once independence has been achieved, those groups cease to be "peoples" under the Banjul Charter, which would be consistent with the "people" in the right to self-determination), but "people" can also be viewed as synonymous with "minority," as practically the same as "the state," or as a general descriptor for all the individuals within a state.[50] Each of these interpretations is hugely significant for how we think of a right to autonomy. If "people" is limited to essentially colonial situations, then there would be very few territories – in sub-Saharan Africa and elsewhere – where the term could be meaningfully applied (Polisario might claim that it applies to Western Sahara, for example). As discussed below, subsequent jurisprudential developments at the African Commission also suggest that this interpretation is overly restrictive. If "people" is treated as synonymous with minority, then every single minority group in a sub-Saharan country could theoretically claim to have the rights enumerated in these articles, which if nothing else would have considerable practical implications. If "people" is treated as synonymous with the state, the contents of "peoples' rights" are effectively eviscerated as rights are claims against the state. And, finally, if "people" is considered merely an aggregate of all individuals in the state, then distinguishing peoples' rights from individual human rights makes little sense other than as an expression of popular sovereignty – which would be consistent with the approach frequently taken in the African Commission's jurisprudence (see below).

A related concern is the nature and extent of self-determination as envisioned by the Banjul Charter. As discussed above, the idea of a right to self-determination has been historically controversial. The African Charter does address self-determination, but in a way that largely puts the focus on the external form of self-determination. Article 20 reads, in its entirety:

1. All peoples shall have the right to existence. They shall have the unquestionable and inalienable right to self-determination. They shall freely determine their political status and shall pursue their economic and social development according to the policy they have freely chosen.
2. Colonised or oppressed peoples shall have the right to free themselves from the bonds of domination by resorting to any means recognised by the international community.
3. All peoples shall have the right to the assistance of the States parties to the present Charter in their liberation struggle against foreign domination, be it political, economic or cultural.

This Article is thus unclear not just in reference to who can claim a right under this article – what is a people – but also what the resulting political arrangement might look like. Taken at face value, the African Charter is thus home to a great deal of ambiguity on autonomy. Fortunately, through its jurisprudence, the African Commission has refined its understanding of people as well as self-determination.

### The African Commission's Case Law on the Right to Autonomy

The African Commission has only heard a handful of communications (the technical term for a case at the ACHPR since, strictly speaking, the ACHPR is not intended as a legal, adversarial, court) relevant to group rights generally and the right to autonomy specifically. Agbakwa's complaint that the African Commission has mostly focused on first-generation civil and political rights remains true to this day.[51] The findings here can largely be divided into two analytical categories: (a) the scope of "people," or, can a sub-national group be classified as a "people"; and (b) do the articles of the Charters give right to autonomy? The answer to the first question is "yes," while the answer to the second question appears to be a qualified "no" in that a right to autonomy as such is not specified, but autonomy is one of several possible arrangements to address a peoples' right to self-determination.

In a general sense, the African Commission has repeatedly argued that a country cannot impose a religion or political system on its citizens. In a series of communications against Sudan, for example, the Commission held that the application of Shari'a must not infringe on the rights of others.[52] More importantly for present purposes, the ACHPR has held that Article 13 – which holds that "[e]very citizen shall have the right to participate freely in the government of his country, either directly or through freely chosen representatives in accordance with the provisions of the law" – in conjunction with Article 20 (the right to self-determination and to determine one's "political status"), means that citizens should be able to determine who governs them.[53] These findings, however, operate firmly with an understanding of "people" as that of all citizens of a country – Nigerians, Gambians, and so on. This is consistent with Kiwanuka's fourth kind of "people," discussed above. In other words, these decisions do not suggest that a sub-national group can claim rights under Article 20 (never mind demanding an autonomy arrangement).

In one of the first major cases concerning Articles 13 and 20, the African Commission had the opportunity to further refine its thinking on the issue of self-determination and peoples' rights. In 75/92 *Katangese Peoples' Congress v. Zaire*, decided in 1995, the ACHPR held:

> In the absence of concrete evidence of violations of human rights to the point that the territorial integrity of Zaire should be called into question and in the absence of evidence that the people of Katanga are denied the right to participate in government as guaranteed by Article 13(1) of the African Charter, the Commission holds the view that Katanga is obliged to exercise a variant of self-determination that is compatible with the sovereignty and territorial integrity of Zaire.[54]

This paragraph is important for three reasons: firstly, it raises the possibility that the Katanga are a people, thus broadening this term's scope to cover sub-national populations, and, secondly, it implies that something along the links of an autonomy regime – as a "variant of self-determination" – is allowable, though not required, under the

Banjul Charter.[55] Thirdly, it confirms the widely held principle that the bar to break away from a state – to violate the territorial integrity of a state – is very high indeed.

In another relatively early case, *155/96 The Social and Economic Rights (SERAC) and the Center for Economic and Social Rights (CESR) v. Nigeria* (decided in 2001), the African Commission held that Nigeria had violated Articles 21 and 24 of the Banjul Charter. Although these are "peoples' rights," the ACHPR did not explicitly address whether or not the Ogoni are in fact a people. Nonetheless, this decision is widely taken as an indication that at least some sub-national groups in Africa can meet the criteria of "people." According to Nwobike, the fact that the Commission even considered the communication, "put beyond question the competence of a group to seek the protection and enforcement of rights."[56] As Murray and Wheatley point out, the ACHPR's phrasing in this decision is also significant. The Commission eschews referring to the Ogoni as a minority or ethnic group, but simply a "people" or in phrases like "the people of Ogoniland."[57] It is worth noting, however, that the Ogoni as a group might be a bit of a special case as they, more so than many other African groups with the possible exception of groups like Maasai, San, and Herero, have been able to assert themselves as substantially distinct from the nation-state in which they reside and not just a "mere" minority. This distinctiveness is the outcome of an aforementioned political branding process and, unlike, say, the San, not the result of a different subsistence strategy.[58]

The Katanga decision has also been re-affirmed and developed. In *266/03 Kevin Mgwanga Gunme et al. v. Cameroon* (decided in 2009), the Commission confirmed that Article 20 does not mean an endorsement of secession but rather envisions alternative forms of self-determination, including autonomy:

> The African Charter cannot be invoked by a Complainant to threaten the sovereignty and territorial integrity of a State party. The Commission has however accepted that autonomy within a sovereign state, in the context of self-government, confederacy, or federation, while preserving territorial integrity of a State party, can be exercised under the Charter.[59]

The Commission also clarified the meaning of people. In brief, the applicant alleged numerous rights violations, including violations of Articles 19, 20, 21, 22, 23.1, and 24. Cameroon responded that the Southern Cameroonians did not have these rights as they are not a people. Cameroon argued that there is no "ethno-anthropological argument" in favor or classifying Southern Cameroonians as a people and that, at any rate, there has been a "remarkable rapprochement at the administrative and legal levels" to the effect that Southern Cameroonians cannot be considered a people distinct from non-Southern Cameroonians.[60] ACHPR rejected this claim and found that Southern Cameroonians are in fact a people because they share "a common history, linguistic tradition, territorial connection, and political outlook ... [They also] identify themselves as a people with a separate and distinct identity. Identity is an innate characteristic within a people. It is up to other external people to recognise such existence, but not to deny it."[61] There are two key implications of this claim: firstly, ethnic distinctions are not required to be a "people," suggesting in turn that an ethnic minority is something different than a people. Secondly, self-identification is re-asserted as primary, suggesting, in a sense, that the burden of proof is on the state alleging that a group is not a people, rather than the other way around.

The Commission did in the end reject the claims of violations of the above articles, which further helps clarify when a right to autonomy might be triggered: first, in its discussion of its rejection of Article 22 violation claims, the African Commission argued that in a developing country, such as Cameroon, the allocation of resources "may not reach all parts of its territory to the satisfaction of all individuals and peoples, hence generating grievances. This alone cannot be a basis for the finding of a violation."[62] Second, in its rejection of the Article 19 and 20 claims, the African Commission re-affirmed that proof of "massive violations of human rights under the charter" are required to trigger the right to self-determination and that

> various forms of self-government ... must take into account the popular will of the entire population [of the state], exercised though democratic means, such as by way of a referendum or other means of creating a national consensus. Such forms of governance cannot be imposed by a state party or a people by the African Commission.[63]

In a different communication, decided in 2015 and brought against Côte d'Ivoire and concerning this country's restrictive laws on citizenship, the ACHPR implied that an ethnic group can be a "people" under the African Charter. The African Commission first held that the

Dioula's are an ethnic group that is an "integral and definitive part of the formation of the Ivorian ethno-cultural landscape."[64] In other words, even if, per *266/03 Kevin Mgwanga Gunme et al. v. Cameroon*, an ethnic identity is not necessary to count as a "people," it is one avenue thereto. Furthermore, the African Commission argued that the individual impact of a rights violation can lead to a violation of a group's rights. Focusing on the alleged violation of Article 22 (right to economic, social, and cultural development – the applicant did not allege violations of any other people's rights), the ACHPR drew on the Inter-American Court of Human Rights' reasoning in *Loyza Tamayo v. Peru* and established that Côte d'Ivoire's failure to recognize Dioulas as citizens negatively impacted an individual's "life plan" which, in turn, led to a "serious violation of the right to development under the provisions of Article 22."[65] The Commission's reasoning was that Côte d'Ivoire's failure to recognize Dioulas as citizens "hinder[ed] every possibility with them to decide with other Ivorians choices relating to the destiny of the Ivorian nation."[66]

In three recent cases the African Commission went further in the direction of a right to autonomy than it has previously done. In *328/06 Font for the Liberation of the State of Cabinda v. Republic of Angola* (decided in 2013), the applicant alleged numerous violations of the Charter, namely Articles 14, 19, 20, 21, 22, and 24. Unlike in the Katanga case, the applicants emphasized in their submission that their desire was "economic self-determination" and not political self-determination of the sort that would threaten the territorial integrity of the state.[67] The applicant also argued that "the people of Cabinda are geographically, politically, linguistically and culturally distinct from Angolans" and that they therefore qualify as a people under Article 20 of the Charter.[68] In response, Angola used an interpretation of Article 20's right to self-determination curtailing it to colonial situations: it submitted that the people of Angola, including the minority in Cabinda, had exercised their right to self-determination upon Angola's independence.[69]

The African Commission found that none of the alleged violations had in fact occurred, but in reaching these findings, several clarifications were made. Firstly, in its consideration of Article 14, it drew a distinction between indigenous peoples and other ethnic minorities, suggesting that a group having a pre-colonial history independent of the country of which it is a part is not sufficient "to sustain a claim for special protection of a distinctive overriding communal right to property under the Charter."[70] In order to qualify as indigenous, the Cabinda would have to claim "strong attachment to their land and their culture." While this finding concerns Article 14, it does suggest a distinction between indigenous people and people, with the former being a narrower version of the latter.

Secondly, the Commission also affirmed that "peoples" in the Charter is in fact sub-national groups but that the fact that a group might be a people may not be sufficient to claim certain rights under the Charter. In case of Article 19, the Commission held that:

> distinct and identifiable groups of "peoples" and communities
> exist within the State Parties to the African Charter and each set of
> "peoples" and communities is entitled to enjoy internal legal equality
> vis-a-vis other "peoples" and communities within the same state. The
> Commission notes that a claim of unequal treatment in violation of
> Article 19 of the Charter requires evidence that a given group or set of
> peoples who is in a position similar to another group or set of people
> has been or is being treated differently or that a given group or set of
> peoples who is in a position different to another group or set of people
> is treated similarly such that the "peoples" complaining suffer unfair
> and unjustifiable disadvantage that amounts to discrimination.[71]

In other words, if this line of reasoning extends to other peoples' rights in the Charter – and the Southern Cameroon case previously discussed suggests that it can – it follows that only people who are treated worse than otherwise equivalent peoples within the same state may claim, say, to exercise its right to self-determination and to freely determine its political status under Article 20.

Finally, the ACHPR once again re-affirmed that self-determination does not lead to a right to violate the sovereignty and territorial integrity of states and that "the right to pursue economic and social development is attainable within the framework of an existing state insofar as different groups and communities are represented in decision-making institutions of the given state."[72]

That sub-national populations can in fact be peoples and that the self-identification criterion is essential was also affirmed by the African Commission in two cases brought against Sudan regarding the conflict in Darfur: *279/03-296/05 Sudan Human Rights Organisation & Centre on Housing Rights and Evictions (COHRE) v. Sudan* (decided in 2009). The applicants alleged numerous violations of the Banjul

Charter, including Article 22. In addressing this allegation, the Commission offered an extended commentary on the meaning of "peoples" in the Banjul Charter, before finding that Sudan had in fact violated this right.

Firstly, the African Commission recognized that the meaning of "peoples" is unsettled – that "jurisprudence in that area is still very fluid."[73] Secondly, while the African Commission listed several attributes that can be used to identify a people (territory, religion, language, etc.), it viewed "the principle of self-identification" as essential.[74] Importantly, the African Commission also argued that in its consideration of the meaning of the term, "it is making a contribution to Africa's acceptance of diversity."[75] This, the African Commission suggested, is in explicit contrast to the "school of thought ... which believes that 'the right of a people' in Africa can be asserted only vis-à-vis external aggression, oppression or colonization."[76]

The final case of note at the African Commission is the Endorois case brought against Kenya in 2003 and decided in 2009. Because this case proceeded to the African Court on Human and Peoples' Rights, it will be discussed in the next section. Before this case is discussed, however, it is appropriate to take stock of the African Commission's jurisprudence to date (save for the Endorois case). Based on this jurisprudence, we can draw two general conclusions:

Firstly, the African Commission has generally broadened the scope of "peoples" both in the sense of allowing that sub-national groups can be peoples and in the sense of the kinds of characteristics that can define a people. In the Cameroon case, it rejected the need for a common ethnic identity specifically and highlighted other points of distinction, including language and political tradition. The outer limits of peoplehood remain somewhat fuzzy, however. That is, would it be sufficient to refer to only one of the criteria listed for Southern Cameroonians? Or are there some criteria that are necessary but not sufficient? Clearly, it is hard to imagine that the African Commission would recognize self-identification as sufficient for peoplehood in the absence of all other possible criteria (e.g. language, subsistence strategy, territorial connection, and so on), but it is nonetheless the case that in its current form the African Commission's jurisprudence is relatively open-ended on this point.

Secondly, it is clear that an autonomy arrangement is a permissible way to satisfy Article 20, but it comes with at least two and possibly three caveats: (a) the arrangement must be established through democratic means, such as a referendum. It cannot be imposed on a people, nor can a sub-national people be granted this arrangement without all citizens of the country concerned being consulted; it is not sufficient to have a referendum, say, in the autonomous-to-be region. To put this in concrete terms, if, say, the San of Botswana were to be given autonomy, not only would the San have to assent to the term, but every citizen of Botswana must have had a say in the matter through the appropriate democratic means. (b) If the findings in the Cabinda case vis-à-vis Article 19 are extrapolated to the other "peoples' rights" in the Banjul Charter, such an arrangement – as one of several possible ways to fulfill the internal right to self-determination – can only be required if the would-be autonomous people are treated differently, in a negative fashion, than otherwise equivalent people. (c) Much of the clarification of the meaning of "people" has hitherto not occurred with explicit reference to Article 20, but to other articles (e.g. Article 22). The assumption herein is that the African Commission is intending a consistent usage of the term with no slippage between articles. This assumption would be supported by the African Commission's statement in the Endorois case (discussed in the next section): "The African Charter in Articles 20 through 24 clearly provides for peoples to retain the rights as peoples, that is, as collectives."[77]

### Indigenous Peoples and the Contribution of the African Court: The Endorois and the Ogiek Cases

The African Court's record on autonomy-related issues is even thinner than that of the African Commission, which is not surprising given its relative youth. It has considered many fewer cases than the African Commission and the vast majority of these cases have not made it past the admissibility stage. But it has considered the issue of indigenous peoples' rights in Kenya, in *2006/2012 African Commission on Human and Peoples' Rights v. Kenya*. This decision largely follows the logic in the earlier referenced African Commission communication, *276/03 Centre for Minority Rights Development (Kenya) and Minority Rights Group (on behalf of Endorois Welfare Council) v. Kenya*. Taken together, these two cases against Kenya constitute the African human rights systems' jurisprudence on indigenous peoples.[78] For present purposes, this jurisprudence has a twofold importance: first, in that it unequivocally asserts the saliency of indigenous peoples' rights – and thus, the concept of indigeneity or indigenous peoples – on the African content. Second, in that it clarifies how indigenous peoples are presumed to be distinct from non-indigenous people (who are still "people").

In 276/03, the African Commission examined the eviction of the Endorois ethnic group by the Kenyan government so that the latter could establish a game reserve. The Commission concluded that the Endorois did meet the criteria of "people" (Kenya had alleged that they did not) and in doing so articulated an understanding of indigenous that prioritized self-identification and a connection between land, culture, and peoplehood over a temporal definition of indigenous as a people inhabiting an area prior to colonialism.[79]

In reaching this conclusion, the African Commission had to engage with the definition of indigenous peoples. Here it drew on the works of its Working Group of Experts on Indigenous Populations/ Communities in asserting four criteria identifying indigenous peoples. These four criteria are: "occupation and use of a specific territory; the voluntary perpetuation of cultural distinctiveness, self-identification as a distinct collectivity, as well as a recognition by other groups; an experience of subjugation, marginalization, dispossession, exclusion or discrimination."[80] It further noted that all African groups (hitherto) recognized as indigenous are hunter-gatherers or pastoralists and that "a key characteristic for most of them is that the survival of their particular way of life depends on access and rights to their traditional land and the natural resources thereon."[81] In other words, the ACHPR concluded, "all attempts to define the concept of indigenous peoples recognize the linkages between peoples, their land, and culture."[82] Taking the above into consideration as well as case law on indigenous peoples from the Inter-American Court on Human Rights, the African Commission concluded:

> [It] is satisfied that the Endorois are a "people," a status that entitles them to benefit from provisions of the African Charter that protect collective rights. The African Commission is of the view that the alleged violations of the African Charter are those that go to the heart of indigenous rights – the right to preserve one's identity through identification with ancestral lands.[83]

The shift from people to indigenous is probably significant here. Throughout the text of the decision, the African Commission is referring to the Endorois as a "people" that has certain rights accruing to "indigenous people." In other words, "indigenous people" appears to be a subset of "people." From the foregoing, and viewed in conjunction with the decisions discussed in the previous cases, two conclusions can be drawn in terms of differentiating the two from each other.

First, marginalization and discrimination are key. Recalling the Southern Cameroons decision, in which the African Commission did not find a violation because of a lack of evidence of marginalization but nonetheless asserted that the Southern Cameroonians are a people for purposes of the African Charter, it appears that marginalization is not a necessary condition of a people (just for claiming rights violations), but it is a necessary condition of indigeneity.

Second, while the African Commission does allow for the possibility that, in the future, indigenous peoples may not be pastoralists or hunter-gatherers, what anthropologists refer to as subsistence strategy and ties to the land appear to be essential to indigeneity (as opposed to "people"). In other words, it appears that the African Commission holds that an indigenous people are a marginalized people with a distinct relationship to the land.

The African Court took a similar approach in *2006/2012 African Commission on Human and Peoples' Rights v. Kenya*. This case was brought to the Court by the African Commission in 2009 after Kenya refused to abide by a provisional order and decided in May of 2017. The circumstances in this case were broadly similar to the Endorois case. According to the Court itself, the central question was whether or not the Ogiek are an indigenous people or not. The applicants argued that the Ogiek are an indigenous people for two reasons (a) they have lived in the Mau Forest "for generations since time immemorial" and (b) "their way of life and survival as a hunter-gatherer community is inextricably linked to the forest which is their ancestral land."[84] The government of Kenya responded to this claim by saying that the Ogiek (a) "are not a distinct ethnic group but rather a mixture of various ethnic communities" and (b) "the Ogieks of today … [have] adapted themselves to modern life and are currently like all other Kenyans."[85]

Like the Endorois, the Ogiek have a long history of marginalization first under the British and later by Kenya and a persistent reluctance by the authorities to recognize the Ogiek as a distinct group. During the colonial era, they were not recognized as a "tribe" because of their geographic dispersion and their sharing a language with neighboring groups. As a result, the Ogiek were frequently lumped together with the

Kalenjin. However, as Lynch points out, many Ogiek have a "historical narrative" of hunting-gathering, suggesting a contrast with the Kalenjin, whose identity largely rests on a pastoral tradition.[86] Nonetheless, during the twentieth century the Ogiek's identity was consistently denied by first the British and later the Kenyan government. In the 1930s the Ogiek were evicted from their traditional homeland in the Mau Forest by the British and subsequent decisions by Kenyan courts confirmed that the Ogiek had no particular rights to the Mau forest.

The African Court found that the Ogiek met the criteria of indigenous people as outlined above, and concluded that the Ogiek are an "indigenous population that is part of the Kenyan people having a particular status."[87] Furthermore, in deliberating on the alleged violation of Article 21, the African Court re-visited the meaning of "people" in the Charter and affirmed that "people" "can be extended to include sub-state ethnic groups ... provided such groups or communities do not call into question the sovereignty and territorial integrity of the State without the latter's consent."[88]

It needs to be noted that Article 20 of the Charter, which arguably is the provision most pertinent to a right to autonomy, was not an issue in either of these cases. However, the ACHPR and ACtHPR did assert the importance of an indigenous people having (a) a right to culture and (b) a say in its development. On the former of these points, the African Court noted in its discussion of the alleged violation of Article 17 (right to education and cultural life):

> [t]he protection of the right to culture goes beyond the duty, not to destroy or deliberately weaken minority groups, but requires respect for, and protection of, their cultural heritage essential to the group's identity. In this respect, culture should be construed in its widest sense encompassing the total way of life of a particular group, including the group's languages, symbols such as dressing codes and the manner the group constructs shelters; engaging in certain economic activities; produces items for survival; rituals such as the group's particular way of dealing with problems and practicing spiritual ceremonies; identification and veneration of its own heroes or models and shared values of its members which reflect is distinctive character and personality.[89]

While this statement does not go quite as far as, nor is as succinct as, Hannum's definition of autonomy as the right to be left alone, it seems that cultural autonomy would be consistent with the state's duty to protect cultural heritage from unwanted interference (that is, unwanted by the people concerned). Indeed, it seems difficult to devise an approach to cultural rights that does not approach cultural autonomy. It is also worth noting that there is nothing in the decision that limits this interpretation of Article 17 to indigenous peoples specifically (this is in contrast to the ACtHPR's discussion of Article 14, or the right to property[90]). It therefore seems to apply to people writ large.

Furthermore, in the Endorois case, the African Commission asserted that the right to development (Article 22) has a procedural and substantive dimension. The procedural dimension means that there can be no pressure or coercion on the Endorois to "buy into" a Kenyan development plan. While the ACHPR and the ACtHPR do not explicitly endorse self-government in the area of development, it seems like a meaningful choice (the procedural dimension) would permit, though not require, some form of autonomy.[91]

The African human rights system's treatment of indigenous peoples, as seen in these two cases, helps flesh out the nature and scope of peoples' rights as discussed in the previous section. For the indigenous subset of people, the African human rights system is more explicit on the non-interfering and protective stance required by a state in certain areas. The African human rights system does not carve out a distinct set of rights specific to indigenous peoples, but rather calls for extra scrutiny of how the existing rights are applied in such contexts.

## Conclusion

In its 30 year existence, the African human rights system has developed a robust jurisprudence in several areas. From this review of its cases, it is clear that it has definitively moved away from an understanding of the right to self-determination as only accruing to colonized populations, for example. But has the African Commission and the African Court created a right to autonomy, be it territorial or cultural?

For the time being, it appears that the answer must be no. There is nothing in the African Commission's jurisprudence that stipulates that territorial autonomy is the required way to address peoples' rights violations. It is, however, a *permissible* way to address these violations. A somewhat more affirmative conclusion can be drawn for cultural autonomy. While, as of yet, there does not appear to be a requirement that a country grants a population cultural autonomy, it does seem that the African Court's findings in the Ogiek's case would go some way in that direction in that it is difficult to envision a non-cultural autonomy approach to cultural rights as defined in the decision.

Other issues remain. For one thing, the African human rights system has broadened the conception of a "people" to a point where a very large number of African groups could conceivably be a people and, given the multi-ethnic composition of virtually all African states, does the African Commission point us in the direction of a future Africa consisting of a patchwork of autonomies within the confines of the current political boundaries? It seems like such a future is theoretically possible but practically unlikely, for three reasons. First is the above caveat that autonomy is a permitted, not required, solution to a peoples' rights violation. Second, such a solution should only be triggered in cases of unequal upholding of rights between the different constituent peoples of a nation. Third, any attempt to establish autonomy would have to be reached through democratic means, meaning that the entire population of Nigeria, say, would have to agree to grant autonomy to the Ogoni (to use an example).

Relatedly, the difference between peoples and indigenous peoples remains somewhat unclear, especially given that the African Commission has held out the possibility that subsistence strategy may not be a key differentiator in the future. Absent this differentiator, it seems like marginalization and inequality are the key differentiators, which would be logically odd. Following the reasoning in the Southern Cameroons case, would the same situation that would give rise to an Article 20 (for instance) violation then also make a people "indigenous"? It is certainly possible that the African Commission would fall back on an element of temporality to avoid such a conclusion, but this speculation nonetheless points to an enduring ambiguity in the assertion of peoples' rights in the African Charter.

## Notes

1 E.g. Horowitz, "Conciliatory Institutions and Constitutional Processes in Post-Conflict States"; Nagle and Clancy, "Constructing a Shared Public Identity in Ethno Nationally Divided Societies"; Simonsen, "Addressing Ethnic Divisions in Post-Conflict Institution- Building"; Wolff, "Post-Conflict State Building."

2 See, for example, Hathaway, "Why Do Countries Commit to Human Rights Treaties"; Risse, Ropp and Sikkink, *The Persistent Power of Human Rights*; Simmons, *Mobilizing for Human Rights*.

3  For example, Nigerian federalism and state creation can be viewed as a not entirely successful effort to use autonomy to prevent conflict (federalism can be viewed as a form of autonomy – see below). See, e.g. Suberu, *Federalism and Ethnic Conflict in Nigeria*.

4  Marchetti and Tocci, "Trapped in the Liberal Peace." Of course, the establishment of a Palestinian state is *not* an example of an autonomy arrangement – but their point is a stand in for a larger one about the attractions of a conflict resolution mechanism premised on specific identitarian politics.

5  On the former point, see Bah, "Introduction"; Duffield, "Social Reconstruction and the Radicalization of Development." On the latter, see Brown, *Regulating Aversion*.

6  Mozaffar and Scarritt, "Why Territorial Autonomy Is Not a Viable Option"; Christin and Hug, "Federalism, the Geographic Location of Groups, and Conflict."

7  Lapidoth, *Autonomy*, 203.

8  See, generally, Murray, *Human Rights in Africa*.

9  Viljoen evocatively describes this transition as growing from "a cat into a lion." See Viljoen, "From a Cat into a Lion?"

10  Warner, "The African Union and Article 4(h)," 183.

11  For a concise overview, see, e.g., Lins de Albuquerque, *The African Peace and Security Architecture (APSA)*.

12  Nathan, "Africa's Early Warning System."

13  Brosig, "The African Peace and Security Architecture and Its Partners," 231.

14  Gruzd, "Peace, Security and the African Peer Review Mechanism."

15  See, for example, Bond, "Removing Neocolonialism's APRM Mask."

16  Manby, "The African Union, NEPAD, and Human Rights."

17  See African Union, *Continental Structural Conflict Prevention Framework*.

18  See Abbas, "The New Collective Security Mechanism of ECOWAS"; Hartmann, "ECOWAS and the Restoration of Democracy in the Gambia."

19  Duffy, "*Hadijatou Mani Koroua v Niger*: Slavery Unveiled by the ECOWAS Court." See, generally, Alter et al., "A New International Human Rights Court for West Africa."

20  See, for example, Nathan, "The Disbanding of the SADC Tribunal."

21  Hannum, *Autonomy, Sovereignty, and Self-Determination*, 4.

22  Ibid.; Kymlicka, "National Cultural Autonomy and International Minority Rights Norms"; Yash Ghai, "Ethnicity and Autonomy." For the sake of simplicity, the terms used herein are "territorial" and "cultural" autonomy.

23  Kymlicka distinguishes between "generic" and "targeted" minority rights for this reason. See Kymlicka, "National Cultural Autonomy and International Minority Rights Norms."

24  One estimate suggests that 75 percent of all autonomous territories in the world are islands. See Ackrén and Olausson, "Condition(s) for Island Autonomy."

25  An-Na'im, *African Constitutionalism and the Role of Islam*, 116.

26  See, for example, Deets and Stroschein, "Dilemmas of Autonomy and Liberal Pluralism"; Kymlicka, *Multicultural Citizenship*.

27  See Hannum, *Autonomy, Sovereignty, and Self-Determination*, 51–73.

28  Musgrave, *Self-Determination and National Minorities*, 208.

29  The literature on self-determination is voluminous. Useful

primers are Cassese, *Self-Determination of Peoples*; Hannum, *Autonomy, Sovereignty, and Self-Determination*; Musgrave, *Self-Determination and National Minorities*; Shaw, *Title to Territory in Africa*.

30  Quoted in Sohn, "Models of Autonomy within the United Nations Framework," 18.

31  Ibid., 21–22.

32  Cassese, *Self-Determination of Peoples*, 352.

33  Shaw notes, however, that the declaration is in fact inconsistent with the UN Charter. For instance, the former's assertion that "the subjection of peoples to alien subjugation, domination and exploitation ... is contrary to the Charter of the United Nations," is in contrast to the inclusion of the trust territory system set up in the latter document. See Shaw, *Title to Territory in Africa*, 77.

34  Quoted in Cassese, *Self-Determination of Peoples*, 72.

35  Quoted in ibid., 88.

36  Quoted in Akhavan, "Self-Determination and the Disintegration of Yugoslavia," 240.

37  See, e.g., Eastwood, "Secession."

38  Murray and Wheatley, "Groups and the African Charter on Human and Peoples' Rights," 219.

39  Cassese, *Self-Determination of Peoples*, 59.

40  See Jackson Preece, *National Minorities and the European Nation-States System*; Musgrave, *Self-Determination and National Minorities*.

41  Nimni, "Nationalism, Ethnicity and Self-Determination."

42  See, e.g., Clifford, *The Marketing of Rebellion*; Lynch, "Kenya's New Indigenes."

43  Chad, Côte d'Ivoire, Equatorial Guinea, Eritrea, Ethiopia, The Gambia, Guinea Bissau, Mauritania, Morocco, Rwanda, São Tomé and Principe, Seychelles, Somalia, Togo, and Uganda were the absent countries.

44  Hodgson, "Becoming Indigenous in Africa." Indeed, the conflict in Côte d'Ivoire illustrates how arguments about autochthony have spurred conflict. See, for example, Bah, "Democracy and Civil War."

45  For a summary of this work, see Murray, "Developments in the African Human Rights System 2003–04." See also Lynch, "Kenya's New Indigenes."

46  Nmehielle, "Toward an African Court of Human Rights." For a more skeptical view, also see: Bekker, "The African Court on Human and Peoples' Rights."

47  Eno, "The Jurisdiction of the African Court on Human and Peoples' Rights." This is important to the present issue if, hypothetically, an African country ratifies a UN treaty that establishes a right to autonomy.

48  The eight countries that have made such a declaration are Benin, Burkina Faso, Côte d'Ivoire, Ghana, Mali, Malawi, Tanzania, and Tunisia. See: http://en.african-court.org/ (accessed May 26, 2017).

49  Kiwanuka, "The Meaning of 'People' in the African Charter on Human and Peoples' Rights"; Murray, *The African Commission on Human and People's Rights and International Law*. On the ACRWC, see Kaime, "The Foundations of Rights in the African Charter on the Rights and Welfare of the Child."

50  Kiwanuka, "The Meaning of 'People' in the African Charter on Human and Peoples' Rights."

51  Agbakwa, "Reclaiming Humanity."

52  *48/90, 50/91, 52/91, and 89/93 Amnesty International, Comité Loosli Bachelard, Lawyers' Committee for Human Rights, Association of Members of the Episcopal Conference of East Africa v. Sudan.*

53  *102/93 Constitutional Rights Project and Civil Liberties Organisation*

*v. Nigeria.* The wording is significant in that the ACHPR states that "Nigerians" (not "people") have this right. The ACHPR has similarly held that military coups are a violation of Article 20. See *147/95 and 149/96 Sir Dawda K Jawara v. The Gambia.*

54   *75/92 Katangese Peoples Congress v. Zaire,* para. 6.

55   See Murray and Wheatley, "Groups and the African Charter on Human and Peoples' Rights," 18–19. It is worth noting that there is scholarly disagreement whether or not the ACHPR here suggests that it might, potentially, accept a right to secession. Okafor argues "there appears to be a point at which the behaviour of an African state towards its constituent groups will enable the ACHPR to call the state's territorial integrity in question" (Okafor, *Re-Defining Legitimate Statehood,* 148), while Pityana, a former member of the African Commission, disagrees: "the African Commission is not ready to interpret the provisions of the [Banjul] Charter in a fashion that embraces the secessionist sentiment in parts of the continent" (Pityana, "The Challenge of Culture for Human Rights in Africa," 233).

56   Nwobike, "The African Commission on Human and Peoples' Rights and the Demystification of Second and Third Generation Rights under the African Charter," 140.

57   Murray and Wheatley, "Groups and the African Charter on Human and Peoples' Rights," 227. It is also possible that this is just the result of inconsistent writing. In *318/06 Open Society Justice Initiative v. Côte d'Ivoire,* for example, the Commission switches between referring to the Dioulas as an "ethnic group" and a "people." In fact, only once in the text of decision does the ACHPR refer to the "Ogoni people" (other than when it refers to the claims of the applicant) and twice as "people of Ogoniland"). See *155/96 The Social and Economic Rights (SERAC) and*

the Center for Economic and Social Rights (CESR) v. Nigeria, paras. 62, 69.

58   Clifford, *The Marketing of Rebellion.*

59   *266/03 Kevin Mgwanga Gunme et al. v. Cameroon,* para. 191.

60   Ibid., para. 168.

61   Ibid., para. 178.

62   Ibid., para. 206.

63   Ibid., para. 199.

64   *318/06 Open Society Justice Initiative v. Côte d'Ivoire,* para. 104.

65   Ibid., para. 186.

66   Ibid., para. 185.

67   *328/06 Front for the Liberation of the State of Cabinda v. Angola,* para. 54.

68   Ibid., para. 62.

69   Ibid., para. 71.

70   Ibid., para. 106.

71   Ibid., para. 114.

72   Ibid., para. 126.

73   *279/03-296/05 Sudan Human Rights Organisation & Centre on Housing Rights and Evictions (COHRE) v. Sudan,* para. 220.

74   Ibid.

75   Ibid.

76   Ibid., para. 222.

77   *276/03 Centre for Minority Rights Development (Kenya) and Minority Rights Group (on behalf of Endorois Welfare Council) v. Kenya.* Curiously, the African Commission quotes its decision in the Ogoni case, though this sentence does not actually appear in the latter.

78   It is also one of the few cases that have been referred to the ACtHPR by the African Commission, suggesting that the former could serve as an "enforcer" of the latter's decisions. See Murray and Long, *The Implementation of the Findings of the African Commission on Human and Peoples' Rights,* 148–61.

79   Ashamu, "*Centre for Minority Rights Development (Kenya) and Minority Rights Group International on Behalf of Endorois Welfare Council v Kenya*: A Landmark Decision from the African Commission.*"

80 *276/03 Centre for Minority Rights Development (Kenya) and Minority Rights Group (on behalf of Endorois Welfare Council) v. Kenya*, para. 150.

81 Ibid.

82 Ibid., para. 151.

83 Ibid., para. 162.

84 *2006/2012 African Commission on Human and Peoples' Rights v. Kenya*, para. 103.

85 Ibid., para. 104.

86 See, e.g., Lynch, "The Wars of Who Belongs Where."

87 *2006/2012 African Commission on Human and Peoples' Rights v. Kenya*, para. 112.

88 Ibid., paras. 198–99.

89 Ibid., para. 179.

90 See Ashamu, "*Centre for Minority Rights Development (Kenya) and Minority Rights Group International on Behalf of Endorois Welfare Council v Kenya*: A Landmark Decision from the African Commission," 307–09.

91 *276/03 Centre for Minority Rights Development (Kenya) and Minority Rights Group (on behalf of Endorois Welfare Council) v. Kenya*, paras. 277–79. See also extensive discussion of this finding in Ashamu.

## References

Abbas, Ademola. "The New Collective Security Mechanism of ECOWAS: Innovations and Problems." *Journal of Conflict and Security Law* 5, no. 2 (2000): 211–229.

Ackrén, Maria and Pär Olausson. "Condition(s) for Island Autonomy." *International Journal on Minority and Group Rights* 15, no. 2 (2008): 227–258.

African Union. *Continental Structural Conflict Prevention Framework: Country Structural Vulnerability and Resilience Assessments (CSVRAs), and Country Structural Vulnerability Mitigation Strategies (CSVMS).* Addis Ababa, Ethiopia: African Union, n.d.

Agbakwa, Shedrack C. "Reclaiming Humanity: Economic, Social, and Cultural Rights as the Cornerstone of African Human Rights." *Yale Human Rights & Development Law Journal* 5, no. 1 (2002): 177–216.

Akhavan, Payam. "Self-Determination and the Disintegration of Yugoslavia: What Lessons for the International Community," pp. 227–248, in *Self-Determination: International Perspectives*, edited by Donald Clark and Robert Williamson. New York: St. Martin's Press, 1996.

Alter, Karen J., Laurence R. Helfer and Jacqueline R. McAllister. "A New International Human Rights Court for West Africa: The ECOWAS Community Court of Justice." *American Journal of International Law* 107, no. 4 (2013): 737–779.

An-Na'im, Abdullahi Ahmed. *African Constitutionalism and the Role of Islam.* Philadelphia, PA: University of Pennsylvania Press, 2010.

Ashamu, Elizabeth. "*Centre for Minority Rights Development (Kenya) and Minority Rights Group International on Behalf of Endorois Welfare Council v Kenya*: A Landmark Decision from the African Commission." *Journal of African Law* 55, no. 2 (2011): 300–313.

Bah, Abu Bakarr. "Democracy and Civil War: Citizenship and Peacemaking in Côte d'Ivoire." *African Affairs* 109, no. 437 (2010): 597–615.

Bah, Abu Bakarr. "Introduction: The Conundrums of Global

Liberal Governance," pp. 1–25, in *International Security and Peacebuilding: Africa, the Middle East, and Europe*, edited by Abu Bakarr Bah. Bloomington, IN: Indiana University Press, 2017.

Bekker, Gina. "The African Court on Human and Peoples' Rights: Safeguarding the Interests of African States." *Journal of African Law* 51, no. 1 (2007): 151–172.

Bond, Patrick. "Removing Neocolonialism's APRM Mask: A Critique of the African Peer Review Mechanism." *Review of African Political Economy* 36, no. 122 (2009): 595–603.

Brosig, Malte. "The African Peace and Security Architecture and Its Partners." *African Security Review* 23, no. 3 (2014): 225–242.

Brown, Wendy. *Regulating Aversion: Tolerance in the Age of Identity and Empire*. Princeton, NJ: Princeton University Press, 2008.

Cassese, Antonio. *Self-Determination of Peoples: A Legal Reappraisal*. New York: Cambridge University Press, 1995.

Christin, Thomas and Simon Hug. "Federalism, the Geographic Location of Groups, and Conflict." *Conflict Management and Peace Science* 29, no. 1 (2012): 93–122.

Clifford, Bob. *The Marketing of Rebellion: Insurgents, Media, and International Activism*. New York: Cambridge University Press, 2009.

Deets, Stephen and Sherrill Stroschein. "Dilemmas of Autonomy and Liberal Pluralism: Examples Involving Hungarians in Central Europe." *Nations and Nationalism* 11, no. 2 (2005): 285–305.

Duffield, Mark. "Social Reconstruction and the Radicalization of Development: Aid as a Relation of Global Liberal Governance."

*Development and Change* 33, no. 5 (2002): 1049–1071.

Duffy, Helen. "*Hadijatou Mani Koroua v Niger*: Slavery Unveiled by the ECOWAS Court." *Human Rights Law Review* 9, no. 1 (2009): 1–20.

Eastwood, Lawrence S., Jr. "Secession: State Practice and International Law after the Dissolution of the Soviet Union and Yugoslavia." *Duke Journal of Comparative and International Law* 3, no. 2 (1993): 299–349.

Eno, Robert Wundeh. "The Jurisdiction of the African Court on Human and Peoples' Rights." *African Human Rights Law Journal* 2, no. 2 (2002): 223–33.

Ghai, Yash. "Ethnicity and Autonomy: A Framework for Analysis," pp. 1–26, in *Autonomy and Ethnicity: Negotiating Competing Claims in Multi-Ethnic States*, edited by Yash Ghai. New York: Cambridge University Press, 2000.

Gruzd, Steven. "Peace, Security and the African Peer Review Mechanism: Are the Tools Up to the Task?" *African Security Review* 16, no. 3 (2007): 53–66.

Hannum, Hurst. *Autonomy, Sovereignty, and Self-Determination: The Accommodation of Conflicting Rights*. Philadelphia, PA: University of Pennsylvania Press, 1996.

Hartmann, Christof. "ECOWAS and the Restoration of Democracy in the Gambia." *Africa Spectrum* 52, no. 1 (2017): 85–99.

Hathaway, Oona A. "Why Do Countries Commit to Human Rights Treaties." *Journal of Conflict Resolution* 51, no. 4 (2007): 588–621.

Hodgson, Dorothy L. "Becoming Indigenous in Africa." *African Studies Review* 52, no. 3 (2008): 1–32.

Horowitz, Donald L. "Conciliatory Institutions and Constitutional Processes in Post-Conflict States."

*William & Mary Law Review* 49, no. 4 (2008): 1213–1248.

Jackson Preece, Jennifer. *National Minorities and the European Nation-States System.* Oxford: Clarendon Press, 1998.

Kaime, Thoko. "The Foundations of Rights in the African Charter on the Rights and Welfare of the Child: A Historical and Philosophical Account." *African Journal of Legal Studies* 3, no. 1 (2009): 120–136.

Kiwanuka, Richard N. "The Meaning of 'People' in the African Charter on Human and Peoples' Rights." *American Journal of International Law* 82, no. 1 (1988): 80–101.

Kymlicka, Will. *Multicultural Citizenship: A Liberal Theory of Minority Rights.* Oxford: Clarendon Press, 1996.

Kymlicka, Will. "National Cultural Autonomy and International Minority Rights Norms." *Ethnopolitics* 6, no. 3 (2007): 379–93.

Lapidoth, Ruth. *Autonomy: Flexible Solutions to Ethnic Conflicts.* Washington, DC: United States Institute of Peace Press, 1997.

Lins de Albuquerque, Adriana. *The African Peace and Security Architecture (APSA): Discussing the Remaining Challenges.* Stockholm, Sweden: FOI, 2016.

Lynch, Gabrielle. "Kenya's New Indigenes: Negotiating Local Identities in a Global Context." *Nations and Nationalism* 17, no. 1 (2011): 148–167.

Lynch, Gabrielle. "The Wars of Who Belongs Where: The Unstable Politics of Autochthony on Kenya's Mt Elgon." *Ethnopolitics* 10, no. 3–4 (2011): 391–410.

Manby, Bronwen. "The African Union, NEPAD, and Human Rights: The Missing Agenda." *Human Rights Quarterly* 26, no. 4 (2004): 983–1027.

Marchetti, Raffaele and Nathalie Tocci. "Trapped in the Liberal Peace: The EU's Approach to Peacebuilding Via Civil Society," pp. 169–197, in *International Approaches to Governing Ethnic Diversity*, edited by Jane Boulden and Will Kymlicka. Oxford: Oxford University Press, 2015.

Mozaffar, Shaheen and James R. Scarritt. "Why Territorial Autonomy Is Not a Viable Option for Managing Ethnic Conflict in African Plural Societies," pp. 230–253, in *Identity and Territorial Autonomy in Plural Societies*, edited by William Safran and Ramón Máiz. London: Frank Cass, 2000.

Murray, Rachel. *The African Commission on Human and People's Rights and International Law.* Oxford: Hart Publishing, 2000.

Murray, Rachel. *Human Rights in Africa: From the OAU to the African Union.* New York: Cambridge University Press, 2004.

Murray, Rachel. "Developments in the African Human Rights System 2003–04." *Human Rights Law Review* 6, no. 1 (2006): 160–175.

Murray, Rachel and Debra Long. *The Implementation of the Findings of the African Commission on Human and Peoples' Rights.* New York: Cambridge University Press, 2015.

Murray, Rachel and Steven Wheatley. "Groups and the African Charter on Human and Peoples' Rights." *Human Rights Quarterly* 25, no. 1 (2003): 213–236.

Musgrave, Thomas D. *Self-Determination and National Minorities.* Oxford: Clarendon Press, 2000.

Nagle, John and Mary-Alice Clancy. "Constructing a Shared Public Identity in Ethno Nationally Divided Societies: Comparing Consociational and Transformationist Perspectives." *Nations and Nationalism* 18, no. 1 (2012): 78–97.

Nathan, Laurie. "Africa's Early Warning System: An Emperor with No Clothes."

*South African Journal of International Affairs* 14, no. 1 (2007): 49–60.

Nathan, Laurie. "The Disbanding of the SADC Tribunal: A Cautionary Tale." *Human Rights Quarterly* 35, no. 4 (2013): 870–892.

Nimni, Ephraim. "Nationalism, Ethnicity and Self-Determination: A Paradigm Shift?" *Studies in Ethnicity and Nationalism* 9, no. 2 (2009): 319–332.

Nmehielle, Vincent O. Orlu. "Toward an African Court of Human Rights: Structuring and the Court." *Annual Survey of International and Comparative Law* 6, no. 1 (2000): article 4.

Nwobike, Justice C. "The African Commission on Human and Peoples' Rights and the Demystification of Second and Third Generation Rights under the African Charter: *Social and Economic Rights Action Center (SERAC) and the Center for Economic and Social Rights (CESR) v. Nigeria.*" *African Journal of Legal Studies* 1, no. 2 (2005): 129–146.

Okafor, Obiora Chinedu. *Re-defining Legitimate Statehood: International Law and State Fragmentation in Africa.* The Hague: Martinus Nijhoff, 2000.

Pityana, Barney N. "The Challenge of Culture for Human Rights in Africa: The African Charter in Comparative Perspective," pp. 219–245, in *The African Charter on Human and Peoples' Rights: The System in Practice, 1986–2000,* edited by Malcolm D. Evans and Rachel Murray. Cambridge: Cambridge University Press, 2002.

Risse, Thomas, Stephen C. Ropp and Kathryn Sikkink (eds.). *The Persistent Power of Human Rights: From Commitment to Compliance.* New York: Cambridge University Press, 2013.

Shaw, Michael. *Title to Territory in Africa: International Legal Issues.* Oxford: Clarendon Press, 1986.

Simmons, Beth A. *Mobilizing for Human Rights: International Law in Domestic Politics.* New York: Cambridge University Press, 2009.

Simonsen, Sven Gunnar. "Addressing Ethnic Divisions in Post-Conflict Institution-Building: Lessons from Recent Cases." *Security Dialogue* 36, no. 3 (2005): 297–318.

Sohn, Louis B. "Models of Autonomy within the United Nations Framework," pp. 5–22, in *Models of Autonomy,* edited by Yoram Dinstein. New Brunswick, NJ: Transaction Books, 1981.

Suberu, Rotimi T. *Federalism and Ethnic Conflict in Nigeria.* Washington, DC: United States Institute of Peace Press, 2001.

Viljoen, Frans. "From a Cat into a Lion? An Overview of the Progress and Challenges of the African Human Rights System at the African Commission's 25 Year Mark." *Law Democracy & Development* 17 (2013): 298–316.

Warner, Jason. "The African Union and Article 4(h): Understanding Changing Norms of Sovereignty and Intervention in Africa through an Integrated Levels-of-Analysis Approach," pp. 167–204, in *Democracy, Constitutionalism, and Politics in Africa,* edited by Eunice N. Sahle. New York: Palgrave Macmillan, 2017.

Wolff, Stefan. "Post-Conflict State Building: The Debate on Institutional Choice." *Third World Quarterly* 32, no. 10 (2011): 1777–1802.

# 3 | DEMOCRACY, POSTWAR TRANSITION, AND PEACEBUILDING IN MUSIC VIDEOS FROM UGANDA

*Okaka Opio Dokotum*

## Introduction

Music videos are audiovisualized poems that articulate the social circumstances of the community and these include the relationship with state and power. Evaluation or critique and praise of democratic and state institutions provide raw material for some of these music videos that in turn provide feedbacks to the power structures of society which are necessary for the reform of those same institutions. These artists cannot avoid ideological entanglement because the challenges in their world demand response that involves taking ideological positions. David Tetzlaff asserts of MTV music videos that, "Pleasure can never be free of ideology, for it can never be totally free of meaning. Fascination represses the signified in favor of the play of signifiers, but it can never eliminate the signified completely. In fact, affective response is heavily dependent on certain meaningful associations."[1] The voiceless in society rely on the artists to articulate their concerns but there can also be a compromise reciprocal celebrity relationship between the artists and the state that champions the idea of peace without questioning the role of the state in undermining peace. It has been argued by some that artists rule the world through the soft power of art. Renowned British poet Percy Bysshe Shelley observed in his famous essay, "A Defence of Poetry" that poets are not just the authors of literature, music, dance, statuary, architecture, and painting, but that they are actually, "the institutors of laws, and the founders of civil society, and the inventors of the arts of life, and the teachers, who draw into a certain propinquity with the beautiful and the true."[2] He argues that in earlier times poets were referred to either as legislators or prophets but that they actually unite both offices. This gives poets the ability to see beyond ordinary men and to legislate through their artistic works. Shelley concludes his essay with these famous lines:

Poets are the hierophants of an unapprehended inspiration; the mirrors of the gigantic shadows which futurity casts upon the present; the words which express what they understand not; the trumpets which sing to battle, and feel not what they inspire; the influence which is moved not, but moves. *Poets are the unacknowledged legislators of the world* [my emphasis].[3]

Poets not only mirror the present, but through their art provide the social, political and cultural barometer that registers shifts in the social and cultural fabric of society and predict the future. They participate in critiquing and improving democratic and cultural power structures. Ugandan poet Okot p'Bitek builds on Shelley's point when he observes that the artist is "the ruler" who "provides and sustains the fundamental ideas, the foundations of society."[4] The artist uses the soft power of art to legislate, unlike the hard oppressive power wielded by politicians. Kenyan author Ngugi wa Thiong'o also weighs in saying that the artists and the politician are products of their social conditioning; that they "trade in words" and address the problems of society.[5] These authors articulate the view that artists are directly engaged in governance through the praise or critique of power systems and structures that call for accountability.

It is important to provide a quick historical overview of conflicts in Uganda as a backdrop to the complexities of post-memory and post-conflict institutional responses to the overwhelming residual political, economic, and psychosocial burdens of the war and its afterlives. Uganda has a history of conflict that stretches back to the 1960s.[6] First were the harbingers of post-independence disillusionment and the clash between powerful age-old cultural institutions – especially the Buganda Kingdom, the biggest of them all – and the new, independent, Western-style postcolonial democratic institution led by the first President of the Republic of Uganda Apollo Milton Obote. The clash led to the storming of the palace of the Kabaka of Buganda by the Uganda Army under the army Commander, Colonel Idi Amin. This event ushered in the abolition of kingdoms in Uganda in 1966. This was followed by the violent military coup of 1971 when General Idi Amin overthrew the elected government of President Apollo Milton Obote. Amin's eight-year dictatorship saw gross violations of human rights on a scale unknown before, and the collapse of economic and social infrastructures as well as basic amenities. The 1979 liberation war also led to massive loss of lives and eventual revenge killings meted on Amin's henchmen by exile returnees. A new scale of massacres and atrocities was reached with the Luwero Triangle war between Yoweri Museveni's National Resistance Army (NRA) rebels and the then Uganda People's Congress (UPC) government of Apollo Milton Obote. Mass graves in Luwero today attest to the traumatic impact of the five-year war which Museveni won in 1986, ushering him into power for decades. But all this would pale in comparison to the devastation, mayhem, and monstrosity of Joseph Kony's Lord's Resistance Army (LRA) war of the late 1980s to 2006. The LRA abducted tens of thousands of children and forced them to commit unspeakable atrocities, conducted epic massacres that are monumentalized in the mass graves and cenotaphs of Atiak, Abia, Amononeno, Barlonyo, and Lokodo in northern Uganda among others. They raped, mutilated their victims, and killed with wicked and unimaginable novelty. The LRA wiped out the populations of entire villages and set their homesteads on fire. The LRA insurgency begun in the Acholi sub-region and the bulk of LRA abductees were Acholi and the neighboring Lango tribe which also suffered the brunt of the LRA war in almost equal measure. Joseph Kony is himself an Acholi from Odek in Gulu District. Contemporary music videos from northern Uganda are in many ways extended discourses on these atrocities and their traumatic post-memory.

In this chapter, I also examine the contributions of Ugandan artists Lucky Bosmic Otim and Master Loketto Lee from northern Uganda, and Robert Kyagulanyi Ssentamu aka Bobi Wine from the south, on the country's effort to promote peace and democracy. Bosmic Otim tends to disarticulate from the political establishment through music activism while Loketto Lee oscillates between the extremes of articulating pro-establishment patronage and meta-anarchism; Robert Kyagalunyi Ssentamu aka Bobi Wine on the other hand takes a post-structuralist position that Emma Mahony calls "interstitial distance," a "disarticulation" from political identification.[7] Kyagulanyi is an award-winning self-styled President of the Ghetto Republic, alluding to his humble rise from a Kampala ghetto to become "one of the most intelligent and most popular musicians."[8] In an effort to remain apolitical, Kyagalunyi finds himself neither here nor there, producing politically apolitical "music that speaks about the many social injustices in Uganda."[9] While he critiques the status quo, he does not necessarily identify openly with opposition parties through his songs and actions.

I examine the 2016 post-election song, "Situka" ["Rise Up"], which though expressing oppositional sentiments, tends to mobilize the fans to shake up the frustrations of the election results that did not favor the opposition and to move on. Kyagalunyi's non-partisan activism consolidated by his election as Member of Parliament of Uganda on an Independent ticket in July 2017 has already provoked heated debates about the divisionary nature of multiparty politics and its focus on the parties and party leaders rather than on the electorate. He is championing reform that takes power away from the center and gives it back to the electorate directly without party mediation.

This chapter also examines how the LRA violence has been captured in contemporary music videos by northern Ugandan artists, represented here by Bosmic Otim and Loketto Lee, where the atrocities are aestheticized as social commentary and entertainment. The music videos record, interrogate, and problematize the war and its aftermath through a delirious aesthetic that tries to make sense of the senseless. The songs also highlight rebel and police brutality calling for reform in the police forces and for electoral reform and peaceful transition of power which is considered the bedrock of political stability. The audiologovisualized song videos become "witnesses" to trauma and avenues for cathartic resolution and restoration.[10] However, democracy is also undermined in some of the videos through celebrity political patronage and the culture of reciprocal tokenism and appeasement as dictated by the political economy of artistic survival. This chapter further examines how democracy is exercised and asserted in northern Uganda through poetic memorialization and critique of the democratic institutions, government agencies, and individuals in power in order to promote democracy, peace building, justice, and human dignity in the decade of postwar transition and reconstruction. The chapter examines this phenomenon through selected music videos from Uganda and how the traumatic experiences are revisited, exposed, analyzed, managed, contested, and even transformed into a celebration of human dignity in light of democracy and human rights. These videos tackle the right to protection of lives and property, the right to education, freedom of the press, and freedom of assembly.

## Theorizing Trauma

Ugandan art generally, and song videos in particular, have become the interactive museum built with bricks of words, sounds, and images, and plastered with pain but painted in beautiful colors of entertainment. It is in this medium that atrocities are recalled, witnessed, and testified to and traumatic history contextualized, interpreted, and contested. It is also through music that democratic processes and institutions are held accountable. In his review of *World Memory: Personal Trajectories in Global Time*, Sam Durrant highlights two kinds of memory. The first is "deep memory," which refers to the "experiences that become 'sedimented into the body'." These are "metaphorical and literal scars" branded on the victims of violence making them living archives and monuments of pain. These scars become transpersonal experiences that amount to collective cultural trauma and affect an entire community or nation. The second form of memory is "common memory," which according to Heidi Grunebaum and Yazir Henri "resides in the intellect, in thought, and in language" as opposed to residing in the physical body.[11] While deep memory is a "non-narratological record of the individual's experience"[12] common memory is found in the national narratives to which poetry belongs. Music videos from northern Uganda become the record of both "deep memory" as a witness of physical and emotional violence meted out to individuals, and "common memory" as the multidisciplinary granary of history that music videos represent, and provide a forum for contextualization and contestation. The music videos are also platforms for resistance to injustice and human rights abuses, and a forum for asserting human dignity. Music is an important avenue for witnessing and dialoguing on the history of Uganda, and realizing psychological and emotional healing; the challenge is how to handle the subject with reverence for the dead and the traumatized. Music videos are especially equipped to distance the reader/viewer from the experience through entertaining techniques while at the same time providing a cathartic escape from negative emotions and rallying the community towards reconciliation. Music videos provide the aesthetic forum for celebrating Ugandan history while highlighting the traumatic fault lines, provoking national debate, celebrating the victims of individual, state-inspired, rebel-induced, and other complex forms of violence. Because of the disruptive nature of trauma, it is inexpressible, but audiologovisualized poetry in the form of music videos uses techniques of distancing, such as euphemisms, irony, satire, denotation, and personification to approach discordant and dissociative subject matter that would be too raw for realism. As Gill Rye observes, "fiction is able to represent what 'cannot be represented by conventional historical, cultural and autobiographical narratives'" and it does this through "mimicking the 'symptomatology' of trauma, by means of 'recurring literary techniques and devices,' such as fragmentation, ellipses, repetition, recurring motifs, tropes etc."[13] As Laury Ocen observes:

> War monuments re-imagine communities in which they are located, in that the memories they create shape particular consciousness on the subject of war, transition, and reform. Through different forms of memorialization such as commemoration, anniversaries, museumization, cultural and artistic performances which are done at memorial sites, these monuments recreate sites, attract interventions, and generate new narratives of wars and life beyond such wars.[14]

As "portable monuments," to borrow Ann Rigney's terminology for literature and its role in shaping cultural memory, music videos participate in democratic debate about war and postwar transition and reform and supports, evaluates and critiques democratic institutions and agencies.[15]

## Textual Analysis of Song Videos

It is important to examine selected song videos from Uganda to establish how the art informs people's understanding and experience of democracy and postwar institutional reforms, which are key elements of peacebuilding in Uganda. The selected song videos are: Lucky Bosmic Otim's "Peace Return" and "Wang Ceng Oter" ["Let the Sun Set with It"], "Peace Anthem" by X-NO P feat. Small Luo, three songs by Master Loketto Lee – "Peace Talks in Juba," "Bigombe," and "We Don't Mind We Don't Care" – and Robert Kyagalunyi Ssentamu aka Bobi Wine's "Situka" ["Rise Up"]. These artists and their songs are representative of a vast array of artists performing for peace whose works cannot be discussed in this chapter for lack of space. Indeed, the most dominant theme in these songs is the search for peace and democracy and postwar transition and electoral reform which challenges government and cultural institutions to uphold the human rights of the people and establish the atmosphere of good governance and peaceful transfer of power. The LRA war destroyed lives, private property, and entire social fabrics of northern Uganda communities. Gross human rights abuses took place during the war many of which went unrecorded except in the psyche of the victims. No song articulates this cry for peace better than Bosmic Otim's "Peace Return," which addresses the LRA leader and his former deputy Vincent Otii directly in Acholi:

| | |
|---|---|
| Kony we, kony duk paco | *Kony please, Kony return home* |
| Kony we, dano mito kuc (× 2) | *Kony please, people want peace (× 2)* |
| Otii Vincent, dug paco | *Otii Vincent, come back home* |
| Otii Vincent, dano mito kuc (× 2) | *Otii Vincent, people want peace (× 2)* |
| Lurok nyero wa, ka gang too do | *Other tribes laugh at us, our home is dying* |
| Lurok cayo w aka waneke. | *Other tribes despise us when we kill ourselves.* |

The song goes on to lament that even the government soldiers who die at the front line fighting the LRA are recruits from Acholi, compounding the tragedy of the sub-region. When Kony's fighters die, they are also *"Leb"* "Luo speakers" (A code for Lango and Acholi people of northern Uganda, and sometimes, the Alur of the West Nile region of Uganda). On the other hand, AIDS is also busy killing hundreds in the congested IDP (Internally Displaced People) camps. The interiorized violence exhibited in the involvement of Acholi and *"Leb"* youth in fighting on both sides of the conflict compounds the tragedy of the LRA insurgency. In the first place, most LRA fighters are abducted children, indoctrinated and transformed into killing machines, yet the bulk of the Uganda People's Defense Forces (UPDF) fighting force deployed in the north is also composed of people recruited from northern Uganda. The forceful resettlement of people in crowded and dilapidated IDP camps has only made the bad situation worse. Collapse of family structures and the associated moral codes of behavior in these camps has led to alcohol abuse, sexual immorality, violence, and starvation. These camps registered the highest HIV AIDS statistics in the country. The video focuses on the failed Juba Peace Talks that ran from July to September 2006 and appeals to combatants to lay down their weapons and embrace peace. The Juba Peace Talks were an excellent opportunity for the government and LRA rebels to sign a lasting peace treaty. This would end the protracted war and the atrocities committed by both sides that led to massive violations of human rights. The treaty would, by the act of being signed, acknowledge the human rights of victims caught up in the conflict and gross violations of this right as a precursor to healing and national reconciliation. A placard held by a school pupil reflects the desperate plea of the civilian population:

> COMBATAN[sic]S, WHY KILL
> INNOCENT PEOPLE?

Another one reads:

> OUR LEADERS
> THINK ABOUT US

The placards challenge both government (which claims to defend the lives and property of the citizens) and the rebels (who claim to fight for justice and the rule of law and of the morality grounded in the Biblical Ten Commandments) to cease being hypocritical and to stop killing innocent people. The artist then casts himself as a freedom fighter through his music; a role that gives him moral superiority over both government and rebel outfits through the song refrain:

> I am a warrior, freedom fighter,
> Lucky Bosmic fighting for freedom.
> Son of the soil, son of Kitgum,
> Lucky Bosmic fighting for freedom.

However, this artistic self-reflexivity shows the triple promotional roles the song video plays. First, it advocates for peace and the restoration of human rights and dignity by critiquing the major players in the insurgency; second, it sells the song and the music video; and third, it markets the artist himself, thus compromising the ability of the music video to provide sincere critique without self-praise and the embedded "iconography of the pop star."[16] Reference to "Son of the soil" apportions heroic stature to the artist. A huge canvas portrait of the artist mounted on a truck together with the artist on top of the same truck, and his self-praise, reinforce the self-reflexivity of the video. This leads to what film scholar Kamilla Elliot calls "de(re)-composition,"[17] a phenomenon whereby the artist and his canvas portrait together with the Rastafarian and Lucky Dube subtexts merge in the viewer's consciousness leading to confusion as to which is which.[18] The appeal to Rastafarian symbols highlights the revolutionary nature of the song and of the artist and the place of music as a third force in democratic discourse. Anne Schumann observes that "Reggae music has come to be regarded as quintessential protest music, both within Africa and globally."[19] Schumann observes further that reggae artists in Côte d'Ivoire, for instance, presented themselves as "the voice of the voiceless,"[20] a posture Bosmic Otim takes in "Peace Return." This accentuates the revolutionary nature of reggae music, and of the role of such music in the search for peace, reconciliation, and propagating human rights and dignity. The music also challenges actors in the war theater of northern Uganda and sets the agenda for postwar institutional reforms. It calls for judicial reform that accommodates indigenous knowledge of jurisprudence, especially the now famous *matto oput* restorative justice as a mechanism for handling the complex legacy of the LRA war.[21]

"Peace Anthem" by X-NO P feat. Small Luo offers a serious critique of government, rebels, and the passivity of Acholi citizens in the diaspora. The biggest weakness with this video is again the overt self-reflexivity of the artist and his attempt to use the serious subject of peace to situate himself as an artist and fighter for peace. It opens like an MTV music video with complete focus on the artists. The back of the artists T-shirt, with his name embedded, provides the establishing shot, which grounds the song performance on the visual iconography of the artist. The opening song line is, "Yeah! Yeah!" followed by a close-up shot of sunglasses, and the unique signature sign with three fingers – one of which is bandaged. A shot of government soldiers on patrol follows. There are portrait shots of worried women and emaciated children, before returning to the artists dressed in typical American bling-bling fashion with ostentatious accessories like imitation gold chains, caps worn backwards, T-shirts, and sunglasses. Then a cut to the chilling metonymic montage of the leg of a presumably dead person with fresh blood oozing. This opening sequence simultaneously establishes the modernist artistic iconography of X-NO P in relation to the international hip-hop landscape, and the raw images of war. The iconography provides artistic authority and prowess to tackle the chilling topic of the destruction of lives in war and the statement that the war must end:

> I am not trying to make a name, I am a no P
> I am trying to be what I am supposed to be
> For me alone as X-No P,

I am saying enough is enough
We need peace

To underscore the last two lines, the imagescape is invoked to reiterate the immediate need for peace. We see a montage of burning houses, a dead woman's body, newspaper headlines saying, "Kony's mother speaks out." Then the singer, passionately in the Acholi language, addresses Acholi people living at ease in New York. The lines emphasize the need for the locals living in the diaspora to stop thinking they have escaped the war, because by association, they are equally affected by the tragedy. The imagescape further shows a montage of religious leaders – symbolizing peace and the peace effort. A visual montage of children's worried faces, people fleeing the war with loads on their heads, and live spine-chilling footage of a girl being bludgeoned on the head follows. Another bloodied dead body is shown, then interview footage of Professor Ogenga Latigo, who argues the case for classifying the tragedy in Acholi as genocide.[22] The singer then gives a historical overview of the war from its inception in 1986, and in another self-reflexive moment he says, "I have one thing to say to you/Through the medium of song and dance," then he talks about the efforts that have been made to stop the war, before launching into a rap refrain:

Let's stop the war we need peace
Let's stop the game, blood flow, blood flow × 2

This is a powerful song video that combines the tripartite audiologo-visualized platforms of words, sound, and images to shock the world with the impact of the war without apportioning direct blame. But the artist minces no words when he says, "Let's stop the war," which shows us this man-made tragedy also has a man-made solution. When he says "Let's stop the game" he attacks the absurd arguments for the war propagated by government, rebels, and war profiteers and calls for an end to the flow of blood. The final dedication says, "A dedication to all those who have been affected by the war in northern Uganda," a fitting tribute to entire people groups in northern and eastern Uganda who were displaced, killed, impoverished, and marginalized by the war. The dedication is followed by the very final close-up shot of X-NO P in the center between two colleagues. The ending shows that the song is as much about the war as about the artist and his band.

*Call for Justice*

While most of the songs call for peace, forgiveness, and reconciliation, especially the now famous *matto oput* traditional mode of justice,
one song "Wang Ceng Oter" ["Let the Sun Set with It"] [literally,
"Let the Sun's Face Take It"] by Lucky Bosmic Otim, however, calls
for swift justice for victims of the LRA insurgency. The song calls for
forgetting the atrocities of the war through the image of the setting sun,
yet it also invokes justice from God for those who are able to escape
justice in courts of law due to their invincibility. Sung exclusively in
Acholi, this music video relies heavily on imagery to project the message of hope, postwar reparation, and restoration. Bosmic opens his
song with the chorus:

| | |
|---|---|
| Wang ceng oter, ojowa, tim aranyi pa joni, | *Let the sun set with it, my people, the atrocities of this people,* |
| Wang ceng oter, lotuwa, tim aranyi pa joni, | *Let the sunset cart it way, the brutality of this people,* |
| Wang ceng ocwal, ojowa, tim aranyi pa joni | *Let the sun set with it, the brutality of this people,* |
| Wang ceng ocwal, lotuwa, tim aranyi pa joni | *Let the sunset cart it way, the callousness of this people.* |

The title simply means, let the sun set with all the atrocities committed during the insurgency. The sunset is also a metaphorical
reference to the end of the long day of bloodshed and the beginning of a new day. The angry opening chorus grounds the song in
the atrocities committed by the insurgents (and counterinsurgents),
specifically highlighting the extreme brutality of the attackers. The
singer then reads out the catalogue of atrocities; the rebels have
destroyed homes, shattered lives, raped, and abused the population
to their heart's content.

Then the singer begins to call for divine justice in verse two (for purposes of illustration I have decided to transcribe the entire sequence):

| | |
|---|---|
| Ai RWOT Rubanga, ngolkop atira | *LORD God, judge righteously* |
| Ai RWOT Lacwec, ngolkop atira, | *LORD God creator, judge fairly,* |
| RWOT Rubanga, ngol kop iwi joni. (× 2) | *LORD God, proclaim judgement on this people. (× 2)* |
| Dano ma yang otimo aranyi ikom wa | *The people who committed atrocities against us,* |
| RWOT Rubanga, ngol kop iwi gi. | *LORD God, pass judgement on them.* |

The judgement extends to those who have tortured and abused innocent people. The singer then goes on to state that God is with the people of Acholi, perhaps to underscore his hope for inevitable justice:

Emmanuel, Emmanuel, God is with us (× 2)

Justice in all its manifestations has been the most elusive pursuit for victims of the fog of the LRA insurgency and counterinsurgency. The artist, while acknowledging that divine justice is the only mode of justice that is inescapable for the atrocious actors in the war, continues to narrate the catalogue of inhumane atrocities committed against innocent civilians in order to prepare for voluntary forgetting of these atrocities as the last phase of mourning in exchange for a new dawn of peace and recovery. In the song, the people of Acholi are metaphorically the people of Israel, the chosen people who can never be annihilated. The people of Israel, chosen by God cannot be reduced in number. The song says even the black ants that crawl on the ground cannot be completely destroyed; neither can white ants (a delicacy in northern Uganda) be completely harvested, because of God's divine plan of regeneration and increase. Even widows and orphans cannot be abused forever because God will inevitably intervene. A people cannot be extinct because grandchildren will grow to become adults. Otim ends by invoking the divine presence of God for protection and for justice. By calling for divine justice for the perpetrators, this song provides a very different take on the war as opposed to the popular emphasis on traditional justice through *matto oput*.

Multiple layers of visual metaphors in this song video underscore poetic realism. The video uses the clouds, the sky, the sun, sunset, the granary, the sorghum field, and the name Emmanuel as audiovisual images for proclaiming the hope of a new, bright, and glorious tomorrow. Justice is assured because none other than God Almighty will bring the perpetrators to book. The establishing shot of the homestead grounds the song in the narrative of reconstruction and restoration. The song underscores postwar peacebuilding and sharp critique of the institutions of democracy and justice. The superimposition of blue clouds sailing low and submerging the singers brightens the mood of the video and points to divine visitation, a Biblical allusion to the transfiguration of Jesus on the Mount where scripture says a bright cloud covered him and his three disciples.[23] The sequences with the artist singing in a ripened sorghum field show fruitfulness, regeneration, and restoration.

It is a time of harvest; a harvest of peace, food, blessings, and prosperity while the season of war is setting with the sun. The repeated shots of the granary also symbolize abundance; the end of famine and lack, and a season of harvest and storage for the future. Low-angle shots of the blue sky naturally make the sky wide and dominant, emphasizing hope. The shots of the sky move from realism to impressionism and to expressionism with the sky changing from white to blue to green. As Mutasem Tawfiq Al-Khader observes of the image of the sky in Coleridge's poetry, "The image of the sky is related to beauty, kindness, hope, and revival. The sky will never be blurred and is synonymous with life itself."[24] The image of the sky is the external expression of internal emotions of happiness and hope for the poet-performer and his people. The sun in rapid stylized motion is black, underscoring the evils with which the sun is loaded as it goes to set, iterating the dusk of the dark day of atrocities. The repeated reference to Emmanuel is a Biblical allusion that grounds their liberation in nothing short of divine intervention (as the Jews waited for the coming of the Messiah) as opposed to state intervention or the intervention of the international community.[25] The same intervention is what will ensure that they escape annihilation but continue to procreate and regenerate. The song video ends with the image of the setting sun to underscore the end of atrocity and suffering, with divine justice assured.

### Political and Artistic Patronage

Perhaps the trickiest music videos are the ones where political and artistic celebrity actors collaborate in iterating the message of peace. These videos provide rare opportunity for these usually strange bedfellows to make one clarion call for peace, yet they also have a tendency to promote the politics of appeasement and patronage. The videos aim at mobilizing popular support from the fanbase of the artists and politicians to support the peace processes. At the height of the LRA conflict, peace initiatives involved politicians, artists, religious leaders, and international NGOs. Although the song videos in this category emphasize the yearning for peace, at the same time, they seek to promote the artists and the politicians they eulogize. These songs are more political than artistic in their excessive praise of politicians. Moreover, visual hobnobbing between the artists and the praised politicians undermines the aesthetic force of the songs, even as they fit the song videos within the traditional African panegyric poetry genre. The artist who best exemplifies this category is Godfrey Onega alias Master Loketto Lee, a tae kwon do star turned musician and his songs "Peace Talks in Juba" and "Bigombe." The opening establishing shot of the first song shows the iconic artist announce himself, "This is Loketto Lee," followed by the dominant portrait of the Honorable Okello Oryem, Minister of State for Foreign Affairs in the Uganda government and a prominent politician from Acholi. There are numerous montage sequences as well as superimpositions of pictures and videos of the minister, and that of the minister with Loketto Lee. The artist receives a trophy from the Honorable Okello Oryem in recognition of his contribution to the peace effort through his songs. We see Loketto Lee shaking hands with the Honorable Ruhakana Rugunda, then Internal Affairs Minister who led the Uganda government delegation to the Juba Peace Talks. The singers appeal to Okello Oryem saying, "Wan omito kuc iyi Acholi" ["We want peace in Acholi"]. A montage of the artist taking a photo with different fans fills the brief visual interlude from the minister's images, followed by a studio shot of musicians playing to the beat. Artillery goes off abruptly, followed by a panning shot of a skull to ground the narrative in the context of war. The visual ordering of shots underscores the collaboration between artistic and political celebrities in drumming out the tune of peace. Rather than the usual cat-and-mouse relationship between politicians and artists, in this song video there is unity, whether it is unity in the search for peace or unity in seeking visibility through music and the reciprocal obligation of fame. Loketto Lee proceeds to thank President Salva Kiir of South Sudan for his role in hosting the peace talks. Fade to Salva Kiir's portrait followed by more praise and pictures of the Honorable Okello Oryem. A gory skull punctuates that sequence before we arrive at a montage of a Ruhakana Rugunda speaking: "We are happy that peace in northern Uganda is becoming a reality. And we are happy that more and more of our people are leaving the camps." A montage of the Honorable Okello Oryem affirming Loketto Lee as an artist and celebrating Lee's songs and their contribution to the peace process follows the Rugunda shot. The metatheatricality of this scene is not lost on the viewer. The montage underscores the shared political and artistic glory. The song then thanks Salva Kiir and then South Sudanese Vice President Ryak Machar in Arabic. The use of Arabic grounds the narrative in the greater regional search for peace. The artist later poses with Ruhakana Rugunda; both of them give the thumbs-up sign. The thumbs could be up for peace; Lee's thumbs could also be up for the photo opportunity with a celebrity politician while Rugunda's could be up for rubbing shoulders with a famous local artist. The thumbs-up sign is also the election symbol for the ruling National Resistance Movement (NRM) party and its deployment in the song video can also be read as a salute by the artists and the politician to the ruling NRM government. The construction of political celebrity and artistic celebrity is evident here as both are products of the culture industry and cash in on the media limelight. As Eric Louw reminds us, "manufacturing successful celebrities is profitable."[26] The sequence also underscores the partnership between government and popular culture icons in promoting peace, democracy, and good governance, while at the same time promoting patronage, which can compromise quality and the content of artistic production. Okello Oryem endorses Lee in another metatheatrical moment in the video when he says; "Many families suffered at the hands of the LRA. The kind of music that Loketto has produced sometimes is counseling, sometimes is [smothering] [sic], sometimes it helps them forget the suffering that they have been through."

Another song video by Loketto Lee that is worth discussing here is "Bigombe," which he dedicates to Honorable Betty Bigome, then Minister of State for Pacification of North and Northeastern Uganda and Head Negotiator between the LRA and the Government of Uganda at the height of the LRA insurgency. Bigombe hails from Acholi. In Lee's own words, he dedicates the song to Bigombe in "appreciation for what you have done for [sic] northern people in Uganda." The refrain goes: "Bigombe we thank you for your efforts/ Bigombe, peace is about to return." Cutaways of Bigombe during the peace process abound. There is footage of Bigombe meeting with Lee. Bigome reciprocates Lee's artistic favor by saying in a superimposed interview in the same video:

> Personally, I am so happy that Loketto Lee has been trying to create awareness among Ugandans about the problem in northern Uganda and the importance of peace. I think this is very critical because it is not only one way of bringing peace [sic]. Spreading the word around helps in confidence building.

The role of the artist in peacebuilding through this music video is evident. It helps in postwar reconstruction as well as strengthening democratic structures. Nevertheless, the endorsement of Lee by the minister in the same song video dedicated to the minister reinforces patronage and shared self-promotion and celebrity image construction and profiting. We later see Bigombe dancing to the same tune praising her; she becomes part of the in-concert performance. The minister moves from being the subject of the song to becoming a part of the song video production, making a rather long metatheatrical cameo appearance, which works as a publicity stunt for the minister, for the song, and for the artist. This reciprocal patronage compromises the critical edge of the artist and even the quality of the art. The artist may not find the moral courage to critique the political establishment that appeases him and gives him visibility.

Loketto Lee's contribution to the peace process has been widely acknowledged in Uganda. As Waswa Deo notes, "his music was very instrumental in the revival of northern Uganda and the LRA peace talks, eventually helping him to win the PAM [Pearl of Africa Music] awards best musician [mid-2000s] northern Uganda." In a dramatic career shift, Loketto Lee joined the Government of Uganda's crime preventers force in 2016 and upgraded to a full police constable shortly after.[27] Lee, whose music is quite popular in South Sudan, with Vice President Salva Kiir being one of his faithful fans, also received a peace award in 2007 and a BBC Peace Award Nomination for his song "Salva Kiir."[28] This shows that the sharply critical artist was able not only to collaborate with politicians and government in the search for peace but to eventually transform himself into a police officer of the Republic of Uganda. On the other hand, it is also possible that Mr. Lee was forced to join the Uganda police due to dwindling cash from his music career. Although Lee cut off his dreadlocks to meet the professional requirements of his new career look, he is known to wear a yellow wig in the evening outside office hours when he goes out to sell his music, a trade he still holds to raise money on the side. "The wig gives him his former stage look every time he goes to perform and [he] puts it off when police duty calls."[29] Although popular song videos can also be apolitical or even anti-establishment, sometimes the search for peace brings government and artists together as is evident in this video.

### Indicting the World

Perhaps the most intense, surreal, and schizophrenic music video about peace discussed in this chapter is Master Dr. Loketto Lee's song "But We Don't Care." In the song video, Lee "expressed his infuriation with the rest of the country for acting unconcerned about the plight of the people in the war-ravaged districts in northern Uganda."[30] The video opens with a bomb blast followed by a thick black mushroom cloud reminiscent of the atomic bomb blasts over Hiroshima and Nagasaki to set the tone, then an eerie sound effect that sets the creepy mood, followed by the opening shot of a wall poster that reads, "Don't cut ears, mouths, hands." The camera cuts to a rotting corpse, then to graffiti that reads, "WE NEED PEACE." A panoramic footage of rotting corpses, war, fleeing civilians, and the lethally wounded follows this visually disorienting shock opening. In one shot, the camera zooms into a raw bullet wound on a leg. Various images of war are found in the video; a manned anti-aircraft gun, images of refugees crossing a river with luggage on their heads, men on their knees shooting at an enemy. This video uses the shock technique to show the viewer the sufferings of the people of the Acholi region of northern Uganda as a way of chastising them for complicity in the atrocities through their silence and indifference. Government, nongovernmental organizations, political leaders, religious leaders and all strata of Ugandan society are challenged by this video to rethink their lack of fellow-feeling for the suffering north. "The suffering of the Acholi people is unspeakable," the opening line of the song says before delving into the details of their suffering:

| | |
|---|---|
| Can marac dong dano too | *It's a terrible tragedy, people die* |
| Can marac dong dano butu ilum (× 2) | *It's a terrible tragedy, people sleep in the bush (× 2)* |
| Nga mayang dong neko ominne | *Who has ever killed his brother?* |
| Nga mayang dong neko lamine | *Who has ever killed his sister?* |
| Nga ma yang dong cobo dud dano | *Who has ever stabbed people's buttocks?* |
| Nga mayang dong ngolo yit dano. | *Who has ever cut off people's ears?* |

The singer then deploys a series of images to describe the pain of their suffering, especially the image of the "bat" who must fly blind and in the night, and the image of "akanyago" (an ugly insect that caries refuse on its back everywhere it goes), before declaring cynically, "We don't mind, we don't care./We don't care, we don't mind." The lines of the song reveal the tragedy of the war in the Acholi region. People die, sleep in the bush, brother kills brother, sister kills sister, there are mutilations. While these atrocities were raging, there were people from other parts of Uganda who felt like the chicken had come home to roost for northerners. This is because northerners have ruled Uganda longer than other regions and are accused of committing atrocities and gross violations of human rights especially during the reign of Idi Amin (1971–1979), Apollo Milton Obote's second term as Ugandan president (1980–1985), and Tito Okello's short term in 1986. As such, the people and institutions that should have helped resolve the LRA conflict were seen as bystanders who cared less if northerners were killing northerners. The tragedy of the north was such that the war increased the prevalence of disease as well. This is captured in the lines of the song below, sung in English for the all country to hear:

> Those guys bring diseases like cholera
> Those guys bring diseases like slim
> Those guys bring diseases like Ebola
> With God on our side, we shall always win them
> With Jesus on our side, we shall always win. (× 2)

"Those guys" refers to northerners as they were collectively called. They are not only war mongers but are responsible for spreading cholera, slim [HIV AIDS], and Ebola. The song video responds to this indifference with corresponding indifference: the refrain of the song clashes with these images headlong: "We don't care, we don't mind/ We don't mind we don't care." Once all the institutions that are supposed to protect the lives and property of the people of Acholi have abdicated their roles, only God is left to take them through their trials. The song expresses faith in God's divine help in the presence of incessant insecurity and the indifference of the government, the people of Uganda, and the international community. To prove that the singer and his band do not care, this music video has some of the most intense erotic dance sequences. The sad lyrics and atrocious visual narrative clash with the gleeful faces of the animated party-scene dancers. The dance reaches climactic deliriousness as the lead queen dancer trembles in *mutuashi* fusion, and others sway and bump to the 1970s bumping hip dance while the lyric repeats "We don't mind, we don't care./We don't care, we don't mind." The combination is a surrealistic montage editing of unrelated clashing shots that underscore the extremes in human experience; extreme aesthetic and erotic pleasure versus extreme violence and tragedy intended to shock the indifferent. This music video is a defiant response to the overwhelming tragedy of war with the singer and dancers asserting their right to happiness and aesthetic pleasure in spite of the deaths and deadly epidemics all around. The music video brought conviction to many in government and civil society in Uganda. Loketto would later compose "We Care Now" as a counterpoint to "We Don't Care" because as Moses Serugo notes, "His opinion has now changed following initiatives to highlight the plight and squalor of folks living in Internally Displaced People's Camps."[31] This video by Lee is considered "close to sounding" like Michael Jackson's controversial video "They Don't Care about Us," directed by Spike Lee, which exposed the crime and poverty in the favela's of Rio de Janeiro. Lee's second song "We Care Now" was part of the Three Hours Away project and the Gulu Peace Concert performed in 2004 that involved several Ugandan artists and aimed at preaching hope in northern Uganda.[32] The song brought immediate improvement in the government's disaster response strategy. Even civil society and international actors were convicted, leading to the adoption of various peace strategies.

### Individual and Institutional Reform

Robert Kyagulanyi Ssentamu aka Bobi Wine is a Ugandan artist who represents the middle ground between artists who openly sing the praises of the government and activist opposition artists who sing oppositional songs. Although he sings a lot about social problems and political oppression, Bobi Wine has refused to throw his lot in with any political party openly in order to act as a mirror reflecting and critiquing democratic processes in Uganda, especially presidential elections – the cornerstone of free and fair political participation. In the last election, although he expressed his admiration for candidate Dr. Kizza Besigye, the presidential nominee for the Forum for Democratic Change (FDC), he did not publicly endorse the FDC party candidate. Kyagulanyi has now joined active politics and was elected Member of Parliament for Kyadondo East Constituency during a by-election in July 2017, having carefully chosen to stand as an Independent candidate unaffiliated with any party. He represents the artist who is disarticulated from all party power centers, government, or opposition, choosing rather to be an Independent politician, artist, and commentator who is free to audit democratic processes in Uganda and to critique its institutions. Kyagulanyi is that artist who is doing what Mahony calls "Taming antagonism and converting it to agonism."[33] As such, he supports opposition sentiments against hegemony but also challenges his audience to go past the rivalry of party politics to instead help build the nation. In fact, Kyagulanyi's message resonated with the voters of Kyadondo East Constituency, who turned up in big numbers for his campaigns and gave him a resounding victory in which he won at all ninety-three polling stations. Kyagulanyi garnered 78 percent of the votes against 22 percent for all the candidates of the major political parties – the ruling National Resistance Movement (NRM) and FDC – combined. Uganda's president threw his weight behind the ruling NRM candidate Sitenda Sebalu, while the FDC President Dr. Kizza Besigye, also known as "The People's President," supported the official FDC candidate Abdu Katuntu. But Kyagalunyi, the self-styled "Ghetto President" beat them all. His popularity was such that opposition party politicians ignored their own candidates and backed Kyagulanyi instead. Kyagalunyi's election is a watershed in Ugandan elections with many already questioning the relevance of multiparty politics, especially in light of its centralized power system of caucuses and jockeying, which leaves the voters out of decision making. Some see Kyagalunyi's entrance into parliament as a transitional moment in Ugandan politics, ushering in "the possibility of a 'third-force' to consolidate a 'political middle,' outside the pro-regime fanatics and the anti-regime radicals."[34] Since his election win, Kyagulanyi has become a prominent challenger to the status quo. He rallies his supporters around his loose "People Power" political pressure group, which mostly appeals to the youth. In August 2018, while campaigning for an Independent parliamentary candidate in Arua Town in West Nile region, Bobi Wine survived an assassination attempt in which his driver, Yasin Kawuma, died. He was later arrested and charged with treason in a Military Court Martial, although the charges of weapons possession were later dropped and a new case of treason preferred against him in a magistrate's court. Bobi Wine, who claims he was tortured during his captivity, later traveled to the United States for treatment and has since become and international personality, even scooping the 2018 African Personality of the Year Award, beating Rwandan President Paul Kagame and Ethiopian Prime Minister Abih Ahmed among other prominent African personalities.[35] Bobi Wine has openly declared his intentions to challenge President Museveni for the highest office in Uganda come the 2021 elections.

Kyagulanyi's post-2016 election song "Situka" ["Rise Up"] is a powerful production that seeks to build consensus on the need to move forward with nation building in spite of the pain of post-election loss, especially for opposition members. He calls for internal reform from within each individual before any electoral reform or transformation in democratic institutions and processes can be expected. The whole song is sung in Luganda but the introduction is in English, perhaps intended to communicate nationally before digging into issues that pertain to the central region, especially Kampala, where the opposition beat the NRM candidate Museveni, who failed to capture power nationally. Below are extracts from the lyrics of Kyagulanyi's pro-reform song "Situka":

> When the going gets tough, the tough must get going,
> Especially when leaders become misleaders, and mentors become tormentors.
> When freedom of expression becomes a target of suppression,
> Opposition becomes our position.

The powerful opening lines in pretty impressive rhyme challenge Ugandans to ignore the failure of the electoral process, brace for the challenges of nation building, and keep moving. Kyagulanyi is an activist singer whose music generally demonstrates what Mahony calls a "non-aligned alignment" with the opposition.[36] As a music activist, it is possible that his definition of opposition transcends the binary opposition-parties-versus-government paradigm – perhaps something much broader including opposition from within the ruling NRM government and internal critique within the opposition in the interest of promoting the national democracy project. The chorus, "Rise up and walk," discourages the destructive logic of anarchy demonstrated by the songs of other radical opposition musicians in Uganda and calls instead for moderation. Unlike 2016 presidential candidates Dr. Kizza Besigye's and Amama Mbabazi's notion of change, which means replacing the man at the top, the singer says change comes from within each citizen:

> What I've just discovered is that the change you desire is right in your hands,
> because the person in whom you have put your hope,
> he has also put his hope in you.

Change therefore should not just be what President Yoweri Museveni famously called "a change of guards" but individual change wherein each citizen seeks to be better and to encourage and inspire others towards doing better for Uganda. He calls on citizens to always know their rights, because knowing one's rights is fundamental to the call for political reform. The persona also makes a plea for national unity:

Don't shy away from working for Uganda,
because it is your own country, even if your boss was not your choice.
Just play your part, because this is your country.

The song attacks injustice but also calls for perseverance on the part of the citizens. It laments oppression but calls for a more radical kind of reform, the individual reform from within, without which no change at the national level can be expected. The song provides a powerful intertextual conversation with some classic texts about the journey of democracy and of endurance. Kyagulanyi paraphrases Martin Luther King's famous 1960 Spelman College Address titled, "Moving from This Mountain" when he says if you can't run, walk, if you can't walk, limp but whatever happens, keep moving.[37] He also borrows verbatim from Billy Ocean's song "When the Going Gets Tough, the Tough Get Going," from the album "Love Zone." In spite of these rather generous borrowings from the said motivational sources, Kyagulanyi's song, composed without any contractual obligation to any political party, provides much needed refreshment in Uganda's music industry in the election and post-election season, when art tends to polarize rather than unite. Kyagulanyi's star attraction has almost everything to do with his musical career and his audience base as a performing artist.

While the song "Situka" tends to be apolitical and calls for personal reform of attitudes towards national development beyond party politics, the video is loaded with images of raw state power and its deconstruction through peaceful protests as well as metaphors of violent resistance. There are several versions of the "Situka" video. The official track with the seal, "Ghetto President," is less political.[38] This version shows a rugged image of Bobi Wine in a blue suit and yellow shirt full of holes. He wears a hanging belt like it was put on in a hurry. He is captured in a combative stride. The most powerful metaphor in the cover image is the shattered chains hanging from his wrists showing his victory over oppression. The neck tie in the colors of the Uganda flag and the national symbol, the crested crane, situate his fight in the arena of politics. The dry leafless trees in the background and the barren rugged terrain also show the state of political barren-ness and the need for political reform and restoration. The second version of "Situka," loaded by Counsellor Mukiibi Williams, is the most political and shows the evolution of the artist's videographic vision of the song to hardcore opposition activism.[39] It is also possible that this video is the post-production studio work of an editing artist with little input from Bobi Wine. Mukiibi's portrait flashes constantly on the lower left corner of the video. Live footage of police brutally during arrests of opposition party supporters, especially the FDC, abound. There is also live news footage from Uganda's National Broadcasting Services (NBS) and Nation Television (NTV) showing police roughing up journalists, which shows the suppression of the free press and the resultant call for press freedom. A screaming NBS news headline tagged "HAPPENING NOW" in "Kasangati/Live" reads "JOURNALISTS ARRESTED." The use of live footage rein-forced by the tag "HAPPENING NOW" shows the reality of police brutality and the need for reform in the police force. The location, Kasangati, is very significant in Ugandan politics because it is the iconic residence of Uganda's famous opposition politician and three-time presidential candidate Dr. Kizza Besigye. This is juxtaposed with the dramatic image of a dirty, half-naked boy contemplating aloud under a tree, "I can be president." The image of poverty, illiteracy, and abandonment that the picture exudes clashes directly with the grand presidential dream.

In the song video, there are several images of especially FDC and Democratic Party (DP) opposition politicians among peaceful protest-ers. Another disturbing superimposed image shows a little boy holding a sachet of Uganda Waragi, a popular local brand of hard liquor, with the writing "Yes" at the back to show the frustrations that have led to unregulated alcohol consumption to the point where near toddlers can be seen drinking hard alcohol drinks. Next to that image is the distraught image of then Inspector General of Police Kale Kayihura in full uniform sitting among a crowd in a contemplative mood as if the power of the masses has hypnotized him and subdued police hardware; this cuts to a group of Ugandans demonstrating in the diaspora with the Uganda flag and with placards reading, "SAY 'NO' TO POLICE

STATE IN UGANDA." One even reads, "HIS EXCELLENCY DR. KIZZA BESIGYE IS UGANDA'S PRESIDENT." The images clash in the Soviet montage fashion highlighting the dialectical class of strong versus weak, state versus citizen. We see opposition politicians who are leading demonstrations being blocked by police. The video shows footage of demonstrators confronting the police. Then a picture of the artist Bobi Wine posing with Dr. Kizza Besigye, his wife Winnie Byanyima, and Waswa Birigwa, an opposition politician. The video then cuts to NTV news footage showing Agaba Maguru of Uganda Human Rights Commission (UHRC) perhaps decrying police brutality and perhaps calling for an investigation into police violence. This is followed by images of opposition leaders with cheerful crowds before the police descend on them, beating, kicking, and butting, followed by a panning shot of FDC supporters flashing the victory sign with one person flying the DP flag. This is followed by the image of a smiling child clad in Dr. Kizza Besigye's campaign poster. Another NBS news headline tagged "HAPPENING NOW" in "Najjanankumbi/ Live" reads, "FDC ANNOUNCES WAY FORWARD." It is not clear what the way forward is, but the next image shows a serious looking bare-chested boy carrying a wooden toy AK 47 assault rifle, perhaps indicating the metaphorical call for a war of peaceful resistance or even a call to violent armed struggle. Images of Besigye abound punctuated by violent images of police arresting demonstrators. A cartoon image of President Yoweri Museveni in army uniform with his neck between the forked head of a claw hammer follows. The image is loaded in many ways. In 2015 President Museveni joked that he was essential to Uganda because he was like the cotter pin that holds the handles of the bicycle crank without which the bicycle (Uganda) cannot move. Opposition politician Dr. Kizza Besigye seized on this to say if Museveni was the cotter pin, he was the hammer that dislodges the cotter pin. The cartoon can be read as the opposition's call for the transfer of power to guarantee political and economic stability with Museveni's long stay in power seen as the single most dangerous cause of instability.

The next image shows dual images of a baby sleeping on stacks of money above a poor little child sleeping on the ground with the captions, "SON OF POLITICIAN" and "SON OF VOTER" respectively. The image reinforces the popular notion in Uganda that all politicians are corrupt, although it does lump all voters into the class of abject poverty. This indictment of politicians is relevant to Kyagalunyi's case because he has argued that what Uganda needs is leaders, not politicians and that is why he offered himself as a leader in joining active politics as opposed to politicians who play the game of politics and its attendant lies, empty promises, sloganeering, corruption, and raw jostling for power. In rapid succession, we see images of FDC leader Dr. Kizza Besigye, followed by a Photoshopped image of President Museveni wearing a yellow prison uniform and eating from a bowl, then the image of President Barack Obama making an emphatic point, followed by the image of a little boy wearing a T-shirt saying "I Can Be President," followed in turn by a daring Photoshopped image of a bare-chested President Museveni between white soldiers, his hands tied with ropes. Below this image is a caption, "WHICH YEAR IS THIS?" followed by another Photoshopped image of a humbled President Museveni carrying a sack of cassava on a bodaboda with an equally humble Janet Museveni riding at the back on top of the sack of cassava.

The concluding image is very significant. Alluding to Leonardo da Vinci's classic fifteenth-century mural painting of the Last Supper, we see a Photoshopped image of President Museveni with his disciples around him. In front of the table is a large image of the symbol of the NRM party, the movement bus. The caption above reads, "IS IT HIS LAST SUPPER, OR THEIR LAST SUPPER?" The last ordering of shots is so daring that it borders on sedition or even treason. The video preempts the possible arrest and incarceration of President Museveni for the perceived atrocities in the earlier part of the video. The image of a humbled Museveni riding a bodaboda anticipates the fall from grace. The image of Museveni arrested by white soldiers perhaps alludes to the International Criminal Court (ICC). Opposition leaders like Dr. Olara Otunu had appealed to the ICC to investigate Museveni and the UPDF for war crimes against humanity, especially for the LRA insurgency and counterinsurgency, a request the ICC declined. This reading is corroborated by the preceding image of President Obama, then leader of the free world, perhaps indicating that American soldiers have or will arrest Museveni. The concluding image speaks for itself. While in the Biblical last supper Jesus ate *"His* Last Supper" before leaving the earth, in the Photoshopped image, the idea is that President Museveni and his political disciples are eating *"Their* Last Supper" before leaving power. The imagescape of Kyagalunyi's song takes a more political tone than the song lyrics. The ordering of shots begins with showing the excesses of the police in particular and the clamp-down on freedom of speech and freedom of assembly. The images get bolder with suggestions that democratic reform is not possible without the peaceful or violent transfer of power. The concluding ordering of shots shows the frustration of the videographer who increasingly calls for the incarceration of President Museveni and preempts his trial at the ICC. The song's lyrics tend to accept the fact that the opposition has lost in the elections and challenge the electorate to move forward for love of Uganda, whether they like the outcome of the election or not. The imagescape on the other hand articulates a more radical political tone that calls for civil and radical disobedience to the point of suggesting a violent transfer of power and indictment of not just President Museveni but his ruling elite as a whole.

## Conclusion

The music videos analyzed in this chapter provide platforms for witnessing the traumas of the LRA violence but also provide catharsis for the victims while evaluating and critiquing the postwar transition. They also interrogate the contradictions surrounding Uganda's con-flicts, especially the LRA war, what Yiju Huang calls, "the internal processes of sense-making; how people derive meaning or fail to do so in the aftermath of a historical catastrophe."[40] These music vid-eos are the afterlives of the war that provide a platform for emotional reparation and transition from the era of war into the era of peace. Laury Ocen has argued that war does not necessarily end with the last gunshot; that "war boundaries transcend the battlefield."[41] Grand historical narratives of the LRA war memorialize the epic massacres through cenotaphs, commemorations, and other such events, yet the victims of the LRA continue to struggle with the "deep memory" of trauma embossed on their bodies and minds. The economic impact of the war in the destruction of livelihoods and traditional cattle econ-omy also compounds the long-term impact of war past the end of gun fire and the LRA's withdrawal beyond the borders of Uganda through the Democratic Republic of the Congo into the jungles of the Central African Republic. The music videos capture the forgotten details of post-memory and how the rank and file victims of the war continue to struggle physically, psychologically, and economically through the transition period. The videos also evaluate and critique transitional mechanisms embedded in democratic institutions that prefer to paint a glossy picture of the vocationalization of northern Uganda, and the narrative of economic reconstruction and atrocity tourism. The positive public reception of the music videos is evident and they impact public discussions as evidenced by Loketto Lee's song video, "We Don't Mind, We Don't" Care" and its sequel, "Now We Care," which capture two different eras in the northern war; first, the time when the north was neglected by citizens of Uganda from other regions, the Uganda government, and international actors; and second, the time of concerted efforts by government, NGOs, religious institutions, and the international community to intervene and end the war. They also offer avenues for postwar psychosocial support and economic recovery.

The strength of the music videos is in creating artistic spaces where what Mbembe calls "repressed topographies of cruelty" are transformed into spatio-temporal theaters for therapy and catharsis – the arena for calling for peace, reconciliation, and justice, or structuring how therapy and emotional healing, or remembrance of the war/trauma is framed.[42] At the same time, the political, social, and humanitarian roles of these artists transcend the music industry; they become political actors and activists for peace and human rights, underscoring the role of the music artist as a voice/vehicle for/of human rights. The failure of the judiciary in Uganda to prosecute LRA war criminals is the rationale for Otim's song calling on God to judge the perpetrators. It also indicts the Ugandan government for its failure to pay reparations to victims. Otim's song as well as Loketto's revert to divine justice and supernatural protection as the only sure way of redress. Kyagalunyi's music activism through his record labels and performances, his star text, and its spillover into competitive parliamentary politics provides a new lens for looking at the phenomenon of political music and its place in upholding democracy, social justice, and human rights. It shows how an artist can transition from music activism to implementing his music vision and speaking practically in parliament for the ghettoized masses. His election also challenges political actors in the government and opposition party trenches to rethink political practice and recenter the citizens who do the voting into decision making. These song videos call for peace, justice, and human rights outside of legal and political frameworks as a form of critical commentary on the failures of government, civil society, and international agencies to deliver justice, peace, and prosperity. The downside of putting faith in these music videos is that these artists may not be reliable orators for peace due to the commercial imperative and ideological entanglements of the celebrity star persona, especially the songs of political patronage. In the case of Bobi Wine, the problem with the political mileage acquired from celebrity star power is that the audiences are not able to distinguish between Bobi Wine the myth, star text, and star persona with all its contradictions and postmodernist fragmentations on the one hand and the Honorable Robert Kyagulanyi Ssentamu, the man who must deliver for his electorate now that he is a member of parliament and presidential aspirant. It also does not show how his music talent and fame will help him in the corridors of power where strategies, compromises, and sometimes downright betrayal abounds, as well as the theatrics of caucuses, trade-offs, bribery, and party-based legislation.

## Notes

1  Tetzlaff, "MTV and the Politics of Postmodern Pop," 85.

2  Shelley, *A Defence of Poetry.*

3  Ibid., 50.

4  Okot p'Bitek, *Artist the Ruler*, 39.

5  Ngugi wa Thiong'o, *Writers in Politics*, 4.

6  Karugire, *A Political History of Uganda*; Adoko, *From Obote to Obote*; Kanyeihamba, *Constitutional and Political History of Uganda from 1894 to the Present*; Reid, *A History of Modern Uganda.*

7  Mahony, "Opening Interstitial Distances in the Neoliberal University and Art School."

8  Larok, "Kyadondo," 14.

9  Ibid., 14.

10  "Audiologovisualization" refers to a production phenomenon wherein a work of art is expressed through a combination of sound "audio," words "logos," and images "visual."

11  Heidi Grunebaum and Yazir Henri, quoted in Durrant, *World Memory.*

12  Ibid.

13  Rye, "The Ethics of Aesthetics in Trauma Fiction," 1.

14  Ocen, "Reading Monuments," 22.

15  Rigney, "Portable Monuments."

16  Vernallis, *Experiencing Music Video*, ix.

17  Elliot, *Rethinking the Novel/Film Debate*, 157.

18  Lucky Philip Dube was the most successful South African reggae musician and Rastafarian and one of the greatest reggae superstars of all time. His musical career spanned twenty-five years with record labels in Zulu, English, and Afrikaans. He died in 2007 after he was shot and fatally wounded by a robber.

19  Schumann, "Music at War," 342.

20  Ibid., 343.

21  *Matto oput*, "to drink a bitter potion made from the leaves of the 'oput' tree," is a traditional Acholi restorative justice ritual which emphasizes forgiveness and reconciliation as opposed to retribution. After a homicide, the victims and perpetrators drink the bitter concoction made from the bitter roots of the plant *oput* in order to find atonement for advertent and inadvertent murder. The guilty party then makes reparation to the aggrieved party to seal the peace made.

22 Professor Ogenga Latigo was Member of Parliament for Agago County, Kitgum District, in northern Uganda from 2008 to 2012. He also served as leader of the opposition in parliament and was very outspoken about government involvement in the atrocities in northern Uganda. By calling for the classification of the killings in Acholi as genocide, the most heinous possible crime against humanity, Latigo sought to invoke the UN Convention on Genocide that would compel UN member states to intervene in stopping the tragedy and bringing perpetrators to justice.

23 Matthew 17:1–8.

24 Al-Khader, "Symbolic Implications."

25 Matthew 1:22; Isaiah 7:14; Isaiah 9:6–7.

26 Louw, "Mandela," 293.

27 Deo, "From the Award Winning Loketo Lee Now a Crime Preventer," 1.

28 Ahimbazwe, "Loketo Lee to Get BBC Peace Award."

29 Brian, "Veteran Singer 'Loketo Lee' Joins Uganda Police Force," para. 4.

30 Serugo, "Uganda"; Mwijuke, "Loketto Lee Out with 'But Now We Care'."

31 Serugo, "Uganda."

32 Ibid.

33 Mahony, "Where Do They Stand?," 58.

34 Larok, "Kyadondo," 14.

35 Nteza, "Bobi Wine Scoops African Personality of the Year Award."

36 Mahony, "Where Do They Stand?," 60.

37 King, "Moving from This Mountain."

38 Sentamu, *Situka*, the official track (February 27, 2016).

39 Sentamu, *Situka*, loaded by Counsellor Mukiibi Williams (March 7, 2016).

40 Huang, "Wounds in Time," 1.

41 Ocen, "Reading Monuments," 107.

42 Mbembe, "Necropolitics," 20.

## References

Adoko, Akena. *From Obote to Obote*. Noida, India: Vikas Publishing House, 1983.

Ahimbazwe, Roderick. "Loketo Lee to Get BBC Peace Award." *New Vision*, March 16, 2007. www.newvision.co.ug/new_vision/news/1168962/loketo-lee-bbc-peace-award.

Al-Khader, Mutasem T. "Symbolic Implications of the Moon and Sky in Coleridge's Poems with Special Reference to 'Dejection: An Ode' and the *Trio*." http://scholar.najah.edu/sites/default/files/conference-paper/symbolic-implications-moon-and-sky-coleridges-poems-special-reference-dejection-ode-and-trio.pdf (accessed April 5, 2014).

Brian, Waiswa. "Veteran Singer 'Loketo Lee' Joins Uganda Police Force." *Enewug.com* 21 (June 2016). www.enewsug.com/veteran-singer-loketo-lee-joins-uganda-police-force/ (accessed May 18, 2017).

Deo, Waswa. "From the Award Winning Loketo Lee Now a Crime Preventer." *Capital FM* 10 (June 2016). http://capitalradio.co.ug/award-winning-loketo-lee-now-crime-preventer/ (accessed May 12, 2017).

Durrant, Samuel. "Postcolonializing Trauma Studies." Review of *World Memory: Personal Trajectories in Global Time*. Ed Jill Bennett and Rosanne Kennedy (Basingstoke and New York: Palgrave Macmillan, 2003). *Postcolonial Text* 1, no. 2 (2005). www.postcolonial.org/index.php/pct/article/view/305 (accessed May 4, 2013).

Elliot, Kamilla. *Rethinking the Novel/ Film Debate*. Cambridge: Cambridge University Press, 2003.

Huang, Yiju. "Wounds in Time: The Aesthetic Afterlives of the Cultural Revolution." PhD diss., University of Illinois at Urbana-Champaign, 2011.

Kanyeihamba, George W. *Constitutional and Political History of Uganda from 1894 to the Present*. Nairobi: LawAfrica Pub, 2010.

Karugire, Samwiri R. *A Political History of Uganda*. Nairobi: Heinemann Educational Books, 1980.

King, Martin Luther. "Keep Moving from This Mountain." The Martin Luther King, Jr. Papers Project (1960). https://swap.stanford. edu/20141218225553/http:// mlk-kpp01.stanford.edu/ primary documents/Vol5/10Apr1960_ KeepMovingfromThis Mountain,AddressatSpelmanCollege. pdf (accessed July 10, 2017).

Larok, Arthur. "Kyadondo: Ghetto President Defeated Uganda's and People's Presidents." *Daily Monitor*, July 4, 2017.

Lee, Loketto. *Bigombe*. Gulu: Keyz Records, DVD (n.d.).

Lee, Loketto. *But We Don't Care*. Gulu: Keyz Records, DVD (n.d.).

Lee, Loketto. *Juba Peace Talks*. Gulu: Keyz Records, DVD (n.d.).

Louw, Eric. "Mandela: Constructing Global Celebrity as a Political Tool," pp. 291–307, in *Celebrity Colonialism*, edited by Robert Clarke. Newcastle-upon-Tyne: Cambridge Scholars Publishing, 2009.

Mahony, Emma. "'Where Do They Stand?' Deviant Art Institutions and the Liberal Democratic State," *Irish Journal of Arts Management and Cultural Policy* 1, no. 1 (2013): 54–63.

Mahony, Emma. "Opening Interstitial Distances in the Neoliberal University and Art School."

*Performance Research* 21, no. 6 (2016): 51–56.

Mbembe, Achille. "Necropolitics." *Public Culture* 15 (2003): 11–40.

Mwijuke, Gilbert. "Loketto Lee Out with 'But Now We Care'." *New Vision* online, May 27, 2005. www. newvision.co.ug/print_article/ new_vision/news/1124301/ loketo-lee-eur-care-eur?print=true (accessed January 2, 2016).

Ngugi wa Thiong'o. *Writers in Politics*. Nairobi: East African Educational Publishers, 1981.

Nteza, Isaac. "Bobi Wine Scoops African Personality of the Year Award." *ChimpReports*, January 1, 2019. https://life.chimpreports. com/bobi-wine-scoops-african-personality-of-the-year-award/ (accessed January 30, 2019).

Ocen, Laury L. "Reading Monuments: The Politics and Poetics of Memory in Postwar Northern Uganda." PhD thesis, Makerere University, Uganda, 2016.

Okot p'Bitek. *Artist the Ruler: Essays on Art, Culture and Values*. Nairobi: East African Education Publishers, 1994.

Otim, Lucky Bosmic. *Peace Return*. Gulu: Hypercom Studios, DVD (n.d.).

Otim, Lucky Bosmic. *Wang Ceng Oter* ["Let the Sun Set with It"]. Gulu: Hypercom Studios, DVD (n.d.).

Reid, Richard J. *A History of Modern Uganda*. Cambridge: Cambridge University Press. 2017.

Rigney, Ann. "Portable Monuments: Literature, Cultural Memory and the Case of Jeanie Deans." *Poetics Today* 25, no. 2 (2004): 361–396.

Rye, Gill. "The Ethics of Aesthetics in Trauma Fiction: Memory, Guilt and Responsibility in Louise L. Lambrichs's Journal d'Hannah."

*Journal of Romance Studies* 9, no. 3 (2009): 48–59.

Schumann, Anne. "Music at War: Reggae Musicians as Political Actors in the Ivoirian Crisis." *Journal of African Cultural Studies* 27, no. 3 (2015): 342–355.

Sentamu, Kyagulanyi R. [Bobi Wine]. *Situka*. (February 27, 2016). www.youtube.com/watch?v=VD3eTlSTDvs (accessed July 13, 2016).

Sentamu, Kyagulanyi R. [Bobi Wine]. *Situka* (March 7, 2016). www.youtube.com/watch?v=QmYbdVzL99M (accessed July 13, 2016).

Serugo, Moses. "Uganda: Sounding Off Loketo Lee Glad 'We Care Now'." *The Monitor* (Kampala), January 23, 2005. http://allafrica.com/stories/200501240289.html (accessed March 1, 2016).

Shelley, Percy. *A Defence of Poetry and Other Essays*. [E-Book]. Project Gutenberg, April 2004, Updated June 16, 2013. www.gutenberg.org/files/5428/5428-h/5428-h.htm#link2H_4_0010 (accessed May 16, 2017).

Tetzlaff, David J. "MTV and the Politics of Postmodern Pop." *Journal of Communication Enquiry* 10, no. 1 (1987): 80–91.

Vernallis, Carol. *Experiencing Music Video: Aesthetics and Cultural Context*. New York: Columbia University Press, 2004.

X-NO P feat. Small Luo. *Peace Anthem*. Gulu: DVD (n.d.).

# 4 | HARNESSING MEMORY INSTITUTIONS FOR PEACE AND JUSTICE: THE CASE OF SOUTH AFRICA

*David Mwambari and Iris Nxumalo*

## Introduction

In post-apartheid South Africa, the quest to address and redress over three centuries of dispossession through settler colonialism, slavery, and apartheid was negotiated through nation-building, unity, and reconciliation initiatives. Of these processes, this chapter seeks to examine attempts to advance a form of restorative justice through the Truth and Reconciliation Commission (TRC), and provide symbolic reparations through community and national memorialization projects. The latter was particularly shaped by the imperative to redress the memory landscape, as "less than one percent of about 4000 declared national monuments in South Africa related to pre-colonial African heritage."[1] Consequently, vigorous debates ensued about the future of existing monuments in the "new" South Africa, with the African National Congress (ANC) opting to retain most of the existing monuments.[2]

The processes of memory and peacebuilding in South Africa are shaped by the negotiated political settlement that anchored constitutional supremacy, human rights, and a liberal political economy as the basis of the post-apartheid state.[3] Despite widespread public participation in the negotiated transition,[4] many have referred to the settlement as an elite compromise that ceded political control to the ANC to secure the capitalist economy.[5] It is within this context that the struggles for recognition, belonging, justice, change, and identity are traversed, often within the bounds of the post-apartheid memory project.

As a new model of transitional justice, the TRC in South Africa, was envisioned as a restorative justice mechanism that engaged with collective memory-making for everyone in society through truth-telling and confessions. However, in practice it became an exercise of political (elite) reconciliation because of its emphasis on proving that violations were politically motivated. The recommendations of this process included the provision of symbolic reparations that saw the creation of collective memory institutions such as museums, monuments, and memorials that would be utilized to redress the memory landscape and advance reconciliation. The evolution of indigenous memory institutions in post-apartheid South Africa enables us to explore how such mechanisms can be utilized for building peace and ensuring justice in deeply divided societies. The focus on memory institutions in post-apartheid South Africa is critical, because of the manner in which the ANC utilized indigenous transitional justice mechanisms to address and redress apartheid within the framework of innovative memory institutions.

This chapter explores the politics of memory and reconciliation in South Africa by centralizing acts of remembering and forgetting as it relates to the use of memory institutions for peacebuilding and justice in South Africa. Although these memory institutions are designed to be repositories of collective memory, this chapter argues that processes of remembering also exhibit acts of forgetting that institutionalize the silencing and erasure of particular historical narratives. It shows that such institutional forgetting and social amnesia undermines the post-conflict institutions-building. By illuminating the ways in which the memory project "achieves status by erasing more complex histories" we seek to demonstrate the bearing that this has on the quest for building sustainable (and positive) peace in South Africa.[6] The cases in this chapter represent the ways in which particular historical narratives are silenced under the weight of reconciliation processes, and how this not only reflects the complex vulnerabilities of those erased but also shapes the engagements of those whose memories are marginalized in the present peacebuilding process. This, we argue, has the potential to generate new grievances and cripple attempts to redress the multiple violences of South Africa's slave, colonial, and apartheid histories through memory institutions.

## Collective Memory and Silence in Peacebuilding and Justice: An African Perspective

The eruption of various conflicts in the 1990s stimulated new forms of knowledge production that sought to understand and explain "new" patterns of violence.[7] The civil wars in Africa and elsewhere had characteristics that were different from earlier wars. First, conflicts in homes, churches, schools, and universities became the new battlegrounds where conflicting parties freely warred against each other.[8] For example, in the African context, these new battlefields were found in conflicts in Angola, Burundi, Congo, Sudan, Liberia, Niger, Rwanda, Sierra Leone, and Somalia in the 1990s. The second feature lay in the kind of stakeholders involved in these conflicts and the resolutions sought. From new militias to the involvement of traditional armies, the theater of warfare did not just consist of their counterparts or mostly male soldiers, but rather an increase of informal militias and other insurgencies who neither waged conventional warfare nor put on uniforms. Fighters now included women, small children, and violent gangs of youth that were politicized and mobilized by either actor.[9] Thus, memorials were no longer built just for soldiers and a few civilians or in specific spaces but there was a need for construction of memorials throughout the social landscape of states that paid tribute to all kinds of contributions and victims.

The lack of understanding and documentation of these new battlefields led to new debates in peace studies. Existing theoretical frameworks try to analyze memory and peacebuilding processes.[10] On a similar note, memory sites and institutions of collective memory have been studied as the intangible aspects of peacebuilding within transitional justice systems.[11] Moreover, the link between collective memory and the institutions is viewed as the basis for maintaining the rule of law in post-conflict countries.[12] Despite the epistemological evolution on this subject, post-conflict scholarship has generally ignored the role of institutions that are created to guard collective memory, memorialization rituals, memorials, and at the same time privilege certain narratives of the past in Africa.[13] As Brett and colleagues have argued, memorials are perceived as "outside the political process – relegated to the 'soft' cultural sphere of art objects, to the private sphere of personal mourning, or to the margins of power and politics."[14] Therefore, in most post-conflict African societies, institutionalized and official memorials "fall between the cracks of existing policies."[15]

Furthermore, debates have shifted to include an understanding that cultural context matters in building long-term peace. Efforts to explore a new framework of "conflict transformation" that combines different actors and considers multi-track approaches that are short, medium, and long term, are critical in addressing the multifaceted nature of conflicts in deeply divided societies.[16] This "holistic" framework builds on the earlier work of Johan Galtung that emphasizes the importance of examining the "root causes" of conflicts with an aim of fostering sustainable peace.[17] Existing literature contends that within the holistic framework, reconciliation is a key component of peacebuilding.[18] Reconciliation is understood to be a long-term process with truth, justice, mercy, and peace at its heart.[19] Individual and collective memory and silence are at the heart of this social transformation. Memories of the past are crucial to both the bearer and those who intervene in reconciliation processes. They allow one to examine the root causes of what occurred, and its consequences, and therefore prevent it from reoccurring. South Africa has based its reconciliation policies of the past two decades on promoting state-led exercises to promote memory as central to national reconciliation while suppressing certain alternative narratives.

One of the recent debates is on the importance of memorialization or social amnesia to achieve peace and reconciliation in post-conflict countries. One side of the debate consists of a school of thought which emphasizes the importance of "emotions, societal beliefs, narratives, and collective memory" in conflicted groups' ability to reconcile and maintain long-term peace.[20] Casey and Winter and Emmanuel understand memory to be an almost universal feature of human society, across time, culture, and geography.[21] These researchers argue that there is a seemingly universal human tendency that seeks to gather "bits and pieces of the past, and joining them together in public."[22] This is to construct a coherent collective memory through private and public events that include, sending condolence messages, visiting the grieving family, or visiting official memorials. The proponents of collective memory therefore argue that memories of the past, whether individual or collective, cannot be imprisoned.[23] The past resists "efforts to make it over."[24] This justification values the importance of building memory institutions as part of reconciliation in post-conflict countries. Hence, we build on this argument to examine the context of South Africa in which collective memory has been included as a state-driven process.

The other school of thought argues that "forgetting" the past or "social amnesia" may be considered as measures of fostering reconciliation amongst former hostile groups instead of remembrance; or that such forgetting can co-exist with memories of a traumatic past.[25] Renan for example argues that those collective memory narratives are also constructed through forgetting or silence.[26] He asserts that a given society "may choose to forget uncomfortable knowledge," for example, the political elites who might have participated in the violence.[27] The phenomenon of forgetting is transformed into what Stanley Cohen calls "social amnesia" or a social process in which members of a community disregards its discreditable past.[28] Hence, collective memory is "intrinsically linked to identity and transmission of memory and history."[29] In addition, social amnesia is also integral to creating new identities in post-conflict societies, a process that is important in reconciliation.[30] The two phenomena comprise the centerpiece of history education in post-conflict countries and therefore shape the future.[31] Both sides of the debate are anchored on a large and broader body of literature that critiques the liberal peace agenda.[32]

Some scholars have pointed out the liberal peace agenda's fundamental shortcomings in addressing post-conflict challenges, while others have proposed ways to renovate the concept and to make it more efficient.[33] The main criticism is that this approach tends to focus "on the development of the liberal state, its institutions and a neoliberal economy" and often ignores the importance of psychosocial support in the reconstruction phase.[34] Others focus on material reconstruction not memory reconstruction.[35] These critics point to its global vision which ignores local factors; worse still, this approach is designed and implemented by international actors at the expense of local actors' interests.[36] However, the case of South Africa reveals the centrality of memorialization in reconciliation processes and problems that arise in building memory institutions that privilege certain narratives in post-conflict societies. Thus, post-apartheid South Africa presents a unique case of a country in Africa that manifests both memorialization and social amnesia in its reconstruction process. For a critical examination of the South Africa case study, this chapter first discusses key memorialization institutions created after apartheid followed by an analysis of alternative narratives silenced in post-apartheid state-driven reconciliation processes.

## Memorialization of South Africa's Apartheid Histories

This section explores the emergence of South Africa's post-apartheid memorialization processes, which excavated hidden or suppressed histories in order to "redress" the memory landscape. This was done, initially, through the work of the Truth and Reconciliation Commission and furthered by museums, monuments, and memorials such as the Apartheid Museum, Robben Island Museum, District Six Museum, and community memorials and monuments. These memory institutions will be critically examined in this section, to shed light on the narratives that are memorialized and its relation to the pursuit of peace and justice in South Africa.

### Truth and Reconciliation Commission

The TRC was established by the Promotion of National Unity and Reconciliation Act, No. 34 of 1995, which sought to establish through statements, hearings, and investigations, "as complete a picture as possible of the nature, causes and extent of gross violations of human rights."[37] The functioning and scope of the TRC reflected the terms negotiated in the settlement, with some arguing that the ANC did not have enough leverage to fight for prosecutions, but had the power to negotiate for the revealing of some truth through this forum.[38] It was this emphasis on bringing lived realities and experiences to the fore that presented one of the most powerful aspects of the TRC experience. The act of bringing to light what was once concealed marked a significant departure from the apartheid past, creating the possibility of testimonies and confessions being a powerful vehicle of closure, reconciliation, anger, self-definition, reopening the wounds, and nation-building and confirming a movement "from repression to expression."[39]

The scope of the TRC was limited to the violations committed between March 1, 1960 and the first democratic elections in 1994 in South Africa, effectively silencing the histories of dispossession, slavery, and the marginalization of the Khoi and San communities.[40] However, scholars like Hamber argued that the narrowed scope of the TRC was for pragmatic purposes, and even though it was narrow in the context of South Africa's history of dispossession, it was much broader than comparable truth commissions at the time.[41] Nonetheless, the continued plight of Khoi and San communities in South Africa and their marginalization from the political processes of nation-building and reconciliation is concerning, despite the pragmatism of the approach. The TRC was envisioned as a restorative justice mechanism that would provide a platform to heal and unite the nation through truth-telling, infused with notions of *ubuntu* and forgiveness to administer "amnesty for perpetrators, truth for the society (not just the victims), and reparations for victims."[42] Between 1996 and 1998, the TRC administered over 21,298 cases and over 7000 amnesty applications were made.[43]

The TRC's engagement with collective memory-making through testimonies and confessions was viewed as a powerful form of alternative historiography that brought to light what was silenced and obscured by the modus operandi of the apartheid state, and included those voices and narratives that were previously excluded from the canons of knowledge.[44] The platform for truth-telling provided by the TRC would then be creating a framework upon which people would pursue reconciliation.[45] It also became a forum where fuller liberation histories could be brought to the fore, as witnessed by the testimonies of ANC members who were imprisoned in Quatro, which served as the movement's detention center in Angola.[46]

However, the narrative of the TRC is not without its limitations. By individualizing the "victims and perpetrators" of apartheid and having to prove that violations were politically motivated, "the Commission rewrote the history of apartheid as one of a drama played out within a fractured political elite."[47] Furthermore, this operationalization neglected the structural, legal, and institutional components of apartheid, which consequently shuffled out the everyday violence of apartheid and excluded most women from contributing to the memory-making mechanism of the TRC. As noted by McEwan, when women did testify, it was about the experiences of males in their families and/ or homes therefore leading to the portrayal of women as "secondary victims" of apartheid abuses.[48] In response to the criticisms of various women's organizations who challenged the gender biases of the process and the gendered partiality of truth created by the TRC's operationalization, the TRC held *three* women-only hearings in Cape Town, Durban, and Johannesburg with negligible media coverage.[49] Unwittingly, as advanced by Mgxashe, the TRC thus "condoned the silencing of women's experience because of the lack of attention to the distinctive ways in which apartheid affected women across all sectors."[50]

While it is important to note that the TRC was one of many mechanisms to advance nation-building, unity, and reconciliation in South Africa, evaluations – then and now – of the efficacy of the TRC reflect concerns about the incongruence between the commission's approach to amnesty and society's widespread need for accountability and justice through retributive justice, perceptions of a forced and hurried process of reconciliation undertaken by the TRC, the reluctance of the state to provide financial reparations, views of reconciliation through amnesty as a sophisticated form of individual and state impunity, and the prevalence of increased criminality in contexts where some form of retributive justice is not practiced.[51] Furthermore, in a context where social reconciliation and transformation is limited, many who participated in the process are starting to feel that they, like the Khulumani Support Group advanced, "have been used in a cynical process of political expediency."[52] As the following sections demonstrate, the use of memory institutions for peacebuilding and justice in South Africa was underpinned by one of the recommendations contained in the TRC report, which called for the use of symbolic reparations (monuments, museums, and memorials) as a measure to assist with reconciliation and to restore the human dignity of survivors of apartheid violence.[53]

### The Apartheid Museum

The Apartheid Museum in Gold Reef City, Johannesburg, is a privately commissioned space of memory that was conceived to secure the bid for Gold Reef City Casino from the Gauteng Gambling Board.[54] Although the site was not commissioned by the state, it reflects the efforts of private entities to engage with and speak to the politics of nation-building and reconciliation in ways that may sometimes reinforce dominant narratives. The Apartheid Museum is a site of reckoning – its design, flow, audio-visual material and structures keep apartheid alive to enable visitors to experience the histories and struggles of South Africa, and emerge to the light (the garden) at the end of the tour, a space envisaged as a site of healing and reflection. As you enter the museum, you encounter the seven pillars of the constitution (democracy, equality, reconciliation, diversity, responsibility, respect, and freedom) in the courtyard, which almost foreground the contrary lived realities that one will encounter as one journeys through the museum. The permanent exhibition consists of these pillars, as well as compartmentalized segments of South Africa's history represented by "photography, film, text, testimony and artefacts."[55] The temporary exhibitions of the museum commemorate the struggle against segregation (with a focus on education), the Freedom Charter, the constitution, the Women's March, the life and death of individuals such as Steve Biko and Ahmed Timol.[56] It is interesting to note the ways in which the temporary exhibitions can also subvert dominant (heteronormative) narratives in peacebuilding and reconciliation in South Africa. This can be seen in the *Journeys of Faith: Navigating Sexual Orientation and Gender Diversity* exhibition that sought to create a space where individuals could explore the reconciliation of their gender and sexual identities with their religious and spiritual beliefs, through their life stories and testimonies.[57]

## Robben Island Museum

The history of Robben Island (which is located in Table Bay in the Western Cape) has constructed this space as a site predominantly known for banishment, isolation, and imprisonment. The island has a rich history with evolving uses and purposes, most popularly known as a maximum-security prison for male political dissidents of color during apartheid.[58] The island now stands as a world heritage site and a national monument, with narratives that frame it as the "university of struggle," but caution should be exercised in deploying these narratives, as it could silence the histories and contributions of those who were imprisoned and/or tortured in other sites during apartheid, especially that of women, who were not imprisoned in Robben Island but in various other sites such as Boksburg, Nylstroom, and Kroonstad, amongst others.[59] An attempt to redress this male-centric prison history is furthered by the Women's Jail at Constitutional Hill in Johannesburg. Robben Island Museum (RIM) balances its conservation, education, and heritage imperatives through its conservation programs, school tours, the African Programme in Museum and Heritage Studies, outreach programs, national education camps, and adult groups.[60]

There are many ways in which the RIM attempted to make the history that they commemorate and memorialize more inclusive, for example, by providing its full history on the website, showcasing the Robert Sobukwe house and naming its catamarans Makana and Autshumato[61] to commemorate and recognize Khoi and Xhosa struggles against colonialism.[62] However, there is a sense, especially on the tour, that these elements provide the build-up to the apex of the tour, which is exploring liberation history through the prison, culminating in the experience of former president Nelson Mandela's prison cell. To this end, many have contested the form of memorialization being advanced by the museum, one that centralizes the liberation narrative of the ANC and almost silences the struggles and contributions of the Azanian People's Organisation (AZAPO), the Pan-African

Congress (PAC), and the Non-European Unity Movement (NEUM), amongst others. Deacon advances, in response to these concerns, that the memorialization of Robben Island will "necessarily be selective in its remembering and forgetting – precisely because of the island's vital role in national reconstruction."[63]

### District Six Museum

Forced removals were an important part of the modus operandi of colonial rule, segregation, and apartheid, which were utilized to dispossess people of color of land and to segregate the South African landscape. Legislation such as the 1913 Land Act and the Group Areas Act of 1950 were utilized in different eras to operationalize forced removals, with the latter having resulted in the forcible removal of over 3.5 million people between 1950 and 1982.[64] These state-led dispossessions occurred throughout the state, in places such as Protea Village, Sophiatown, and Cato Manor. The forced removals that occurred within District Six (located in Cape Town) both predated the 1910 "Union" of South Africa (by 1901 all black people were removed after the area was declared a colored area) and were executed by the apartheid government, to convert its declaration of District Six as a white area into reality by forcibly removing coloreds between 1966 and 1981.[65]

District Six Museum is a people's museum because it was estab-lished by former residents who sought to "repossess the history of the area as a place where people lived, loved and struggled."[66] The aim was thus not to recreate District Six, but to populate this seemingly empty space with the memories, stories, homes, streets, pictures, and voices of former residents and tourists who had lived, worked, and traveled to District Six. It seeks to portray some of the lives and histories of the community before the forced removals by using a form of reflective nostalgia to reflect inconsistences, contradictions, and empty spaces.[67] The museum is in the former Methodist Church in Buitekant, Cape Town and acquired a second building in the same street, which is now referred to as the Homecoming Centre. Per the District Six Museum website, the Homecoming Centre is a part of the cultural heritage pre-cinct found in District Six, and is envisaged as a space for "education and memory work," providing rental spaces for events, a book shop, and a coffee shop.[68]

One of the most interesting facts about the District Six Museum is that it became a Land Claims Court in 1997, which not only saw the establishment of protocol for land restitution claims but also eventually administered these processes by becoming a space where resettlement into District Six and financial compensation was decided on individual claims.[69] Naidu advances that the practices of the museum have provided a methodology of work regarding how museums can strategically position themselves to mediate the past in the present.[70] This is evidenced by their engagement with diasporic District Six former residents and the broader Western Cape community, youth and public education programs, as well as their positioning to engage in the politics of land restitution and return to District Six. This engagement, the museum advances, is anchored in the exploration of the "relationship between landscapes and memorialisation in support of human rights, urban justice and the creation of a more just and inclusive civil society."[71]

### Community Memorials and Monuments

One of the localized ways in which symbolic reparations were created in South Africa was through community memorials. These memorials were designed to commemorate acts of apartheid violence in specific communities, to build trust and to reconcile parties who may have fought on different sides during the struggle. This is the case for memorials and monuments such as the Thokoza Monument and Thembisa Monuments – both found in Ekurhuleni Municipality in Gauteng – to commemorate the lives lost in the political violence between ANC and Inkatha Freedom Party supporters, and memorials such as the Sharpeville Massacre Memorial and the Duncan Village Massacre Memorial to commemorate state-sanctioned massacres in response to widespread protest action. These initiatives are typically funded by local and/or provincial government structures, "to provide a public, symbolic gesture of compensation in the absence of tangible financial assistance for individual victims."[72] Community reception of these initiatives reveals they were not always welcome, with some acts of memorialization seen to be hugely inappropriate and badly received, with a lack of consultation and local ownership, widespread vandalism and sites not reaping the economic and developmental benefits anticipated or promised by government.[73] It is interesting to note that despite the mass efforts that have been made to restore human dignity through memorialization, Naidu's research indicates that these gestures were mechanisms to divert people's attention from "more significant forms of reparation, such as financial reparations or land restitution" and are seen to thus pose a danger to the nation-building and peacebuilding process.[74]

## Effect of Silences and Institutional Forgetting on Peacebuilding and Justice

Institutional forgetting linked to South Africa's gendered and sexualized histories reflects the diverse experiences and complex vulnerabilities of gender and sexual minorities that traverse notions of belonging, citizenship, freedom, justice, and visibility within the framework of South Africa's heteronormative nation-building project. The prevalence of sexual and gender-based violence as expressed through the increase of corrective rape as a political tool to discipline performances of non-heterosexual sexualities, murder, ostracization, and discrimination on the basis of gender and sexual orientation in schools, churches, hospitals, police stations, and communities reflects the limited freedoms available in the post-apartheid era.

The near exclusion of gender and sexuality in South Africa's memory project reflects the politics that shape access to belonging, services, opportunities, citizenship, and the political community more broadly – and also shapes the preservation of life and how individuals may live or die.[75] This reflects not only the unfinished work of memory institutions in the quest for peacebuilding and justice in the country, but also the complex ways in which intersectional forms of oppression interact and shape the compromised forms of citizenship in post-apartheid South Africa. This section explores how particular forms of historical memory are silenced through social amnesia and institutional forgetting, by exploring the memorialization of South Africa's slave histories and the contributions of women and members of the LGBTQIA+ community in the anti-apartheid struggle.

### South Africa's Slave Histories: Race, Gender, and the Khoi and San Peoples

Pumla Dineo Gqola, reflecting on Wicomb's work, *David's Story*, which brings to the fore the challenges of historicizing and story-telling, shares the profound difficulties of so doing "when there is no dependable narrative, only the coloniser's written form."[76] This problem rings true in multiple ways for the indigenous people of South Africa, the Khoi and the San, who have endured genocide, enslavement, oppression, and non-recognition for centuries.

Even though the TRC could not address the gross human rights violations against the Khoi and the San in the time of colonialism and slavery, the post-apartheid era has provided a space where the hidden histories of the Khoi-San and of slavery could be brought to light in museums, school curricula, and memorials. Not only was South Africa's slave history absent from these spaces in former times, but it was also absent from the lexicon of the liberation struggle, as it was considered divisive.[77] The project of remembering generally and with reference to the indigenous peoples of South Africa and experiences of slavery are profoundly gendered, racialized, and sexualized.[78] This is shaped not only by the erasure of women from these histories, but also by the patriarchal empire-building project that inscribed meaning upon bodies and used the bodies of Southern African women to shape the language of scientific racism.[79] No better is this demonstrated than in the case of Sara Baartman as depicted in "I Have Come to Take You Home."[80] The repatriation and burial of Sara Baartman will thus be examined to demonstrate the gendered and racialized ways in which the memory project is utilized for nation-building in South Africa.

### The Reparation and Burial of Sara Baartman

Narratives and memorials of the nation tend to emphasize the corporeality of women to symbolize the nation and to invent and reinvent identities in the present. One such example of the latter is found in re-inventions of post-apartheid Afrikaans identity, which makes claims to Krotoa, an enslaved Khoi woman who married a Dutch settler, as their founding mother to establish a foundation for notions of African authenticity and indigeneity. It is important to challenge, as Gqola and Coetzee do, the appropriations of the herstories of enslaved women, because of the very troubling gendered ways in which their bodies are dismembered and the violence of their herstories are silenced for political and economic purposes.[81] Another such attempt was made by using the repatriation and burial of Sara Baartman to construct symbolic links to nation-building and the restoration of the dignity of indigenous peoples and women.

The herstories of Sara Baartman reflect the contradiction of simultaneously having volumes of work written on her corporeality, yet very little is known about *her*. Sara Baartman was an enslaved Khoi woman sent to London and Paris to be paraded, abused, displayed in museums, and subsequently taken away from public view. Unsuccessful attempts were made to repatriate Sara's remains by former president Nelson Mandela (1994) and by Alfred Nzo and Ben Ngubane, ministers of the Foreign Affairs and Arts and Culture ministries respectively, in 2000.[82] Other parties involved in the negotiations included the Griqua National Council, Musée de l'Homme (where the cast of her body and her remains were stored), and the French government. The quote mentioned in this sub-section's title, is found in a poem written as a tribute to Sara Baartman by Diana Ferrus, which later spurred a French senator to translate and present the poem to Senate to motivate for the passing of a bill that ensured the repatriation of Sara Baartman.[83] Despite claims that her remains were lost,[84] her remains were eventually repatriated to South Africa in 2002. This process was constructed as an important part of South Africa's nation-building project, and as argued by Samuelson, recast her body to project images of a restored and united body politic through modes of decolonial self-writing that did not destabilize the terms of respectability, decency, and domesticity upon which Baartman's corporeality was written about.[85] Her remains were laid to rest in Hankey, Eastern Cape. Although it was declared in 2002 that her burial site was to be made a national heritage site, it was only officially acknowledged as such from 2008.[86] The construction of the Sarah Baartman Centre of Remembrance, which is located close to her burial site, has experienced significant delays and has been a site for protest action due to low and late pay.[87]

### The Memorialization of Women's Contributions to the "Liberation" Struggle

*Despite* the South African government's political commitment to gender equality, the memorialization projects pursued by the government have failed to reflect this commitment and the mass involvement of women in different South African eras. This is largely significant, as the gender biases and the lack of representivity hinder reconciliation, erase and forget the important contributions made by women to South Africa's history, and compromise women's citizenship in the nation-building process. So dire is the situation that some have lamented the

"Great Man character" of the present memorialization project, with Miller probing us to think deeply about the costs associated with the erasure of women's activism and political agency in South Africa by asking, "what happens when national pride, or revolutionary success, is equated with male leadership?"[88]

At present, the majority of the memorials erected to honor women's contributions have been privately sponsored, with the exception of the National Monument to the Women of South Africa, the Gugu Dlamini Memorial to commemorate the life and HIV/AIDS activism of Dlamini, and the Women's Jail in Constitutional Hill, Johannesburg. The remainder of this section will briefly look at the National Monument to the Women of South Africa to speak to the gendered acts of memorialization which privilege male contributions, and also the inaccessibility of the monument as representative of the erasure and silencing of women's activism in the struggle and their compromised citizenship today.

The National Monument to the Women of South Africa is significant because it was the first national-level attempt to memorialize women's activism and vast contributions to the struggle.[89] The monument is located at the Union Buildings in Pretoria, which is strategically important because it can be seen as the locus of government and presidential power in South Africa. The bidding, deliberation, and design of the monument reflected feminist interventions on memorialization, which sought to resist the grandeur and monumentality of patriarchal expressions of power and importance by imbibing a different set of notions and standards, sometimes anchored in understatement and humility.[90] The winning design had at its center a grinding stone called *imbokodo*, with an interactive sound experience of chants used by the women who participated in the 1956 Women's March. Despite the fact that many of the activists loved the memorial because of the way it integrated the politics of the everyday into the struggle against apartheid, many heavily criticized it particularly because they struggled with its lack of monumentality, and deemed it to be neither empowering nor affirming to the women who risked their lives in acts of mobilization akin to treason at the time.[91] Although the intention of the monument was for it to be publicly accessible, it remains largely inaccessible due to the inaccessibility of the Union Buildings, and the closing down of public space for people to access the monument. The monument is no longer accessible to individuals unless authorization is obtained from the highest levels, and demonstrates the very intricate ways in which "the work of forgetting happens."[92] The work of remembering as a form of resistance is thus taken up through localized memory projects such as Amazwi Abesifazane, Ministries of the Christian Development Agency for Social Action, Khulumani Groups, and the Direct Action Centre for Peace and Memory, which politicizes and recognizes the continuum of apartheid violences through "radical oral history projects, autographical accounts by women and life histories of communities lost or destroyed under the apartheid removals, and radical art projects."[93] These projects represent notions of a postcolonial archive which seeks to include excluded peoples, questions silences and marginalization, brings to the fore erasures, and prioritizes examinations of power and its effect in shaping the archive, memorialization, and historical narratives.

### Queering and the "Liberation" Struggle: Contesting Heteronormative Erasure

The erasure of black queer histories is the most sustained form of silence and institutional forgetting that pertains to historical narratives and the use of memory institutions to redress colonialism, slavery, and apartheid histories in South Africa today. Despite the gains secured through LGBT activism that not only advanced the anti-apartheid struggle but also advocated for legal reform and redress through recognition, equal treatment, and protection under the law in post-apartheid South Africa, there is no state-driven initiative to memorialize the contributions of the LGBT community to South Africa's history. Despite widely held views that homosexuality is un-African, it has long been established that "[n]ot only did queerness exist in Africa before colonialism but it did so in many variations that reflect the diversity of Africa's cultures with fluidity: weaving itself in and out of gender norms, social institutions, moral censure and even social utility."[94] This positioning becomes central because it reflects the centrality of the colonial civilizing missions of the British, Dutch, and the Afrikaner Nationalist Party in criminalizing, othering, and pathologizing non-heterosexual relationships and acts of intimacy with the use of Christian doctrine.[95]

Queer people and their histories are thus, an integral part of South Africa's histories of colonialism, slavery, and apartheid – and as such – their liberation is intricately bound to the liberation of others.[96] Despite the prevalence of narratives that frame apartheid solely as a racial project, apartheid was a regulatory regime that sought to control all areas of life – and was deeply invested in exercising power and control over inter-personal relationships and performances of gender and sexuality in South Africa through various forms of legislation and policing. Examples of this are found in the Immorality Act of 1957, the Sexual Offences Act of 1957, the Mixed Marriages Act of 1959, and the Immorality Act of 1950, the Immorality Amendment Act of 1969, and the Immorality Act of 1988, which imposed harsher sentences than earlier pieces of legislation.

Within this brief *longue durée* of queer histories, individuals in the LGBT community also experienced forms of human rights violations such as multiple forms of discrimination, torture, imprisonment, and death (some because of their anti-apartheid and LGBT activism and orientation) that should have been considered by the TRC – but was not because of the limited framing of the TRC discussed earlier in this chapter.[97] The advocacy of white gay associations that took no stance against apartheid – such as Law Reform and the Gay Association of South Africa (GASA) – to the broad-based black associations that aligned with the ANC and the United Democratic Front – such as Gay and Lesbians of the Witswatersrand (GLOW), the Organisation of Lesbian and Gay Activists (OGLA), and the National Coalition for Gay and Lesbian Equality (NCGLE) – was especially absent from popular narratives. Thus, multiple forms of silences exist: erasure in historical narratives, transitional justice mechanisms, anti-colonial and anti-Apartheid memorialization, and liberation narratives.

It is for this reason that Marion Drew implored readers to challenge their conceptions of freedom in South Africa by asking, "How many battles do people have to fight to be free?"[98] This rings especially true for gender and sexual minorities, whose "struggles in South Africa have generally been marginalised in organisations, movements and discourses that ostensibly focus on struggles for human dignity, equality and justice."[99] Acts of self-remembering and archiving thus become deeply political forms of resistance that challenge the heteronormativity of the present memory project. Such acts of remembering are found in Gay and Lesbian Memory in Action (GALA) for example, which has positioned itself as "an important destination for people interested in the study, promotion and preservation of the history, culture and contemporary experiences of LGBTI people in Africa."[100]

## Conclusion

This chapter has explored the varied ways in which the past is remembered, memorialized, and deployed in the service of reconciliation and peacebuilding in South Africa. Because these processes of peacebuilding and memorialization are deeply political, grievances may arise that speak to fundamental contestations of power, belonging, and identity in the "post"-conflict moment. Placing processes of remembering within a context of power becomes imperative, as it enables us to explore what is remembered, how it is remembered, and the modes of silencing and forgetting that accompany the institutionalization of memory within memory institutions. It is within this context that we argue that the narratives that regimes privilege and silence are significant, as they shape the course of peacebuilding in divided societies and attempts to advance sustainable peace.

This chapter has sought to make an argument for the centrality of the politics of memorialization and memory institutions in the context of conflict transformation through peacebuilding and justice mechanisms in post-conflict and divided societies. By placing memory institutions at the heart of political processes, we place significance on the historical narratives utilized that shape notions of remembering and institutional forgetting in South Africa. Further to this, we argue that what is not remembered (and is therefore excluded) from the memory project hinders the ability of these mechanisms to address the root causes of historical injustices, and provides the basis for new forms of grievance and struggle.

As reflected in the memory projects pursued by South Africa in the service of nation-building, reconciliation, peacebuilding, and justice, silences and omissions "assume presence and speak volumes"[101] and reflect the variety of purposes that these serve. Not only do the present silences in the memory project in South Africa legitimize those in power with liberation narratives, but they are also utilized by individuals and communities to navigate the politics of survival and identity formation in post-apartheid South Africa. Furthermore, the narratives and silences witnessed in the above memory project also speak to a sense of exclusion – not only in historical narrative but also in imaginations of the "new nation," revealing the compromised forms of citizenship and marginalization that characterize such silences.

Where is the space, then, for reconciliation and sustainable peace amidst silence and institutional forgetting? Is it possible to build these new societies with the weight of the silences that have bearing on livelihoods, belonging, and the configuration of power in the present? We find that in this case, the road to reconciliation and justice as pursued within the memory project is turbulent and contentious, and inscribes boundaries on who belongs and which struggles are recognized, prioritized, and addressed within the infrastructure of peacebuilding. Not only does this reflect the importance of memory institutions in the quest of peacebuilding and justice, but it also demonstrates how memory institutions and historical narratives can serve or hinder the quest for an inclusive and just society after conflict. What the discussion above also reveals is how contentious issues of local ownership are – even when the memory and peacebuilding work is led by the state. It reminds us that these processes are also political, and evaluations of such work are not served by placing memory and memorialization on the margins of the political process.

## Notes

1   Davison, "Museums and the Reshaping of Memory," 150.

2   Coombes, *History after Apartheid*, 19–23.

3   Wilson, *The Politics of Truth and Reconciliation in South Africa*, 3–6.

4   Barnes, *Owning the Process*.

5   See for example Southall, "The Power Elite in Democratic South Africa."

6   Okoye, "The Limits of Representation?," 11.

7   See for example Williams, who in his book *War and Conflict in Africa* argued that the causes of conflict and their nature were not exclusively linked to "colonialism, postcolonial elites, ethnicity and greedy criminals," 7. He identifies the survival of weak states as the main thread that links these new conflicts in Africa. However, Ali Mazrui disagrees and instead traces the new conflicts to colonial legacies in various countries. He identifies many factors such as artificial colonial borders, altered new social identities in post-colonial Africa as examples of the colonial legacy. See Mazrui, *Conflict in Africa*. Other scholars such as Rick Auty (*Sustaining Development in Mineral Economies*), Ian Gary and Terry Lynn Karl ("Bottom of the Barrel"), and Michael L. Ross ("Oil, Drugs, and Diamonds") argue that oil and diamonds in particular are to blame for the rise of conflicts in Africa. Similarly, others explained that these wars are influenced by economic factors, see Collier and Hoeffler, "On Economic Causes of Civil War." On conflicts that instrumentalize ethnicity in Africa see Nnoli, *Ethnic Conflicts in Africa*. Other researchers such as Abu Bakarr Bah argue that state decay is a much "more useful concept for examining the conditions that lead to civil wars and state failure in Africa." See Bah, "State Decay."

8   Kaldor argues that "the new wars can be contrasted with earlier wars in terms of their goals, the methods of warfare and how they are financed." Kaldor, *New and Old Wars*, 6.

9   See for example ibid.; Coulter, "Female Fighters in the Sierra Leone War"; and Drumbl, "She Makes Me Ashamed to Be a Woman." Also for

a discussion on distinction of actors see Bah, *Civil Non-State Actors in Peacekeeping and Peacebuilding in West Africa*.

10   Charbonneau and Parent, *Peacebuilding, Memory and Reconciliation*.

11   Barsalou, "Situated Conceptualisation"; Barsalou and Baxter, *The Urge to Remember*; and Naidu, *Ties that Bind*.

12   Minow and Rosenblum, *Breaking the Cycles of Hatred*.

13   Meierhenrich, *Topographies of Remembering and Forgetting*.

14   Brett et al., *Memoralisation and Democracy*, 2.

15   Ibid.

16   Paffenholz, "International Peacebuilding Goes Local."

17   Galtung, *Peace, War and Defense*.

18   Bar-Tal and Bennink, "The Nature of Reconciliation as an Outcome and as a Process"; Lederach, *Building Peace*; and Ross, "What Do We Know about Natural Resources and Civil War?"

19   Lederach, *Building Peace*.

20   Keynan, "Between Past and Future," 20.

21   Casey, *Remembering*, 1; Winter and Emmanuel, *War and Remembrance in the Twentieth Century*.

22   Ibid.

23   Ševčenko and Russell-Ciardi, "Sites of Conscience," 9.

24   Schudson, "The Present in the Past versus the Past in the Present," 105.

25   Renan, *What Is a Nation?*; and Cohen, *States of Denial*.

26   Renan, *What Is a Nation?*, 8.

27   Ibid.

28   Cohen, *States of Denial*, 138.

29   Ibid.

30   Naidu et al., *History on Their Own Terms*, 29.

31   Cole, "Transitional Justice and the Reform of History Education."

32   For example Richmond, "Failed Statebuilding versus Peace Formation"; Doyle and Sambanis, *Making War and Building Peace*; and Mac Ginty, "Indigenous Peace-Making versus the Liberal Peace."

33   Doyle and Sambanis, *Making War and Building Peace*; Paris, *At War's End*; Paris, "Saving Liberal Peace Building."

34   Richmond, "Peace during and after the Age of Intervention," 6.

35   See for example works of Bah, "People-Centered Liberalism"; Bah, "The Contours of New Humanitarianism."

36   Bah, "The Contours of New Humanitarianism."

37   Government of the Republic of South Africa, *Promotion of National Unity Act N°34 of 1995*, Chapter 2, Section 3(1a), 4.

38   Hamber, "Remembering to Forget," 6.

39   Ndebele, "Memory, Metaphor, and the Triumph of Narrative," 20; Bremner, "Memory, Nation-Building and the Post-Apartheid City."

40   Mamdani, "Amnesty or Impunity?"; Robins, "Silence in My Father's House."

41   Hamber, "Remembering to Forget."

42   Ibid., 54.

43   Wilson, *The Politics of Truth and Reconciliation in South Africa*, 22–23.

44   See for example Stanley, "Evaluating the Truth and Reconciliation Commission"; Marschall, "Memory and Identity in South Africa"; and Coombes, "Witnessing History/Embodying Testimony."

45   Naidu, *Symbolic Reparations*, 15.

46   Cleveland, "We Still Want Truth."

47   Mamdani, "Amnesty or Impunity?," 56.

48   McEwan, "Building a Postcolonial Archive?"

49   Ibid., 745.

50   Coombes, "Witnessing History/ Embodying Testimony," S94.

51   Wilson, *The Politics of Truth and Reconciliation in South Africa*, 25; Hamber, "Remembering to Forget," 6; Stanley, "Evaluating the Truth and Reconciliation Commission," 525; Borneman, *Settling Accounts*, 71.

52   Khulumani Support Group Press Release, dated October 27, 1999; quoted in Wilson, *The Politics of Truth and Reconciliation in South Africa*, 22.

53   Naidu, *Ties that Bind*.

54   Bremner, "Memory, Nation-Building and the Post-Apartheid City," 100.

55   Ibid., 88.

56   Apartheid Museum, "Exhibition Archive."

57   Apartheid Museum, "Journeys of Faith."

58   Deacon, "Remembering Tragedy, Constructing Modernity."

59   Coombes, *History after Apartheid*; Coombes, "Witnessing History/Embodying Testimony."

60   Robben Island, "Education at RIM."

61   Makana – also written Maqana and Makhanda – was a Xhosa prophet-chief who was imprisoned on Robben Island after he led his people in a series of rebellions against British invasion, occupation, and colonialism. Autshumato was a Khoi leader who worked as a translator for the Dutch East India Company. Also referred to as Harry de Strandloper, he initially worked on the island and was later imprisoned. He is also known for having escaped the island with a fellow prisoner but was later found.

62   Robben Island, "Education at RIM."

63   Deacon, "Remembering Tragedy, Constructing Modernity," 178.

64   South African History Online, "Forced Removals in South Africa."

65   De Kok, "Cracked Heirlooms."

66   Coombes, *History after Apartheid*, 120.

67   Ibid., 123–131.

68   District Six Museum, "The Homecoming Centre."

69   Coombes, *History after Apartheid*.

70   Naidu, *Ties that Bind*.

71   District Six Museum, "Restitution in District Six."

72   Marschall, "Memory and Identity in South Africa," 194.

73   It is interesting to note that in the case of the Duncan Village Massacre Memorial, the symbol of a warrior with a spear and shield was utilized to spark the remembering of a broader history of resistance, by placing the massacre within this context of a broader anti-colonial and liberation struggle. However, the community felt that the symbol was more representative of Xhosa anti-colonial resistance, which they felt was improper given the context of the massacre. Another interesting way residents felt that their pain was appropriated inconsiderately was with the memorial built in Mamelodi to commemorate the disappearance of political activists during apartheid. The ANC built a memorial stone and called it the Stanza Bopape Memorial (prominent ANC activist who disappeared during the struggle). This caused grave dissatisfaction amongst the families of other activists who were not similarly commemorated, and felt like their loved ones had been excluded from the memorial. See Kgalema, *Symbols of Hope*, 18–20.

74   Naidu, *Ties that Bind*, 1.

75   Livermon, "Queer(y)ing Freedom."

76   Gqola, *What Is Slavery to Me?*, 73–74.

77   Ward and Worden, "Commemorating, Suppressing, and Invoking Cape Slavery."

78  Gqola, *What Is Slavery to Me?*, 12–13.

79  See for example Abrahams, "The Great Long National Insult"; Boehmer, "Transfiguring"; Bradford, "Women, Gender and Colonialism"; Hendricks, "'Ominous' Liaisons"; Ramaswamy, "Body Language."

80  Ferrus, "A Poem for Sarah Baartman."

81  Gqola, *What Is Slavery to Me?*, 61–104; Coetzee, "Krotoa Remembered."

82  Setshwaelo, "The Return of the 'Hottentot Venus'."

83  Ibid.

84  Gqola, *What Is Slavery to Me?*, 63.

85  Samuelson, *Remembering the Nation, Dismembering Women?*, 85–118.

86  South African Heritage Resources Agency, "Hottentot Venus Declared National Heritage Site in April 2008."

87  Chirume, "Labour Disputes Delay the Construction of R164-million Sarah Baartman Centre."

88  Miller, "Selective Silence and the Shaping of Memory in Post-Apartheid Visual Culture."

89  Ibid., 297.

90  Marschall, "How to Honour a Woman."

91  Miller, "Selective Silence and the Shaping of Memory in Post-Apartheid Visual Culture," 297–306.

92  Ibid., 315.

93  McEwan, "Building a Postcolonial Archive?," 746.

94  Mwikya, "Unnatural and Un-African."

95  Drew, *A Different Fight for Freedom*, 6–11; and South African History Online, "The History of LGBT Legislation."

96  McCaskell, "Queers against Apartheid."

97  Drew, *A Different Fight for Freedom*, 11.

98  Ibid., 30.

99  Hames, "The Women's Movement and Lesbian and Gay Struggles in South Africa."

100  Gay and Lesbian Memory in Action, "Background & Origins."

101  Motsemme, *"The Mute always Speak": On Women's Silences at the Truth and Reconciliation Commission*, quoted in Gqola, *What Is Slavery to Me?*, 71.

## References

Abrahams, Yvette. "The Great Long National Insult: 'Science', Sexuality and the Khoisan All in the 18th and Early 19th Century." *Agenda* 32 (1997): 34–48.

Apartheid Museum. "Exhibition Archive." http://apartheidmuseum.org.www17.jnb1.host-h.net/exhibition-archive (accessed January 12, 2017).

Apartheid Museum. "Journeys of Faith: Navigating Sexual Orientation and Gender Diversity." http://apartheidmuseum.org.www17.jnb1.host-h.net/journeys-faith (accessed January 30, 2017).

Auty, Richard. *Sustaining Development in Mineral Economies: The Resource Curse Thesis*. New York: Routledge, 1993.

Bah, Abu Bakarr. "State Decay: A Conceptual Frame of Failing and Failed States in West Africa." *International Journal of Politics, Culture, and Society* 25, no. 1–3 (2012): 71–89.

Bah, Abu Bakarr. "Civil Non-State Actors in Peacekeeping and Peacebuilding in West Africa." *Journal of International Peacekeeping* 17, no. 3–4 (2013): 313–336.

Bah, Abu Bakarr. "The Contours of New Humanitarianism: War and Peacebuilding in Sierra Leone." *Africa Today* 60, no. 1 (2013): 2–26.

Bah, Abu Bakarr. "People-Centered Liberalism: An Alternative Approach to International State-Building in Sierra Leone and Liberia." *Critical Sociology* (2015): 1–19.

Barnes, Catherine. *Owning the Process: Public Participation in Peacemaking*, no. 13. Durban: ACCORD, 2002.

Barsalou, Judy, and Victoria Baxter. *The Urge to Remember: The Role of Memorials in Social Reconstruction and Transitional Justice*. Washington, DC: United States Institute of Peace, 2007.

Barsalou, Lawrence. "Situated Conceptualization," pp. 620–651, in *Handbook of Categorization in Cognitive Science*, edited by Henri Cohen and Claire Lefebvre. Oxford: Elsevier, 2005.

Bar-Tal, Daniel, and Gemma Bennink. "The Nature of Reconciliation as an Outcome and as a Process," pp. 11–38, in *From Conflict Resolution to Reconciliation*, edited by Yaacov Bar-Siman-Tov. Oxford: Oxford University Press, 2004.

Boehmer, Elleke. "Transfiguring: Colonial Body into Post-Colonial Narrative." *Novel: A Forum for Fiction* 26, no. 1 (1992): 268–277.

Borneman, John. *Settling Accounts: Violence, Justice and Accountability in Post-socialist Europe*. Princeton, NJ: Princeton University Press, 1997.

Bradford, Helen. "Women, Gender and Colonialism: Rethinking the History of the British Cape Colony and Its Frontier Zones, c. 1806–70." *Journal of African History* 37, no. 3 (1996): 351–370.

Bremner, Lindsay G. "Memory, Nation-Building and the Post-Apartheid City: The Apartheid Museum in Johannesburg," pp. 85–104, in *Desire Lines: Space, Memory and Identity in South Africa*, edited by Noeleen Murray, Nick Shepherd and Martin Hall. New York: Routledge, 2007.

Brett, Sebastian, Louis Bickford, Liz Ševčenko, and Marcela Rios. *Memorialisation and Democracy: State Policy and Civic Action*. Conference Report. Santiago, Chile, 2007.

Casey, Edward S. *Remembering: A Phenomenological Study*. Bloomington, IN: Indiana University Press, 1987.

Charbonneau, Bruno, and Genevieve Parent, eds. *Peacebuilding, Memory and Reconciliation: Bridging Top-Down and Bottom-Up Approaches*. Routledge: London.

Chirume, Joseph. "Labour Disputes Delay the Construction of R164-million Sarah Baartman Centre." *GroundUp*, August 26, 2016. www.groundup.org.za/article/labour-disputes-delay-construction-r164-million-sarah-baartman-centre/.

Cleveland, Todd. "We Still Want Truth: The ANC's Angolan Detention Camps and Post-Apartheid Memory." *Comparative Studies of South Asia, Africa and the Middle East* 25, no. 1 (2005): 63–78.

Coetzee, Carli. "Krotoa Remembered: A Mother of Unity, a Mother of Sorrows," pp. 112–119, in *Negotiating the Past: The Making of Memory in South Africa*, edited by Sarah Nuttall and Carli Coetzee. Cape Town: Oxford University Press, 1998.

Cohen, Stanley. *States of Denial: Knowing about Atrocities and Suffering*. Cambridge: Polity Press, 2000.

Cole, Elizabeth A. "Transitional Justice and the Reform of History Education." *The International Journal of Transitional Justice* 1, no. 1 (2007): 115–137.

Collier, Paul, and Anke Hoeffler. "On Economic Causes of Civil War." *Oxford Economic Papers* 50, no. 4 (1998): 563–573.

Coombes, Annie. *History after Apartheid: Visual Culture and Public Memory in a Democratic South Africa.* Durham, NC: Duke University Press, 2003.

Coombes, Annie. "Witnessing History/ Embodying Testimony: Gender and Memory in Post-Apartheid South Africa." *Journal of the Royal Anthropological Institute* (2011): S92–S112.

Coulter, Chris. "Female Fighters in the Sierra Leone War: Challenging the Assumptions?" *Feminist Review* 88, no. 1 (2008): 54–73.

Davison, Patricia. "Museums and the Reshaping of Memory," pp. 143–160, in *Negotiating the Past: The Making of Memory in South Africa*, edited by Sarah Nuttall and Carli Coetzee. Cape Town: Oxford University Press, 1998.

de Kok, Ingrid. "Cracked Heirlooms: Memory on Exhibition," pp. 57–72, in *Negotiating the Past: The Making of Memory in South Africa* edited by Sarah Nuttal and Carli Coetzee. Cape Town: Oxford University Press, 1998.

Deacon, Harriet. "Remembering Tragedy, Constructing Modernity: Robben Island as a National Monument," pp. 161–179, in *Negotiating the Past: The Making of Memory in South Africa*, edited by Sarah Nuttal and Carli Coetzee. Cape Town: Oxford University Press, 1998.

District Six Museum. "The Homecoming Centre." www.districtsix.co.za/ Content/Museum/About/ HomecomingCentre/index.php (accessed December 20, 2016).

District Six Museum. "Restitution in District Six." www.districtsix. co.za/Content/Museum/About/ Restitution/index.php (accessed December 20, 2016).

Doyle, Michael W., and Nicholas Sambanis. *Making War and Building Peace: United Nations Peace Operations.* Princeton, NJ: Princeton University Press, 2006.

Drew, Marion. *A Different Fight for Freedom.* Braamfontein: Gay and Lesbian Memory in Action, 2008.

Drumbl, Mark. "She Makes Me Ashamed to Be a Woman: The Genocide Conviction of Pauline Nyiramasuhuko." *Michigan Journal of International Law* 34, no. 3 (2013): 559–603.

Ferrus, Diana. "A Poem for Sarah Baartman." October 20, 2013. http://peacebenwilliams. com/a-poem-for-sarah-baartman- by-diana-ferrus-read-the-poem-that- helped-bring-her-home/.

Galtung, Johan. *Peace, War and Defense.* Copenhagen: Christian Ejlers, 1976.

Gary, Ian, and Terry Lynn Karl. "Bottom of the Barrel: Africa's Oil Boom and the Poor." Catholic Relief Services, 2003. www.crs.org/sites/default/files/ tools-research/bottom-of-the-barrel. pdf (accessed December 20, 2016).

Gay and Lesbian Memory in Action. "Background & Origins." www.gala. co.za/about_us/background_and_ origins.htm (accessed July 1, 2017).

Government of the Republic of South Africa. *Promotion of National Unity Act No. 34 of 1995.* Pretoria: Government Printers, 1995.

Gqola, Pumla Dineo. *What Is Slavery to Me? Postcolonial/Slave Memory in Post-Apartheid South Africa.* Johannesburg: Wits University Press, 2010.

Hamber, Brandon. "Remembering to Forget: Issues to Consider When Establishing Structures for Dealing with the Past," pp. 56–78, in *Past Imperfect: Dealing with the Past in*

*Northern Ireland and South Africa.* Derry/Londonderry: INCORE/UU, 1998.

Hames, Mary. "The Women's Movement and Lesbian and Gay Struggles in South Africa." *Feminist Africa* 2 (2003): 1–4.

Hendricks, Cheryl. "'Ominous' Liaisons: Tracing the Interface between 'Race' and Sex at the Cape," pp. 29–44, in *Coloured by History, Shaped by Place: New Perspectives on Coloured Identities in Cape Town*, edited by Zimitri Erasmus. Cape Town: Kwela and South African History Online, 2001.

Kaldor, Mary. *New and Old Wars: Organized Violence in a Global Era.* Second Edition. Cambridge: Polity Press, 2006.

Keynan, Irit. "Between Past and Future: Persistent Conflicts, Collective Memory, and Reconciliation." *International Journal of Social Sciences* 3, no. 1 (2014): 19–28.

Kgalema, Lazarus. *Symbols of Hope: Monuments as Symbols of Remembrance and Peace in the Process of Reconciliation.* Cape Town: Centre for the Study of Violence and Reconciliation, 1999.

Lederach, John Paul. *Building Peace: Sustainable Reconciliation in Divided Society.* Washington. DC: United States Institute of Peace Press, 1997.

Livermon, Xavier. "Queer(y)ing Freedom: Black Queer Visibilities in Postapartheid South Africa." *GLQ: A Journal of Lesbian and Gay Studies* 18, no. 2–3 (2012): 297–323.

Mac Ginty, Roger. "Indigenous Peace-Making versus the Liberal Peace." *Cooperation and Conflict* 43, no. 2 (2008): 139–163.

Mamdani, Mahmood. "Amnesty or Impunity? A Preliminary Critique of the Report of the Truth and Reconciliation Commission of South Africa." *Diacritics* 32, no. 4 (2002): 32–59.

Marschall, Sabine. "How to Honour a Woman: Gendered Memorialisation in Post-Apartheid South Africa." *Critical Arts* 24, no. 2 (2010): 260–283.

Marschall, Sabine. "Memory and Identity in South Africa: Contradictions and Ambiguities in the Process of Post-Apartheid Memorialisation." *Visual Anthropology* 25, no. 3 (2012): 189–204.

Mazrui, Ali Al'amin. "Conflict in Africa: An Overview," pp. 36–50, in *The Roots of African Conflicts: The Causes and Costs*, edited by Alfred Nhema and Paul Tiyambe Zeleza. Oxford: James Currey, 2008.

McCaskell, Tim. "Queers against Apartheid: From South Africa to Israel." *Canadian Dimension*, July/August 2010. https://canadiandimension.com/articles/view/queers-against-apartheid-from-south-africa-to-israel (accessed July 3, 2017).

McEwan, Cheryl. "Building a Postcolonial Archive? Gender, Collective Memory and Citizenship in Post-Apartheid South Africa." *Journal of Southern African Studies* 23, no. 2 (2003): 739–757.

Meierhenrich, Jens. *Topographies of Remembering and Forgetting: The Transformation Lieux de Mémoire in Rwanda.* Madison, WI: University of Wisconsin Press, 2011.

Miller, Kim. "Selective Silence and the Shaping of Memory in Post-Apartheid Visual Culture: The Case of the Monument to the Women of South Africa." *South African Historical Journal* 63, no. 2 (2011): 295–317.

Minow, Martha and Nancy L. Rosenblum. *Breaking the Cycles of Hatred:*

*Memory, Law and Repair*. Princeton, NJ: Princeton University Press, 2002.

Mwikya, Kenne. "Unnatural and Un-African: Contesting Queerphobia by Africa's Political Leadership." *Feminist Africa* 19 (2015): 98–105.

Naidu, Ereshnee. *Symbolic Reparations: A Fractured Opportunity*. Cape Town: Centre for the Study of Violence and Reconciliation, 2004.

Naidu, Ereshnee. *Ties that Bind: Strengthening the Links between Memorialisation and Transitional Justice*. Cape Town: Centre for the Study of Violence and Reconciliation, 2006.

Naidu, Ereshnee, Yolelwa Mbanjwa, and Cyril Adonis. *History on Their Own Terms: The Relevance of the Past to a New Generation*. Cape Town: Centre for the Study of Violence and Reconciliation, 2007.

Ndebele, Njabulo. "Memory, Metaphor, and the Triumph of Narrative," pp. XX–XX, in *Negotiating the Past: The Making of Memory in South Africa*, edited by Sarah Nuttal and Carli Coetzee. Cape Town: Oxford University Press, 1998.

Nnoli, Okwudiba. *Ethnic Conflicts in Africa*. Dakar: CODESRIA, 1998.

Okoye, Ikem Stanley. "The Limits of Representation?" *Art Journal*, no. 66 (2007): 11–18.

Paffenholz, Thania. "International Peacebuilding Goes Local: Analysing Lederach's Conflict Transformation Theory and Its Ambivalent Encounter with 20 Years of Practice." *Peacebuilding* 2, no. 1 (2014): 11–27.

Paris, Roland. *At War's End: Building Peace after Civil Conflict*. Cambridge: Cambridge University Press, 2004.

Paris, Roland. "Saving Liberal Peace Building." *Review of International Studies* 36, no. 2 (2010): 337–365.

Ramaswamy, Sumathi. "Body Language: The Somatics of Nationalism in Tamil India." *Gender and History* 10, no. 1 (1998): 78–109.

Renan, Ernest. "What Is a Nation?" pp. 8–22, in *Nation and Narration*, edited by Homi K. Bhabha. New York: Routledge, 1990.

Richmond, Oliver P. "Failed Statebuilding versus Peace Formation." *Cooperation and Conflict* 48, no. 3 (2013): 378–400.

Richmond, Oliver P. "Peace during and after the Age of Intervention." *International Peacekeeping* 21, no. 4 (2014): 509–519.

Robben Island. "Education at RIM." www. robben-island.org.za/learn#education (accessed December 30, 2016).

Robins, Steven. "Silence in My Father's House: Memory, Nationalism, and Narratives of the Body," pp. 120–140, in *Negotiating the Past: The Making of Memory in South Africa*, edited by Sarah Nuttal and Carli Coetzee. Cape Town: Oxford University Press, 1998.

Ross, Michael. "Oil, Drugs and Diamonds: The Varying Role of Natural Resources in Civil Wars," pp. 47–70, in *The Political Economy of Armed Conflict: Beyond Greed and Grievance*, edited by Karen Ballentine and Jake Sherman. Boulder, CO: Lynne Rienner Publishers, 2003.

Ross, Michael L. "What Do We Know about Natural Resources and Civil War?" *Journal of Peace Research* 41, no. 3 (2004): 337–356.

Samuelson, Meg. *Remembering the Nation, Dismembering Women? Stories of the South African Transition*. Scottsville: University of Kwa-Zulu Natal Press, 2007.

Schudson, Michael S. "The Present in the Past versus the Past in the Present." *Communication* 11, no. 2 (1989): 105–112.

Setshwaelo, Marang. "The Return of the 'Hottentot Venus'," February 14,

2003. web.mit.edu/racescience/in_media/baartman/baartman_africana.htm.

Ševčenko, Liz, and Maggie Russell-Ciardi. "Sites of Conscience: Opening Historic Sites for Civic Dialogue: Foreword." *The Public Historian* 30, no. 1 (2008): 9–15.

South African Heritage Resources Agency. "Hottentot Venus Declared National Heritage Site in April 2008," March 27, 2015. www.sahra.org.za/sarah-baartman-burial-site/.

South African History Online. "Forced Removals in South Africa." www.sahistory.org.za/article/forced-removals-south-africa (accessed January 15, 2017).

South African History Online. "The History of LGBT Legislation." www.sahistory.org.za/article/history-lgbt-legislation (accessed July 1, 2017).

Southall, Roger. "The Power Elite in Democratic South Africa: Race and Class in a Fractured Society," pp. 17–38, in *New South African Review 3: The Second Phase – Tragedy or Farce?*, edited by Devan Pillay, John Daniel, Prishani Naidoo, and Roger Southall. Johannesburg: Wits University Press, 2008.

Stanley, Elizabeth. "Evaluating the Truth and Reconciliation Commission." *The Journal of Modern African Studies* 39, no. 3 (2001): 525–546.

Ward, Kerry, and Nigel Worden. "Commemorating, Suppressing, and Invoking Cape Slavery," pp. 201–218, in *Negotiating the Past: The Making of Memory in South Africa*, edited by Sarah Nuttall and Carli Coetzee. Cape Town: Oxford University Press, 1998.

Wicomb, Zoe. *David's Story*. Cape Town: Kwela, 2000.

Williams, Paul D. *War and Conflict in Africa*. Cambridge: Polity Press, 2011.

Wilson, Richard A. *The Politics of Truth and Reconciliation in South Africa: Legitimizing the Post-Apartheid State*. Cambridge: Cambridge University Press, 2011.

Winter, Jay, and Emmanuel Sivan. *War and Remembrance in the Twentieth Century*. Cambridge: Cambridge University Press, 2000.

# 5 | NATURAL RESOURCE REFORMS IN POSTWAR LIBERIA AND SIERRA LEONE: CONTRADICTIONS AND TENSIONS

*Michael D. Beevers*

## Introduction

Peacebuilding emerged during the 1990s with the objective of bringing peace and stability to the developing world's war-torn societies, which were viewed as detrimental to national, regional, and international security. The objective of peacebuilding is to remake states by addressing the lack of state institutions and governance failures that make states fragile and conflict prone. Since war-torn states are inherently thought to be incapable of reconstructing themselves, international actors intervene until they are stable and able enough to govern themselves. Peacebuilding operations focus on rehabilitating the sovereign authority of the state and rebuilding state institutions so that war-torn states have the renewed legitimacy to establish or alter the rules, institutions, and processes that govern political and economic decisions, and structure state–society interactions.[1] Peacebuilding also emphasizes the peace-enhancing traits of democracy and a free-market economic system, both of which are believed to foster peace and reduce the risk of future conflict.[2]

Whether a war-torn society can sustain peace after armed conflict depends on a host of interrelated factors, including the conditions that led to the onset of war, the character of the precious conflict, and the nature of the peace settlement.[3] Peace and stability are also influenced by the extent of both United Nations involvement and international intervention.[4] Peacebuilding was initially a short-term project concerned with negotiating peace agreements, monitoring ceasefires, provisioning humanitarian aid, providing electoral assistance, and overseeing the disarmament of combatants, although this did not appear adequate to pave the way for a durable peace.[5] In response, a broadened concept of peacebuilding shifted to incorporate and address a range of issues including traditional development goals of poverty alleviation and economic growth, violations of human rights, transparent and accountable governance, promotion of democracy, rule of law, religion, ethnicity, and resources and environmental issues.[6]

One area that has received significant attention in contemporary peacebuilding operations is natural resources as scholarship began to suggest they play a vital role in the transition from war to peace. One influential strand of research, for example, argued that an abundance of natural resources was associated with the onset and duration of civil conflict since reliance on valuable commodities like timber, diamonds, minerals created a form of dependence that undermined governments, made them corrupt and less accountable, increased poverty, and led to economic decline.[7] Related scholarship suggested that civil conflict was motivated by access to wealth derived from the trade in natural resources, which combatants (rebels and governments) could use to enrich themselves and buy weapons that would fuel and prolong violence.[8] Evidence that natural resources were funding and fueling violent conflict resulted in policy interventions such as UN sanctions and international initiatives aimed at limiting the trade in "conflict resources" to end and mitigate conflict. As Carolyn McAskie, the former UN Assistant Secretary-General for Peacebuilding Support noted in 2007, "where resources exploitation has driven war or served to impede peace, improving governance capacity to control natural resources is a critical element of peacebuilding."[9] In war-torn societies, improving natural resource governance is often done under the rubric of "reform" that involves substantial intervention by international actors to establish and alter laws, regulations, institutions, policies, and practices that in principle determine how people should behave relative to natural resources.

Despite an increasing awareness that well-governed natural resources may help consolidate peace and the proliferation of natural resources reforms in war-torn societies, we are still learning how such reforms shape peacebuilding. This chapter examines recent efforts to govern forests in Liberia and diamonds and minerals in Sierra Leone.[10] This is particularly salient because in both countries natural resources have been recognized as a contributing factor to a decade or more of violent conflict. Liberia is often associated with "conflict timber," and Sierra Leone remains forever linked to so-called "blood diamonds." Since the conflicts ended in 2002 and 2003, respectively, there has been substantial effort to reform how resources are governed so that they can help foster peace rather than conflict. What I find, first, is the extent governance reforms in Liberia and Sierra Leone are analogous. More specifically, a set of factors shape the trajectory of post-conflict natural resources governance by placing it on the international agenda and providing a rule-making and institution-building blueprint. This blueprint emphasizes economic explanations of violent conflict and places an emphasis on the extraction and export of natural resources as a foremost peacebuilding strategy. Put another way, natural resource governance not only shapes peacebuilding but peacebuilding influences what is in the "realm of the possible" in terms of natural resources governance. While this is not a problem in and of itself, I argue that it has the possibility to exacerbate problems that undermine the consolidation of peace and long-term development.

## Liberia and Sierra Leone: Natural Resources and Violent Conflict

Scholars and commentators alike have tried to understand the causes of the civil wars in Liberia and Sierra Leone.[11] Despite the diversity of competing and interrelated narratives, attention has been focused on the economic motives of the combatants and the role of the resource trade in funding these conflicts. This is despite evidence that the looting of the resources was nothing new and that patronage and grievances had historically been a deep source of violence and contention in both countries.

### The Liberian Conflict

In Liberia, the conflict was framed around Charles Taylor, first as a rebel leader and later as president, who used the control and exploitation of, and trade in resources such as diamonds, iron ore, rubber, and timber to amass power and personal wealth.[12] Taylor was not only able to establish control over Liberia's vast natural resources but by bringing conflict into Sierra Leone was able to control its productive diamond mines. Between 1991 and 1994, Taylor amassed upwards of $100 million annually from these activities.[13] These vast sums allowed him to supply weapons to his rebel army as well as the Revolutionary United Front (RUF) in Sierra Leone, and grease networks of patronage both inside and outside Liberia. Taylor's looting of Liberia also made it easier to overlook his primary goal for starting the conflict, which was a desire for political change after a century or more of authoritarian governments in Monrovia. Regardless, the war came to resemble a strategic stalemate that increasingly looked like a conflict motivated by greed. Any moral or political motivation for fighting diminished as economic or profit motives grew.

In 1995, the Abuja Accords were negotiated and elections brought Taylor to power. Taylor quickly established state control over the formal economy and cut deals that benefited political and business patrons. The Liberian Resources Corporation was granted all of Liberia's mineral rights, the Oriental Timber Company was given the largest timber concession in the country, and Taylor's brother was appointed to head the Forest Development Authority.[14] What is interesting is that the state efforts to control the natural resource trade was not unusual in the history of Liberia, given that those in power have often used the considerable revenues to dispense patronage and consolidate political power. What was different was that the revenue went to purchase weapons and to finance a continuation of violence and human rights abuses not only in Liberia, but also in Sierra Leone.[15] The UN passed resolution 1306 in 2000 banning the importation of all diamonds from Sierra Leone. With revenues from the diamond trade greatly reduced, Taylor turned aggressively to the timber industry. In 2001, the value of Liberian timber exports was estimated to be about $100 million, and "conflict timber" had replaced "diamonds as the new source of funding for conflict in Liberia."[16] The UN Security Council placed a ban on the export on all round logs and timber products originating in Liberia in July 2003. By mid-2003, Taylor faced a military defeat by rebel factions, and the vast sums of wealth leveraged to buy weapons and dispense patronage had been diminished. Moreover, pressure on Taylor to leave the country increased in light of war crimes indictments by the Special Court of Sierra Leone. In August 2003, Taylor went into exile, an interim transitional government was appointed, efforts were made to disarm and demobilize combatants, and elections were scheduled for 2005. The UN also established a 15,000 UN peacekeeping force to improve the security situation.

It should be said that the framing of the conflict, especially early on, was largely in economic terms (either focused on Taylor or rebel groups), or as competition over the trade in natural resources. However, this simplistic analysis overlooks the more complex socio-political and economic roots of the conflict, and how these are connected to natural resources. In fact, the conflict was enabled by deep resentment toward a long line of oligarchic, dysfunctional, and oppressive governments, of which Taylor's was the newest. Liberia's natural resources had long been a source of tension due to a history of unfair land ownership and tenure rights devised in the 1800s.[17] These rules allowed certain groups the right to own land while forcing the indigenous population to remain tied to communal systems. These dynamics persisted in the 1950s and 1960s as Liberia opened up its forests and minerals to international markets, and the government moved to consolidate control over the most valuable lands with the benefits accumulating to a small group of national and foreign elites. These "concessionary" arrangements left most of the country underdeveloped and a large segment of the population disenchanted, with few opportunities and little access to land. Therefore, while those rebels recruited by Taylor and other rebel factions may have resorted to looting as the war continued, these political grievances played a significant role.

Framing the conflict in economic terms also overlooks the fact that the Liberian conflict was predominantly a political struggle that had a long history. For instance, one could view the conflict through the lens of patronage, which involves political elites diverting state revenues into personal networks to gain support and maintain power. Systems of patronage are political practices that can undermine the state by diverting revenues to political supporters instead of provisioning for basic services, and marginalizing particular groups.[18] Networks of patronage are essential for political power and financially dependent on natural resources. Such networks tend to thrive in places like Liberia where a majority of revenues come from natural resources, and agreements and concessions are arranged with little transparency or accountability. A focus on patronage also better explains Taylor's motives, which were not primarily about personal enrichment, but capturing political power in Monrovia. In fact, economic and political motives – rather than separate and isolated – are deeply intertwined, and Taylor's looting of the country's natural resources was not only to buy weapons, but also to dispense patronage. In sum, a more accurate account of the conflict and its links to natural resources should emphasize both patrimonial-resource linkages and grievances linked to land ownership that led to "state decay," rather than exploiting timber and other resources solely for economic motives.[19]

*The Sierra Leone Conflict*

The Sierra Leonean conflict, like the Liberian case, was similarly portrayed as a resource conflict or "diamond war" directly fueled and prolonged by the availability of these valuable global commodities.[20] While Taylor amassed a fortune from Sierra Leonean diamonds and was able to buy weapons and dispense patronage, the RUF and its leaders in Sierra Leone also fought to control diamond areas. Beyond that, there was collusion between the rebels, rogue government soldiers (commonly known as Sobels), and others to control $250 million in potential diamond revenue annually.[21] This collusion provided little impetus to "fight for peace" as the chaos enabled by the conflict virtually guaranteed financial benefits to combatants. The irony is the government of Sierra Leone was also dependent on diamond revenues for sustaining the armed forces and supporting networks of patronage on which political authority depended.[22]

Deprived of diamond revenues Sierra Leone's government began to implode leading to a coup, which brought army Captain Valentine Strasser to power and began the four-year reign of the National Provisional Revolutionary Council (NPRC) in 1992. Unfortunately for Strasser and the NPRC government control of diamonds remained elusive, and the looting of rutile and bauxite mines further limited the potential for government revenue, which was needed to fight the war. These dynamics led the government to hire South African mercenaries Executive Outcomes (EO) in 1995 to help bring order to Freetown, secure mining interests, and reestablish control of eastern diamond fields. Despite nefarious links between EO and foreign business interests, the presence of EO did give the government of Sierra Leone some military victories. As the security situation improved, international pressure for peace negotiations increased, leading to the Abidjan Accords and setting the stage for elections in 1996. Although Strasser was overtaken in a coup, a vote was held (without the RUF participating), and Tejan Kabbah was elected as president. The Kabbah government continued to rely on mining concessions for revenue and private firms for security. However, with stability restored and a democratically elected government in power, popular dissatisfaction led to the departure of EO. This had the effect of placing corrupt government forces back in control of the country, and leaving diamond areas unprotected from large-scale exploitation, collusion, and competition.[23] With a large-scale military advance against the RUF pending, a military coup against

Kabbah was successful in May 1997, placing Johnny Paul Koroma of the new Armed Forces Ruling Council (AFRC) in power. Koroma invited the RUF to join the government, which only led to the looting and brutalization of Freetown and triggering massive human displacement. The deteriorating situation led to an expanded military role for the Economic Community of West African States Monitoring Group (ECOMOG), which was to enforce law and order and restore the previous government.

International pressure for a peace settlement culminated with the July 1999 Lomé Agreement. However, the hastily arranged settlement fell apart as Charles Taylor, now president of Liberia, continued to supply arms to the RUF through the diamond trade. Fighting resumed and the RUF, controlling an estimated 90 percent of the country, took 500 peacekeepers hostage and started to move toward Freetown in May 2000. The international "spotlight" at this time focused on the role of diamonds in fueling and prolonging the war leading to UN Security Council Resolution 1306 prohibiting the direct or indirect import of rough diamonds from Sierra Leone and required the government to establish a certificate of origin for trade in diamonds.[24] With the UN force compromised and pressure for direct intervention mounting, the British introduced a military force to provide security. With the British forces on the ground and the United Nations Mission in Sierra Leone (UNAMSIL) increasing its peacekeeping contingent to 17,000 troops, the situation stabilized. By the end of 2000, the RUF had begun to disarm and demobilize.[25] Although an isolated and depleted Taylor was still in power in Liberia, the government held successful national elections in which Kabbah was voted president in May 2002.

The focus on the economic motives of the combatants as well as the focus on "conflict diamonds" in fueling the war, however, overlooked the conflict's roots, including a long history of patronage and grievances associated with natural resources that made the rebellion possible.[26]

The widespread lack of development for a great majority of Sierra Leoneans generated resentment based on a historical pattern of undemocratic government.[27] These resentments were deepened by Sierra Leone's natural resources because the population was aware of the country's "abundance," but also aware it did not benefit from them.[28] Land availability was also a source of conflict, as the availability of land for agriculture and other livelihoods had to compete with other uses such has diamond mining, which was controlled by elites and favored wealthy entrepreneurs.[29] Young rural males, in particular, had little access to productive land and few employment opportunities other than ending up as diamond miners. As such, recruitment was motivated, at least at the outset of the conflict, by much more than the "spoils of war."

Grievances over land and underdevelopment also stem from a historically unjust and corrupt political system, beginning with British colonialism. The system is based on networks of patronage dedicated to exploiting the country's resource base in order to gain political currency. A colonial policy of patronage, for example, was characterized by paying off local chiefs in exchange for stability and relative control of diamond areas. This played a significant role in marginalizing large parts of the population and undermining government authority. Setting the stage for conflict and the process of "state decay" was also Sierra Leonean President Siaka Stevens (1968–1985) who instituted a one-party state and centralized control of diamond mining to consolidate political power. This exacerbated already exploitative land relationships and made illegal the small-scale diamond mining many people relied upon for their livelihoods. Under Steven's autocratic rule, diamond revenue was diverted from state institutions into networks of patronage, leading to economic decline. This dynamic produced political (rather than simply economic) motives for war and a disenfranchised group of young men that could easily be recruited into the RUF.[30]

### Liberia and Sierra Leone: Natural Resources and Peacebuilding

Given the conflicts in Liberia and Sierra Leone came to be framed as "resource conflicts" in which timber or diamonds played a large part it is no wonder that reform of the natural resource sectors were an international peacebuilding priority. However, despite more than a decade of reform substantial problems remain in both countries where restarting extraction of natural resources has remained mired in controversy over the granting of concessions to extractive companies and disputes with local communities.

#### Forests and Peacebuilding in Liberia

Despite the importance of Liberia's forests to sustaining livelihoods and evidence that the war led to considerable damage to the forest resources on which communities depend, efforts by international actors were focused on establishing forest reforms.[31] The reforms were intended to reconstitute state control over forest resources and ensure timber revenue contributed to the rebuilding of the country. International actors stressed reform as a prerequisite for lifting the UN sanctions and efforts began to develop a set of internationally acceptable reforms to harness the full potential of Liberia's forest resources for peacebuilding. The sanctions demanded that Liberia gain "full authority and control of timber producing areas" and take "all necessary steps to ensure that government revenues ... are not used to fuel conflict."[32] The sanctions mandated systems of transparency and accountability to ensure timber revenues "benefit the Liberian people, including development," and environmentally sustainable business practices, legal reforms, and a review of concessionary agreements.[33] To assist the government and help build the institutional capacity of the Forest Development Authority, the Liberia Forest Initiative was created.[34]

International actors understood that timber extraction was important, if not crucial, for Liberia's postwar development and economic recovery. The trade in timber had helped to fuel the conflict, but stagnant economic growth was seen as a threat because without perceptible progress people might rebel. The problem was that the Liberian Forest Concession Review Committee (FCRC) uncovered a decades-long pattern of mismanagement, abuse, and corruption. The committee found that concessions allocated by the government equaled more than twice the amount of land available for timber extraction.[35] In addition, most taxes owed the government were never paid by the timber companies, and many of them severely damaged the livelihoods of communities.[36] Based on the findings, international actors called for the revocation of past timber concessions and the passage of genuine forest sector reforms to address corruption and illicit timber extraction. They also recommended establishing the Governance and Economic Management Assistance Program (GEMAP) that put an international adviser in place to "protect revenue streams of key revenue generating agencies and institutions" and among other things assist the Liberian government with the granting of concessions.[37]

In a first step toward reform, newly elected President Ellen Johnson Sirleaf issued Executive Order #1 in early 2006 canceling all forest concessions and placing a moratorium on commercial timber harvests.[38]

The UN acknowledged Liberia's progress and conditionally lifted the sanctions in June 2006 (UNSC 2006). Permanent lifting was to occur only if comprehensive forest reforms passed within ninety days, subject to review by the Security Council. After three months of stakeholder consultations, the Government of Liberia enacted the National Forestry Reform Law (NFRL). The NFRL represented a package of reforms that ostensibly emphasize the government's authority over forests. The reforms reasserted that the government not only holds in trust all forestlands for the Liberian people, but is the sole authority over all matters concerning their use.[39] The reforms were oriented around the "three 'C's" concept of forest management – commercial, community, and conservation. The "three 'C's" provided something for all stakeholders by acknowledging the multiple uses and values of Liberia's forests and highlighting the importance of sustainable forests and sustainable benefits for the people.[40] The NFRL also recognized that "past instances by both Liberian and non-Liberians of political patronage, corruption, tax evasion, violations of the rights of local communities and lack of transparency have resulted in the unsustainable management of forests, and even fueling conflict."[41]

Given the significance of economic growth and development to the logic of peacebuilding, and the centrality of raw materials to jump-starting post-conflict economies, timber extraction received the lion's share of attention in the reform process.[42] Liberia's "conflict to development" strategy stressed the necessity of resuscitating the economy, creating employment opportunities, rebuilding infrastructure, and supplying basic services by fast-tracking productive economic sectors.[43] The objective was to alleviate poverty, which emerged in the peacebuilding discourse as the most prominent source of renewed conflict in war-torn societies.[44] In Liberia, economic growth was to enable a sustained peace by "reviving the traditional engines of growth" and restructuring the economy with the assistance of foreign investment and exports thus alleviating any motive to reignite conflict.[45] Indeed, Liberia's forests represented an enormous opportunity for a cash-strapped country ravaged by years of conflict and institutional decay. However, because of Liberia's history of corruption and economic malfeasance the reforms pursued by international actors emphasized "good governance" measures, including transparency, accountability, and the rule of law. The NFRL mandated safeguards designed to improve transparency and accountability by monitoring concession agreements, implementing chain-of-custody contracts, and tracking timber revenues. The law acknowledged the historical lack of benefits for the Liberian people and the necessity of having local communities "fully engaged in the sustainable management of forests" and "communities ... equitably participate and ... benefit from ... forests."[46] While public participation is a global norm for forest governance, there was a genuine fear that if communities did not obtain a portion of the benefits from resources, then hostilities and instability would follow.

On paper, the NFRL was comprehensive and described by a staff member of an international organization as "cutting edge." However, despite the implementation of forest reforms, not to mention the tens of millions spent by international actors, the process has been problematic The government, for example, has been criticized for slow progress in realizing financial returns from timber extraction. Initial projections estimated that the sector would generate $24–36 million and create employment in forest areas.[47] However, to date virtually no timber has been legally exported and little revenue has been collected. Part of the problem stems from difficulties awarding concessions to reputable companies. All companies bidding for large forest concessions in 2008 were unqualified, with no significant experience in timber extraction, and no discernable capital to carry out operations. Not only does this suggest such companies will fail to meet mandated obligations in terms of paying royalties and taxes, but also that they were "shell companies" that, if allowed to do business, would increase the risk of corruption. Where companies bidding on forest concessions were known, it was also risky. In 2009 allegations surfaced that the Liberian authority responsible for approving forest concessions may not have followed the law in approving a timber company accused of illegal logging in other parts of the world.[48] There was also a mounting number of "improprieties" in the awarding of concessions that raised questions about the government's commitment to transparency and accountability. According to the UN Panel of Experts, the FDA altered forest management contracts that would have amounted to lost revenue of $50 million over a twenty-five-year period to Liberia while benefiting the companies.[49] There have been persistent reports of altered forest contracts and a "fixed" bidding process that benefited certain companies.

The lack of extraction led to the widespread use of Private Use Permits (PUP) that many viewed as a loophole in the NFRL.[50] Between

2010 and 2012, approximately seventy PUPs were issued covering roughly 40 percent of the country's forest lands, and comprising three-quarters of its timber exports.[51] PUPs allowed private landowners to sell timber to companies. While PUPs required social agreements and environmental assessments, unlike conventional timber contracts on "public lands," no payments to the government or local communities were required, In addition, there was no open bidding process or plan for sustainable management. Investigations, however, exposed that most PUPs were actually bogus.[52] Most, if not all, were signed with little or no community involvement and there was no compensation for local communities. The PUPs portended serious consequences for the overharvesting of Liberia's forests. Governmental officials, including the head of the FDA, were indicted for illegally granting the PUPs.[53] In 2013, President Sirleaf declared a moratorium on the granting of PUPs, and any related timber extraction.

Problems have been compounded by what is best characterized as a backlash against the "timber-centric" agenda. The perception is that local community objectives have been subordinate to timber extraction and the reforms fail to address historical grievances related to access, exclusion, and land ownership. According to a member of Liberian civil society, "fast-tracking timber has eroded the trust between the government and communities and ... a more deliberate set of rules of how communities would be integrated into commercial activities needs to be discussed." There is a view that definitional issues, such as clarity over land ownership and tenure rules, and legitimate conflict resolution structures should be established before, not after, commercial forestry begins in order to mitigate any potential conflict. The view among international and Liberian advocacy organizations was that moving too fast to extract timber, or even having inflated expectations for timber extraction, will only undermine efforts to establish the rule of law. As the member of a civil society organization noted, such practices could "plunge some communities into conflict when timber harvests do start." These same organizations were also questioning whether timber extraction can actually alleviate poverty or be a catalyst for peace. Instead, they say that extraction promotes conflict since it fosters a culture of patronage, consolidates old rivalries over resources and agitates grievances among the population. In numerous interviews with members of civil society organizations and local groups, both worried that a rush to extract timber ignored Liberia's long history of exploitation, in which the people did not benefit but became poorer. Timber extraction is perceived as the state, once again, trying to assert its control and authority over forests at the expense of communities and the population. Recently, there is a growing movement to place the rights and livelihoods of people at the center of land and hence forest policy.[54] A Land Rights Act is pending that would presumably grant communities title to their land and ultimately empower them to make decisions about how their land is used.[55]

*Diamonds, Minerals, and Peacebuilding in Sierra Leone*

Diamonds were perceived as the biggest threat to peace and security in Sierra Leone, and the result there was vigorous effort by international actors to reform the diamond sector. Understanding that, as one person working on the reforms mentioned, "all eyes are on Sierra Leone" and there is a great amount of pressure to get diamond reforms "right" and make sure the era of "blood diamonds" is finished. Initial initiatives to leverage diamonds for peace was the passing of UN sanctions to limit the ability of combatants to use the revenues to wage war. Similar to Liberia, governance reforms focused on the reestablishment of state control over diamond producing areas and measures to ensure that smuggling was reduced and revenues brought into formal channels to benefit the Sierra Leonean people. As a consultant for the government put it, the international community required "more supervision, more regulation and more education" when it came to reviving the diamond sector. At the urging of the international community, the government also passed a number of legal and regulatory reforms to bring consistency to the diamond industry. This included the Diamond Trading Act, Alluvial Diamond Mining Amendments to the Mines and Minerals Act of 2009, Mines and Minerals Regulations, and the Diamond Cutting and Policy Act. More importantly perhaps, was the implementation of the Kimberly Process Certification Scheme (KPCS) designed to ensure that the production of diamonds can be traced from the "mine to the point of export" (i.e. chain of custody), and exports tracked and accompanied by a "certificate of origin" to ensure they do not originate from conflict areas.[56] The KPCS was intended to disincentivize the illicit smuggling that had occurred before and during the war by improving transparency, and increasing the export of diamonds through official government channels.

Indeed, by one measure governance reforms of the alluvial diamond sector have been successful. Since the end of the war diamond exports and revenues have increased. Diamond mining continues to provide livelihoods to an estimated 250,000 people and outside of agriculture is the country's principal employer.[57] Official export revenues from alluvial diamonds increased to over $109 million in 2010, which amounted to approximately $3 million in royalties for the government.[58] Recapturing state control and revenue from the diamond sector, however, is also problematic because lives have not improved for the miners and diamond "diggers." One of the criticisms of the KPCS and other "good governance" reforms is that they did not address working conditions, poverty, and other inequalities.[59] This was particularly important because the alluvial nature of these diamonds make them particularly important for the livelihoods of miners and a nomadic group of diggers whose livelihoods depend on small-scale mining. Moreover, diggers (disproportionately young and uneducated) were easily recruited by the RUF to fight in the civil war since they lacked other opportunities and were historically exploited. The sector is highly exploitative and diamond mining areas are more susceptible to poverty, disease, and death compared to the population as a whole. Diggers, who are enticed by the promise of substantial "winnings," are generally not employed as wage laborers, but work under a profit-sharing arrangement with the miner and earn approximately $1 per day.[60] As diamonds move up the value chain their price increases exponentially, perhaps by as much as 800 percent.[61]

Several governance reforms were introduced to address the exploitation of diggers and miners including efforts to improve working conditions and increase pay. The Integrated Diamond Management Program established cooperatives to provide a higher price for diamonds given it was structured to bypass the dealers where a majority of the profit of the diamond trade is made.[62] Still, miners often rely on dealers for food and equipment to mine an area so it is difficult to make the process work. The project stalled after one year as allegations of corruption by financiers and little, if any profit was made by the fifty or so cooperatives.[63] Another project initiative provided training to diggers and miners so they can better value diamonds and equip them to negotiate a fair return from local dealers. While 800 diggers were trained, the project ended with little evidence that the diggers realized any additional benefits since the diamond market operates much like a cartel.[64] The Diamond Area Community Development Fund (DACDF) was also initiated to provide communities with a portion of export taxes. The DACDF, was concerned primarily with empowering mining communities to make their own community development decisions through the allocation of a small portion (0.75 percent) of the government's 3 percent export tax. The DACDF is also concerned with providing incentives to miners and chiefdoms to curtail smuggling and engage in legal mining activities since it would result in revenue for the community. Although revenue has been dispersed to communities, questions remained as to whether community projects reflected the wishes of communities.[65]

What is important as well is that diamond mining is in decline in Sierra Leone and despite programs to improve the lot of diggers and communities, nothing will restore diamonds to the ground. Many working in the diamond field harbor dreams of "getting rich" but most recognize the inability of the deposits to meet livelihood needs and provide future opportunities. In addition, the government's pursuit of revenue has led to a crackdown on "illegal mining" reducing even further the livelihood opportunities, and fostering resentment. Interviews in mining communities, in fact, suggest that many want to move into subsistence agriculture, but have limited opportunities to do so. This is mostly due to exclusive land ownership and tenure rights that make acquiring land for farming and agricultural production almost impossible for diggers (or unemployed youth, more broadly). Land in Sierra Leone was either owned by powerful elites or administered by local chiefs, and both had incentives to control land. Put simply, this has the potential to foster resentment and contention as the youth population continues to grow and opportunities for sustainable livelihoods shrink.

Attention to the security threat posed by alluvial diamonds dominated international policy discussions following the conflict. Nevertheless, the emphasis quickly shifted to exploiting Sierra Leone's vast deposits of rutile, bauxite, iron ore, gold, and kimberlite diamonds. The widespread view was that the restoration and expansion of large, industrial mineral exploration and exports were critical to economic recovery and poverty alleviation. As an international consultant working to reform the mineral sector told me, greater industrial capacity and "increasing the size of the mineral pie" was not only good for development, but long-term peace and security. Given the significance of rebuilding the economy in war-torn societies, and the centrality of raw materials to jump-starting economic growth, it is not surprising that mineral exports were viewed as critical for this task. Indeed, Sierra Leone's vast mineral deposits offered the opportunity to rebuild the economy, create employment, and provide basic services to the population. Sierra Leone's peacebuilding strategy emphasized the importance of economic growth, youth employment, and acquiring state revenue based on rebuilding the country's mining (and agricultural) sector. The government's post-conflict development strategy, *Agenda for Change*, suggests that only a "transformation of the economy" will be able to set the country on a path to peace.[66] Peacebuilding reforms suggested that foreign investment in mineral extraction would be able to provide the revenue and employment necessary.[67]

Since corruption has historically been associated with the use of mineral resources, the *Agenda* stressed the need for governance improvements, including in transparency, accountability, and the rule of law. This led to reforms of the country's mining laws and reviews of past mining agreements. The Mines and Mineral Act for example was lauded as a comprehensive attempt to establish more efficient state control of mineral resources, capture fiscal revenue, increases royalty rates, tighten reporting requirements, and addresses environmental protection and community benefits. Despite these optimistic changes, the Act remains controversial given the relative lack of participation by civil society in the reform process and the likely difficulty of implementation.

Regardless, between 2005 and 2009, some 150 prospecting and exploration licenses were granted to an estimated 100 private mining companies, which has signaled to the world that the country is "open for business."[68] According to some estimates, mining licenses are held on nearly 80 percent of Sierra Leone's surface area.[69] Sierra Rutile (e.g. Titanium Resources Group) operates one of the largest deposits of rutile and ilmenite in the world. Octea Diamond Group (formerly Koidu Holdings) runs the country's only kimberlite diamond mine and produces almost 30 percent of the country's diamonds. Sierra Minerals Holdings (e.g. Vitemco Investment Group) presently accounts for 1 percent of the total global production of bauxite, with this number expected to grow. The greatest share of Sierra Leone's mineral sector, and the basis of untold optimism about a new "resource boom," are iron ore deposits that are some of richest in the world. UK-based

London Mining recently negotiated a twenty-five-year lease to redevelop the Marampa mine, and new investments are expected to substantially increase output. African Minerals, also UK-owned, was similarly granted a twenty-five-year lease on what has been described as one of Africa's largest mining operations.[70] Total exports from African Minerals alone are projected to reach $1 billion and at its peak generate $3 billion a year.[71] African Minerals also expects to employ 10,000 directly or indirectly at the mining site, which would make it the largest employer in the country.[72]

Despite the good news, controversy over the transparency of agreements and revenues suggests that problems that have historically been rampant in the mining sector have begun to resurface. Sierra Leone was suspended from the Extractives Industry Transparency Initiative for a time because mining companies and government entities did not report revenue payments as required.[73] Agreements between the government and mining companies were negotiated behind closed doors and contained overly generous clauses and tax rates. Sierra Rutile, for example, negotiated a tax rate of 0.5 percent on "turnover" even when the Income Tax Law required a rate of 3.5 percent.[74] This seemingly small difference meant that the government would forego $10 million between 2009 and 2014. Lease agreements with London Mining and African Minerals have also been deemed illegal because contrary to the tax rate of 37.5 percent stipulated in the Mines and Mineral Act of 2009, the agreement set rates of 6 percent and 25 percent, respectively.[75] This drastically reduced revenue intended for the government and mining communities. Mining companies and the government suggest that generous tax rates are necessary incentives to attract foreign investors. Others, however, argue that it undermines negotiations on mining contracts. As I was told in an interview, "why spend vast sums of donor money on reforming the mineral sector and passing new laws, if they are only to be ignored."[76]

There are also increasing tensions related to poor working conditions, environmental impacts, high unemployment, and the cost of basic commodities, issues of displacement and resettlement, impacts on arable land, and a general lack of promised benefits in mining communities.[77] In almost all instances, workers and community members also feel a lack of inclusion and engagement in decisions related to mining and that promises made by mining companies are not taken seriously.[78] More concerning is a trend of violence in communities that threatens not only mining operations, but also peace and stability itself. Operations at Koidu Holdings (now Ocetea) were halted in 2007 after police killed two people protesting the lack of compensation to landowners, problems with resettlement, and the lack of employment opportunities for local people.[79] More deaths were reported during a worker strike in 2012.[80] Violence has also erupted at an African Minerals site as workers were demanding better pay and working conditions. In this case, police shot one bystander and left dozens injured.[81] A Human Rights Commission investigation found that police used disproportionate force, employed arbitrary arrests, destroyed property, and engaged in inhuman and degrading treatment of the protestors, but none of the police involved were prosecuted.

Of course, civil society groups and activists question the long-term development prospects of mineral exploitation and whether the benefits from mineral resources can really be the key to post-conflict peace and development. From this perspective, minerals offer little hope to the people given that Sierra Leone, which has been mining diamonds for three-quarters of a century, remains one of the most impoverished countries in the world. In addition, the country has a checkered history with diamond mining, including exploitation of workers, human rights abuses, and war. The notion that better governance and more efficient state control over resources can transform decades of mismanagement, patronage, and corruption into prosperity in a matter of years is met with genuine cynicism.

### Natural Resource Governance in Liberia and Sierra Leone: A Blueprint?

Based on the above discussion, it appears that reforms in the forest sector in Liberia and diamonds and mineral sectors in Sierra Leone are analogous. Natural resource governance in both countries appears to be written according to a certain rule and institution-building blueprint about how to leverage natural resources for peacebuilding. The purpose of this section is to examine reasons why this might be the case.

One critical factor that helped to determine the salience of natural resources in both Sierra Leone and Liberia was how the conflicts were framed. In spite of the variety of causes linked to the onset and continuation of both conflicts, a majority of attention focused on the presumed economic motivations of the combatants, including most prominently Charles Taylor. Starting at a time when the international system was in flux and pronouncements of a "new world order" were common, both conflicts appeared to commentators and the media as irrational, brutish, and chaotic. The only explanation seemed to be "greed" and the self-enrichment of "bandits," rather than a competition for political power or societal grievances. Once economic motives became the defining characteristic of the conflicts, scholars and commentators began looking for the profitable assets over which the combatants were fighting. Since Liberia and Sierra Leone both contained vast amounts of globally valuable natural resources, this narrative gained prominence and offered a parsimonious explanation for conflicts difficult to explain.

While narratives of natural resource conflict helped to place natural resources on the international peacebuilding agenda, they also led to actual practices about how natural resources should be governed in war-torn societies. Both countries for example, emphasized the reestablishment of state control over the resource base and improved state institutional capacity and authority so that natural resources were made "governable." The underlying presumption was that the conflict undermined the state's institutional ability to govern its natural resources (and its revenues) and therefore must be rebuilt. It also presumed that the state and its agencies were the appropriate entity to govern natural resources on behalf of society because the state alone has the sovereign right to do so. Not surprisingly then, post-conflict natural resources governance was fundamentally state-centric in its approach.

Post-conflict natural resources governance also places a high priority on the significance of leveraging the economic benefits of natural resources in order to rebuild the country and set it on a path to peace and prosperity. As the above cases clearly show, post-conflict governance in the natural resource sectors described is predominantly concerned with exporting timber, diamonds, or minerals so as to foster economic growth and increase state revenue and employment opportunities. The emphasis on "fast-tracking" export strategies and foreign direct investment was based on the conventional wisdom that natural resources form the backbone of development and provide the essential building blocks of economic growth, poverty reduction, and social stability.[82] Such rationale was fundamentally constructed not only on the perceived peace-enhancing traits of international trade, but the assumption deeply embedded in the logic of peacebuilding that poverty and a "failure of economic development" is the biggest risk factor for renewed conflict.[83] In theory, if natural resources can be governed well they can work to revive the economy to "buy confidence in the peace process."[84]

While the focus on leveraging the economic development to the state is deeply embedded in post-conflict peacebuilding, there is a recognition that market-oriented policies and natural resource extraction may increase – not decrease – conflict in fragile states and war-torn societies.[85] To mitigate the potential problems with leveraging the economic benefits from timber and diamonds, the view was that state institutions must be effectively reassembled and reestablished in order to ensure natural resources are governed in accordance with the norms of good governance, including transparency, accountability, and the rule of law. Because both Liberia and Sierra Leone have historically granted concessions and contracts to businesses "under the table," and revenues from natural resources have never trickled down to the population, economic oversight was required by international actors in order to help secure the natural resources base for the population. The perception was that if the population does not quickly see tangible and direct benefits (e.g. basic services, infrastructure) from the government in the aftermath of war, grievances could swiftly turn into instability and conflict.

## Peacebuilding and Natural Resource Governance: Contradictions and Tensions

What does all this mean and why might it be important? First, a focus on the economic motives of combatants and the natural resource dimensions of conflict tends to oversimplify the causes and conditions that led to conflict in the first place. These analyses overlook that the Liberian conflict was enabled by grievances in reaction to oppressive governments or the result of historically unfair land ownership arrangements that enriched a few and left the population underdeveloped. Likewise, in Sierra Leone, a historical pattern of undemocratic governments, underdevelopment, and a lack of land formed a set of political grievances that only intensified with the one-party state. The larger point is that in both Liberia and Sierra Leone grievances and struggle over natural resources were largely about land and a failure to benefit directly from their vast natural resources. What is problematic for natural resources governance, which remains focused on governing natural resources for state revenue and economic growth, is that international actors may not address land-related issues that concern and affect much of the population. In fact, there is a real threat that extraction of minerals and timber could exacerbate already existing tensions with regard to land.

Focusing on economic motives also renders invisible the ways in which political and economic dimensions are linked via systems of patronage. Networks of patronage are essential for political power and financially dependent on natural resources. Taylor's motives were essentially political although they involved looting the country's natural resources to buy loyalty and dispense patronage. The same dynamics explain the patrimonial system in Sierra Leone, whereby diamond revenue was funneled into informal rather than formal state channels in order to maintain power and pay off emerging warlords. In essence, political power in Liberia and Sierra Leone has historically required the leveraging of the economic benefits of natural resources, and this often presages agreements, concessions, and resources management policies that are arranged without genuine inclusiveness, transparency, or accountability. The difficulty is that these practices can undermine conventional statebuilding by diverting revenues away from the provisioning of basic services, marginalizing certain populations, and creating conditions that give rise to "spoilers." Problems with timber contracts and PUPs have raised questions about transparency and accountability in Liberia. Conversely, in Sierra Leone reports that mineral agreements and concessions are negotiated behind closed doors raises concerns that historical patterns of corruption are still alive and well. If reforms only rebuild previous patronage-resource structures they can legitimize and deepen systems of patronage and work to weaken government and divert revenues away from peacebuilding priorities. Therefore, post-conflict natural resource governance must not simply rebuild state institutions but actually alter pre-war social, economic, and political structures.

While fostering economic growth, providing employment, and generating state revenue have their challenges and are certainly important, they tend to dominate discussions and crowd out other factors vital for the consolidation of peace. Environmental issues related to water, sanitation, shelter, food, and energy supplies are almost overwhelmingly overlooked. Moreover, they can lead to tunnel vision that risks overlooking the sustainable livelihoods of communities more broadly.

Unfortunately, the result of a comprehensive focus on sustainable livelihoods related to agricultural production and the use of forest products is that they are often labeled as part of the "informal" economy or as low-stakes issues, and do not receive sufficient attention in peacebuilding efforts. The factors that habitually impede communities from meeting their livelihoods, including perverse land ownership or grievances and resentment related to extraction, are not adequately addressed. Indeed, interviews in both countries turn up a widely held perception that livelihoods and communities are being left behind in the peacebuilding process. An emphasis on economic growth, foreign direct investment, and fast-tracking natural resource extraction has also resulted in contentious political struggle. In Liberia the "backlash" stems from a perception that community objectives are subordinate to the governments and international actors' timber-producing priorities while failing to address historical grievances over land ownership and community rights. There is little confidence based on historical experience that communities will benefit directly through the government's commercial forestry activities and that a development model based on timber exports will genuinely help communities. At the same time, Sierra Leone's miners as well as communities adjacent to mining areas continue to feel exploited by more powerful actors.

However, this does not have to be the case. The findings in this chapter provide several insights that can help to open up new opportunities for governing natural resources in post-conflict settings. First, it should be noted that economic narratives of conflict are often exaggerated, which can lead to reforms that address only economic-based solutions like limiting trade on natural resources or mandating good governance of resource wealth. While transparency of resource revenues, government accountability, and new laws and regulations to manage resource extraction are vitally important, such initiatives must be accompanied by genuine efforts to deal with the politics of control that surround natural resources and the deep-seated grievances of the population and local communities. Peacebuilding investments at the local level, which include genuinely incorporating the desires of local communities in reforms, are generally slower and small in financial terms but can pay significant peace dividends. Second, reforms that place economic growth and the export of natural resources at the apex of peacebuilding risk recreating the very structures that historically provided massive profits to the few while doing little to improve the lives of local communities and the population as a whole. The concessionary model, for example, leaves most decision making in the hands of government authorities and dismisses the idea that local communities have the right to decide how their resources are managed. The peacebuilding agenda needs to explore strategies that affirm the rights of local people and open up the possibility of new models of grassroots development that can have positive repercussions for peace. The focus on "fast-tracking" resource extraction can also lead to the exclusion of other problems. This is evident in Liberia and Sierra Leone where problems of land ownership, community rights, and an availability of alternative livelihoods have the potential to undermine peace. Finally, although leveraging natural resources can be important as a source of revenue, exaggerated expectations only help to undermine confidence in peacebuilding. As a result, there needs to be a concerted effort to bring expectations in line with reality. In sum, natural resources can assist the difficult task of building peace, but only if post-conflict natural resource reforms instill confidence, foster cooperation, and heal the wounds of the past.

## Notes

1 Call, *Building States to Build Peace.*

2 Paris, *At War's End*; Bah, *International Security and Peacebuilding.*

3 Stedman et al., *Ending Civil Wars*; Fortna, "Scraps of Paper?"; Hartzell et al., "Stabilizing the Peace after Civil War."

4 Doyle and Sambanis, *Making War and Building Peace.*

5 Collier et al., *Breaking the Conflict Trap.*

6 Boutros-Ghali, *An Agenda for Peace*, 4; UN Security Council, "Peacebuilding," 1–2.

7 Ross, "How Do Natural Resources Influence Civil War?"

8 Collier and Hoeffler, "Greed and Grievance in Civil War."

9 McAskie, "The Peacebuilding Natural Resource Nexus."

10 The chapter is based on fieldwork and documentary evidence gathered in Liberia and Sierra Leone between 2008 and 2015. Over 100 interviews were conducted with government officials, international organizations, civil society groups, local communities, and others familiar with natural resource issues. The interviewees were granted anonymity given the sensitive nature of this research.

11 Levitt, *The Evolution of Deadly Conflict in Liberia*; Sawyer, *The Emergence of Autocracy in Liberia*; Bah, "State Decay"; Richards, *Fighting for the Rainforest*; Reno, *Corruption and State Politics in Sierra Leone*; Keen, *Conflict and Collusion in Sierra Leone.*

12 Reno, *Warlord Politics and African States*; Smillie et al., *The Heart of the Matter*; Global Witness, *A Rough Trade*; New York Times, "The Business of War in Africa."

13 Ellis, *The Mask of Anarchy*, 90–91.

14  Global Witness, *Logging Off*; UN Panel of Experts, S/2000/1195, 12.

15  Smillie et al., *Heart of the Matter*.

16  Global Witness, *Logging Off*.

17  Levitt, *The Evolution of Deadly Conflict in Liberia*.

18  Reno, "Shadow States and the Political Economy of Civil Wars."

19  Bah, "State Decay."

20  Smillie et al., *Heart of the Matter*; Rupert, "Diamond Hunters Fuel Africa's Brutal Wars"; Junger, "The Terror of Sierra Leone."

21  Reno, *Warlord Politics and African States*, 126; Keen, *Conflict and Collusion in Sierra Leone*.

22  Reno, *Warlord Politics and African States*.

23  Ibid.; Keen, *Conflict and Collusion in Sierra Leone*.

24  Smillie et al., *Heart of the Matter*; UN Security Council, Resolution 1306.

25  Keen, *Conflict and Collusion in Sierra Leone*, 267–276.

26  Richards, *Fighting for the Rainforest*; Bangura, "Political and Cultural Dynamics of the Sierra Leone War."

27  Keen, *Conflict and Collusion in Sierra Leone*, 9.

28  Ibid., 8.

29  Reno, *Warlord Politics and African States*.

30  Abdullah, *Between Democracy and Terror*.

31  Save My Future Foundation, *Plunder*, 2.

32  UN Security Council, Resolution 1478.

33  Ibid.

34  McAlpine et al., "Liberia."

35  FCRC, "Forest Concession Review," 35–37.

36  Ibid., 37.

37  "About GEMAP," www.gemap-liberia.org/about_gemap/index.html (accessed March 15, 2017).

38  The Forest Concession Review Committee recommended canceling all forest concessions.

39  Government of Liberia, *An Act Adopting the National Forestry Reform Law*.

40  Ibid., 6.

41  Ibid., 6.

42  International Monetary Fund, *Liberia*.

43  Government of Liberia, *Interim Poverty Reduction Strategy Summary*.

44  Collier et al., *Breaking the Conflict*.

45  International Monetary Fund, *Liberia*, 21.

46  Government of Liberia, *An Act Adopting the National Forestry Reform Law*, 34–35.

47  International Monetary Fund, *Liberia*, 64.

48  Global Witness, "Liberia Poised to Hand Forests to Timber Pirates."

49  UN Panel of Experts, S/2008/785.

50  Beevers, "Securing Forests for Peace and Development in Postconflict Liberia."

51  Global Witness, "Signing Their Lives Away."

52  Ibid.

53  Special Independent Investigating Body, "Report on the Issuance of Private Use Permits."

54  Beevers, "Forest Governance and Post-Conflict Peace in Liberia."

55  Liberian Governance Commission, "Land Rights Law and the Constitution."

56  Grant, "The Kimberley Process at Ten."

57  World Bank, "Sierra Leone Mining Sector Reform"; UNEP, *Sierra Leone*.

58  NACE, "Sierra Leone at the Crossroads."

59  Partnership Africa Canada, "Killing Kimberley?"

60  World Bank, "Sierra Leone: Tapping the Mineral Wealth."

61  Levin and Gberie, "Dealing for Development," 29.

62  Ibid., 9.

63  Cooper, "As Good as It Gets," 111.

64  Ibid., 112.

65  Maconachie, "Diamond Mining."

66  Government of Sierra Leone, "The Agenda for Change," 1.

67  World Bank, "Sierra Leone: Tapping the Mineral Wealth."

68  NACE, "Sierra Leone at the Crossroads," 5.

69  Ibid.

70  Stearns, "Sierra Leone Hopes to Become Africa's Biggest Exporter of Iron Ore."

71  Manson, "Sierra Leone's War Trauma Gives Way to Resource Bonanza."

72  MacNamara, "African Minerals in $1.5bn China Pact."

73  Berger, "Sierra Leone Declared EITI Compliant."

74  NACE, "Sierra Leone at the Crossroads."

75  DanWatch, "Not Sharing the Loot."

76  Interview with member of Sierra Leonean advocacy organization, 2012.

77  UNEP, *Sierra Leone*; Human Rights Watch, *Whose Development?*

78  Interviews with people living and working in numerous mining communities, 2008, 2009, and 2012.

79  NACE, "Sierra Leone at the Crossroads."

80  *Reuters*, "Violent Strike Halts Work at Sierra Leone Koidu Diamond Mine."

81  Human Rights Watch, *Whose Development?*

82  Bannon and Collier, *Natural Resources and Violent Conflict*; del Castillo, *Rebuilding War-Torn States*; UNEP, *Sierra Leone*.

83  Paris, *At War's End*.

84  Woodward, "Economic Priorities for Successful Peace Implementation," 344.

85  Paris, *At War's End*; Ross, "How Do Natural Resources Influence Civil War?"

## References

Abdullah, Ibrahim. *Between Democracy and Terror: The Sierra Leone Civil War*. Dakar: CODESTRA, 2004.

Bah, Abu Bakarr. "State Decay: A Conceptual Frame for Failing and Failed States in Africa." *International Journal of Politics, Culture and Society* 25 (2012): 71–89.

Bah, Abu Bakarr. *International Security and Peacebuilding: Africa, the Middle East and Europe*. Bloomington, IN: Indiana University Press, 2017.

Bangura, Yusuf. "The Political and Cultural Dynamics of the Sierra Leone War," pp. 13–40, in *Between Democracy and Terror: The Sierra Leone Civil War*, edited by Ibrahim Abdullah. Dakar: CODESTRA, 2004.

Bannon, Ian, and Paul Collier. *Natural Resources and Violent Conflict*. Washington, DC: The World Bank, 2003.

Beevers, Michael D. "Forest Governance and Post-Conflict Peace in Liberia: Emerging Contestation and Opportunities for Change." *The Extractive Industries and Society* 3 (2015): 320–328.

Beevers, Michael D. "Securing Forests for Peace and Development in Postconflict Liberia." *African Conflict and Peacebuilding Review* 6 (2016): 1–24.

Berger, Christina. "Sierra Leone Declared EITI Compliant." April 10, 2017. https://eiti.org/news/sierra-leone-declared-eiti-compliant.

Boutros-Ghali, Boutros. *An Agenda for Peace: Preventative Diplomacy, Peacemaking and Peacekeeping.* New York: United Nations, 1992.

Call, Charles. *Building States to Build Peace.* Boulder, CO: Lynne Rienner, 2008.

Collier, Paul, and Anke Hoeffler. *Greed and Grievance in Civil War.* Washington, DC: World Bank, 2000.

Collier, Paul, V.L. Elliott, Håvard Hegre, Anke Hoeffler, Marta Reynal-Querol, and Nicholas Sambanis. *Breaking the Conflict Trap: Civil War and Development Policy.* Washington, DC: World Bank, 2003.

Cooper, Neil. "As Good as It Gets: Securing Diamonds in Sierra Leone," pp. 103–118, in *Whose Peace: Critical Perspectives on the Political Economy of Peacebuilding*, edited by Michael Pugh, Neil Cooper, and Mandy Turner. London: Palgrave, 2008.

DanWatch. "Not Sharing the Loot: An Investigation of Tax Payments and Corporate Structures in the Mining Industry of Sierra Leone." 2011.

del Castillo, Graciana. *Rebuilding War-Torn States: The Challenge of Post-Conflict Economic Reconstruction.* Oxford: Oxford University Press, 2008.

Doyle, Michael W., and Nicholas Sambanis. *Making War and Building Peace: United Nations Peace Operations.* Princeton, NJ: Princeton University Press, 2006.

Ellis, Stephen. *The Mask of Anarchy: The Destruction of Liberia and the Religious Dimension of an African Civil War.* New York: New York University Press, 1991.

Forest Concession Review Committee (FCRC). "Forest Concession Review: Phase III." May 31, 2005.

Fortna, Virginia Page. "Scraps of Paper? Agreements and the Durability of Peace." *International Organization* 57 (2003): 337–372.

Global Witness. *A Rough Trade: The Role of Companies and Governments in the Angolan Conflict.* London: Global Witness, 1998.

Global Witness. *Logging Off: How the Liberian Timber Industry Fuels Liberia's Humanitarian Disaster and Threatens Sierra Leone.* London: Global Witness, 2002.

Global Witness. "Liberia Poised to Hand Forests to Timber Pirates." Briefing Document, July 15, 2009.

Global Witness. "Signing Their Lives Away: Liberia's Private Use Permits and the Destruction of Community-Owned Rainforest." Briefing Document, September 3, 2012.

Government of Liberia. *An Act Adopting the National Forestry Reform Law.* 2006.

Government of Liberia. *Interim Poverty Reduction Strategy Summary.* 2006.

Government of Sierra Leone. "The Agenda for Change: Second Poverty Reduction Strategy." 2008.

Grant, J. Andrew. "The Kimberley Process at Ten: Reflections on a Decade of Efforts to End the Trade in Conflict Diamonds," pp. 159–179, in *High-Value Natural Resources and Post-Conflict Peacebuilding*, edited by Päivi Lujala and Siri Aas Rustad. New York: Earthscan, 2012.

Hartzell, Caroline, Matthew Hoddie, and Donald Rothchild. "Stabilizing the Peace after Civil War: An Investigation of Some Key Variables." *International Organization* 55 (2001): 183–208.

Human Rights Watch. *Whose Development? Human Rights Abuses in Sierra Leone's Mining Boom.* Washington, DC: Human Rights Watch, 2014.

International Monetary Fund. *Liberia: Poverty Reduction Strategy.* Washington, DC: IMF, 2008.

Junger, Sebastian. "The Terror of Sierra Leone." *Vanity Fair,* December 6, 2000.

Keen, David. *Conflict and Collusion in Sierra Leone.* New York: Palgrave, 2005.

Levin, Estelle A., and Lansana Gberie. "Dealing for Development: The Dynamics of Diamond Marketing and Pricing in Sierra Leone." Diamond Development Initiative, March 2006.

Levitt, Jeremy. *The Evolution of Deadly Conflict in Liberia.* Durham, NC: Caroline Academic Press, 2005.

Liberian Governance Commission. "Land Rights Law and the Constitution." Policy Brief 2, 2015.

MacNamara, William. "African Minerals in $1.5bn China Pact." *Financial Times* [London], July 13, 2010.

Maconachie, Roy. "Diamond Mining, Urbanization and Social Transformation in Sierra Leone." *Journal of Contemporary African Studies* 30 (2012): 705–723.

Manson, Katrina. "Sierra Leone's War Trauma Gives Way to Resource Bonanza." *Financial Times* [Freetown], April 13, 2012.

McAlpine, Jan L., Peter A. Donohue, and Oliver Pierson. "Liberia: Forests as a Challenge and Opportunity." *International Forestry Review* 8 (2006): 83–92.

McAskie, Carolyn. "The Peacebuilding Natural Resource Nexus, Annex to Meeting Report of Managing Natural Resources in Post-Conflict Societies: Lessons in Making the Transitions to Peace." September 2007.

National Advocacy Coalition on Extractives (NACE). "Sierra Leone at the Crossroads: Seizing the Change to Benefit from Mining." March 2009.

New York Times. "The Business of War in Africa." August 8, 1999.

Paris, Roland. *At War's End: Building Peace after Civil Conflict.* Cambridge: Cambridge University Press, 2004.

Partnership Africa Canada. "Killing Kimberley? Conflict Diamonds and Paper Tigers." Occasional Paper 15. November 2006.

Reno, William. *Corruption and State Politics in Sierra Leone.* Cambridge: Cambridge University Press, 1995.

Reno, William. *Warlord Politics and African States.* Boulder, CO: Lynne Rienner, 1998.

Reno, William. "Shadow States and the Political Economy of Civil Wars," pp. 43–68, in *Greed and Grievance: Economic Agendas in Civil War,* edited by Mats Bergdal and David Malone. Boulder, CO: Lynne Rienner, 2000.

*Reuters.* "Violent Strike Halts Work at Sierra Leone Koidu Diamond Mine." December 21, 2012.

Richards, Paul. *Fighting for the Rainforest: War, Youth and Resources in Sierra Leone.* Oxford: James Currey, 1996.

Ross, Michael. "How Do Natural Resources Influence Civil War? Evidence from Thirteen Cases." *International Organization* 58 (2004): 35–67.

Rupert, James. "Diamond Hunters Fuel Africa's Brutal Wars." *Washington Post,* October 16, 1999.

Save My Future Foundation (SAMFU). *Plunder: The Silent Destruction of Liberia's Rainforests.* Monrovia: SANFU Foundation, 2002.

Sawyer, Amos. *The Emergence of Autocracy in Liberia.* San Francisco, CA: Institute for Contemporary Studies, 1992.

Smillie, Ian, Lansana Gberie, and Ralph Hazelton. *The Heart of the Matter: Sierra Leone, Diamonds, and Human*

*Security.* Ottawa: Partnership Africa Canada, 2000.

Special Independent Investigating Body. "Report on the Issuance of Private Use Permits (PUPs)." December 19, 2012.

Stearns, Scott. "Sierra Leone Hopes to Become Africa's Biggest Exporter of Iron Ore." *Voice of America News* [Dakar], February 17, 2010.

Stedman, Stephen John, Donald Rothchild. and Elizabeth Cousins. *Ending Civil Wars: The Implementation of Peace Agreements.* Boulder, CO: Lynne Rienner, 2002.

UN Environment Programme (UNEP). *Sierra Leone: Environment, Conflict and Peacebuilding Assessment.* Geneva: UNEP, 2009.

UN Panel of Experts. "Report of the Panel of Experts Pursuant to Security Council Resolution 1306." S/2000/1195. December 2000.

UN Panel of Experts. "Report of the Panel of Experts Submitted Pursuant to Security Council Resolution 1819." S/2008/785. December 2008.

UN Security Council. Resolution 1306. S/RES/1306. 2000.

UN Security Council. "Peacebuilding: Toward a Comprehensive Approach: Statement by the President of the Security Council." S/PRST/2001/5. February 2001.

UN Security Council. Resolution 1478. S/RES/1478. 2003.

Woodward, Susan. "Economic Priorities for Successful Peace Implementation," pp. 183–214, in *Ending Civil Wars: The Implementation of Peace Agreements*, edited by Stephen John Stedman, Donald Rothchild, and Elizabeth M. Cousens. Boulder, CO: Lynne Rienner, 2002.

World Bank. "Sierra Leone: Tapping the Mineral Wealth for Human Progress." Report No. 26141-SL. July 25, 2005.

World Bank. "Sierra Leone Mining Sector Reform: A Strategic Environmental and Social Assessment." Report No. 44655-SL. July 10, 2008.

# 6 | DEVOLUTION AND ELECTORAL VIOLENCE IN KENYA

*Aditi Malik*

## Introduction

Following the 2007–2008 post-election crisis in Kenya, in 2010, 67 percent of the country's voters voted in favor of a new constitution. By then demands for constitutional reform in Kenya were not novel; they had been placed before different administrations for several decades. Decentralization, for instance, was something that smaller ethnic communities had advocated for ever since independence. Following the restoration of multiparty competition and the initiation of political liberalization in the early 1990s, moreover, such demands had gained momentum.[1] However, successful Kenyan governments had blocked constitutional change, and for over forty years, ruling elites had maintained the status quo through a largely centralized and clientelistic state apparatus. As such, the mere passing of the new constitution was a significant event in Kenya's political history. This constitution ushered in a series of important reforms, which included implementing a new threshold for the presidency (changing the previous plurality requirement to a simple majority), enhancing the range of rights for women and minorities, requiring that all electoral coalitions register themselves three months before a presidential election, and creating regional governments in the form of forty-seven newly created counties.[2]

Today, Kenya's counties wield significant political, administrative, and fiscal powers. For one, they receive funds from the national government – in the form of unconditional grants – to use for developmental purposes. They also have their own assemblies as well as a county governor. The decision to create these counties, however, was not simply motivated by the objective of promoting development and providing opportunities for local-level political participation. In fact, according to Article 174 of the new constitution, devolution in Kenya was implemented to realize several different objectives, which included, promoting democratic and accountable exercise of power, fostering national unity amidst diversity, enabling self-governance of the people towards their interrogation of the [s]tate, recognizing the right of communities to self-management and development ... ensuring equitable sharing of national and local resources, rationalizing further decentralization of [s]tate organs, and enhancing checks and balances.[3]

In the run-up to the 2013 elections, numerous stakeholders on the ground were of the opinion that devolution would also serve to prevent a recurrence of electoral violence in the country.[4] Simply put, this expectation held that by devolving political authority to the local level, the new constitution would dampen the "winner-take-all" nature of Kenya's presidential elections and thereby contribute to the maintenance of peace.

This chapter assesses the effects that devolution has had on patterns of election-related conflict in Kenya. In doing so, it considers the relationship between post-conflict institutional design on the one hand and electoral violence – at both the national and sub-national levels – on the other. Recent studies of the Kenyan county system have shed light on the ways in which devolution has affected rent-seeking and patronage.[5] However, research on the effects that the county system has had, and is likely to have, on incentives for, and patterns of electoral violence is still incipient.[6] Drawing on evidence from three counties – all of which experienced conflict in association with their local elections in 2013 – this chapter makes the case that devolution has been a partial success in Kenya: while it has reduced elites' incentives to instrumentalize violence around presidential elections, the county system has simultaneously created high-stakes elections at the *local* level, around which such conflict could be organized in the future. Simply put, the project finds that increased ethnic competition *within* counties has generated several new drivers of election-time violence in the country. In making this argument, the research makes two key contributions. First, it proposes an original theory about how decentralization reforms can actually contribute to a continuation – albeit localized – rather than an elimination of conflict in post-violence developing democracies. Second, and with regard to Kenya, the research combines original quantitative event data with in-depth interviews and evidence from case studies to identify different pathways through which electoral violence occurred around the 2013 elections.

At its broadest level, this study seeks to contribute to theory-building. Consequently, rather than comparing violent and peaceful counties, the chapter deliberately focuses on three counties that experienced conflict in 2013. This approach makes it possible to tease out the causal mechanisms through which devolution gave rise to local-level violence while at the same time mitigating conflict around the 2013 presidential election.

The chapter is organized as follows. I begin by providing historical background about agitations for constitutional reform in Kenya, focusing particularly on the period since the re-instatement of multiparty competition. Next, I discuss the literature on the relationship between decentralization and violent conflict. The following section describes the key features of decentralization in Kenya and introduces the three cases that are at the heart of this study – namely, Tana River, Marsabit, and Isiolo – all of which experienced violent conflict in association with their county-level elections in 2013. The section also specifies the causal mechanisms that drove electoral violence in each of these places, and demonstrates how these processes were spawned by decentralization reforms. Finally, I comment on the implications of this study, and briefly discuss what future patterns of election-related conflict under Kenya's new constitution could look like. I suggest that the results so far are mixed: while devolution has dampened the drivers of election violence at the national level, by shifting the locus of electoral competition to the local level, it has created a new set of high-stakes elections around which such clashes are likely to occur in the future.

### Kenya's 2010 Constitution

Following independence, the first generation of Kenyan politicians oversaw a series of steps that contributed to the creation of a centralized state.[7] This early concentration of power at the center was maintained through successive presidents' clientelistic networks, which were often used to favor and reward co-ethnics.[8] Nonetheless, and especially since the re-introduction of multiparty politics in the 1990s, local activists began to advocate that a new constitution be passed. The focus of these agitations was twofold: to reduce the power of the presidency and to implement decentralization reforms. However, and as a leading scholar on the subject has noted, until 2010, "power holders successfully blocked all attempts" to bring about constitutional change in Kenya.[9] Among the many thwarted efforts, perhaps the biggest disappointment was the rejection of the "Bomas" draft, which sought to rein in the powers of the president through several different mechanisms including separating powers, introducing checks and balances, and implementing devolution.[10] Unfortunately, the version of the constitution – known as the "Wako" draft – which was eventually put to a referendum in 2005, was a significantly diluted version of the Bomas draft, and it "restored full executive powers to the president."[11] As such, it is not surprising that 58 percent of Kenya's voting population subsequently voted against the Wako draft.

In one sense, the fact that numerous attempts at constitutional reform were blocked by ruling Kenyan politicians tells a discouraging story about the entrenched nature of elite power in the country. At the same time, the rejection of the Wako draft was generally seen as a "positive step toward democratic consolidation in Kenya" and one that "raised hopes for the future."[12] Put simply, through their rejection of this draft, Kenyan voters made it clear that they would not be satisfied with cosmetic changes to the country's institutions. While this rejection was a necessary step on the road to achieving constitutional reform in Kenya, it was by no means sufficient. Rather, it was the post-election violence of 2007–2008, which brought Kenya to the brink of a civil war, that heightened the need for far-reaching institutional change. Specifically, the post-election crisis – the third case of widespread electoral conflict to have broken out in the country since the restoration of multiparty competition – made it amply clear that Kenya was, and had been, in a state of institutional decay for some time.[13]

To bring an end to the violence in 2008, several rounds of negotiations were held between Mwai Kibaki (the incumbent who had been declared the winner of the election) and Raila Odinga (the leading opposition candidate, who had alleged electoral fraud). One of the key results of these negotiations was the creation of the post of prime minister for Odinga. Subsequently, the terms of a power-sharing agreement between Kibaki and Odinga were formalized and a Grand Coalition government was crafted. The peace negotiations also mandated that the question of constitutional reform be revisited, and by November 2009, a new draft of Kenya's constitution was prepared. Following a few minor modifications, the draft was passed by the country's MPs and August 4, 2010 was set as the date for the constitutional referendum. As stated above, the constitution subsequently received support from a majority of the voting public.

For several different reasons, Kenya's new constitution has come to be understood as a vital corrective to previous watered-down proposals. Moreover, its peaceful passing has been seen as an encouraging signal as to "the increasing institutionalization of political power" in sub-Saharan Africa.[14] Yet, existing research on the *effects* that the new constitution has had – on patronage, executive power, and the quality of elections – suggests that Kenya has seen little meaningful change with regard to these important matters.[15] Along similar lines, this research finds that the effect of decentralization – on elites' incentives for violence – has been only partially successful. Positively, there are important reasons to expect that election-related conflict in Kenya will be more diffuse going forward, as the new constitution has lowered the stakes of presidential elections. At the same time, however, it does not appear that constitutional reform has rendered the option of driving violence to win votes entirely obsolete. On the contrary, evidence from 2013 suggests that devolution has intensified intra-county ethnic com-petition and has thereby merely altered the kinds of elections – from national to local – around which the use of conflict makes electoral sense. To understand why this is the case, a closer examination of the theoretical relationship between decentralization and violent conflict, as well as its specific manifestation in the selected Kenyan counties, is necessary. The forthcoming sections of this chapter address these important questions.

### Decentralization and Violent Conflicts: What Is the Link?

In the scholarship on constitutional design, devolution is frequently prescribed as a way to manage violent conflict. Decentralization pro-ponents claim that there are several different means through which devolving power to sub-national units can serve to contain violence.[16] First, devolution is understood to bring the government closer to the people and thus improve the distribution of public goods and services at the local level. In addition, decentralization creates opportunities for local-level representatives, who are more in tune with the challenges in their areas, to take up political office and improve sub-national outcomes. When achieved, these improved outcomes are believed to thwart local-level grievances that could be mobilized for violent ends. Finally, decentralization allows citizens – including "territorially con-centrated minority groups [– to] control … their own political, social, and economic affairs."[17]

At the same time, however, recent research has uncovered that decentralization is not a magic bullet and that, under certain conditions, it can actually lead to a continuation of, or even an increase in, violent conflict. The most powerful reason uncovered for this association is related to the rise of regional parties. Simply put, when decentralization brings about a proliferation of regional parties – which advocate for narrow regional policies – then rather than stemming conflict, such reforms have been found to exacerbate violence.[18] Admittedly, however, and especially in places like Kenya, where political parties are typically formed on the basis of ethno-regional criteria, the mechanisms and pathways through which devolution could serve to increase political violence are likely to be different. Some potential mechanisms that could bring about this outcome include creating new high-stakes elections, "reinforcing regionally-based identities, producing legislation that discriminates against certain ethnic or religious groups in a country, supplying groups at the regional level of government with the resources [and reasons over which] to engage in … conflict," carving out new ethnic minorities, shifting the composition of electoral fault-lines, encouraging the construction of new electoral alliances, and rendering pre-existing regional cleavage structures electorally relevant and manipulable.[19]

Forthcoming sections of this chapter will demonstrate how different combinations, constellations, and sequences of these mechanisms affected the timing and targets of electoral violence in Tana River, Marsabit, and Isiolo around Kenya's 2013 elections. For the moment, however, the purpose of this chapter is to draw attention to the fact that the long-reigning theoretical expectation, which held that the introduction of decentralization is a useful way to reduce violent conflict, has come under significant scrutiny in recent scholarship. Indeed, the fact that the implementation of sub-national governance provides only a partial solution for ebbing violent conflict has already been observed in cases such as Nigeria and India.[20] In places like Indonesia, furthermore, research has shown that decentralization has created new arenas for the organization of election-related violence.[21] Building on these insights, this chapter teases out the varying effects that devolution has had on national and local-level competition in Kenya. It shows that by providing unprecedented access to developmental funds, decentralization reforms have contributed to new patterns of local-level election-time violence in the country while at the same time decreasing the risks of widespread electoral violence occurring in relation to presidential elections.

## Devolution and Electoral Violence in Kenya

Compared to 2007–2008 as well as the elections of the 1990s, Kenya's 2013 presidential election concluded relatively peacefully. At the same time, however, to say that the 2013 elections were entirely peaceful would be inaccurate. According to recent scholarship on the topic, violent events that occur six months before and three months after an election can be classified as being electoral in nature.[22] In association with the 2013 Kenyan elections, and in late 2012 and early 2013 alone, 477 individuals were killed and another 118,000 were displaced in incidents of communal conflict.[23] Much of this violence, moreover, was tied to competition over newly created county-level positions.

This research focuses on three counties – Tana River, Marsabit, and Isiolo – which experienced conflict in relation to the 2013 elections. These sites are appropriate for a theory-building exercise such as this one for several reasons. To begin with, Tana River, Marsabit, and Isiolo are among the ten poorest counties in all of Kenya.[24] As such, the comparative component of this research is based on a selection of like, and therefore comparable, cases. Furthermore, and as with other forms of violence – including civil wars – recent research on electoral violence has shown that poverty is a major driver of such conflict.[25] Consequently, the selection of Tana River, Marsabit, and Isiolo makes it possible to investigate the link between poverty and electoral violence under Kenya's new constitution. Third, the selected counties are diverse and ethnically heterogeneous, and in keeping with previous patterns of electoral violence in Kenya, election-related conflict in each of these places manifested itself along ethnic lines. Finally, the three sites are well-suited for a comparative analysis because, despite their shared characteristics and initial conditions, the violence that broke out here displayed important differences in terms of its dynamics. Two key differences are particularly noteworthy. First, and as summarized in Table 6.1, the timing of the conflicts varied considerably: Tana River fell prey to pre-vote violence, Marsabit experienced clashes after the conclusion of its county-level elections, and Isiolo witnessed both pre- and post-vote clashes. Second, distinct causal pathways contributed to election-related clashes in each of these sites. Thus, the selection of these three cases allows for a comprehensive probe into the questions of *why*, *how*, and *when* decentralization reforms can contribute to election-time violence in developing democracies.

Before this research can delve into a detailed discussion of the violence that occurred in Tana River, Marsabit, and Isiolo, however, it is vital to shed some light on the key attributes of Kenya's county system. It is to this task that the remainder of this section is dedicated. Devolution, which created forty-seven new counties in Kenya, was one of the central reforms that emerged out of the new 2010 constitution. The axes of devolution in the country, moreover, are threefold: administrative, political, and fiscal. For the purposes of better understanding incidents of election violence around the 2013 elections, it is crucial to pay attention to this composite set of powers that county representatives now enjoy. This is because it is these enhanced responsibilities that have rendered the county-level elections to be high-stakes contests. Consequently, it is the county-level elections around which it makes sense for politicians to organize conflict. As the forthcoming discussion will illustrate, it is also around these local contests that voters can be mobilized to participate in violence.

Each of Kenya's forty-seven counties houses a county assembly. Members of the county assemblies (MCAs) are elected at the ward

TABLE 6.1 Variations in Timing and Causal Pathways of Electoral Violence

| Case | Timing of Violence | Mechanism(s) and Purpose of Violence |
|---|---|---|
| Tana River | Pre-election violence | Pre-existing ethnic cleavages rendered electorally salient and manipulable → creation of new cross-ethnic alliance; violence used to overthrow long-standing power-holders |
| Marsabit | Post-election violence | Change in composition of electoral fault-lines → creation of new multi-ethnic alliance that ousted long-time power-holders; violence as a reaction to this reshuffling |
| Isiolo | Pre and post-election violence | Pre-existing ethnic cleavages rendered electorally salient and manipulable → contributed to pre- and post-election violence<br>Competition for development projects along new electoral fault-lines → contributed to post-election violence |

level and there are 1450 wards across the country. In addition, each county elects a women's representative and a senator who represents the interests of the county in the Senate, which is the upper house of Kenya's parliament. Finally, through a gubernatorial election, county residents elect a governor, who is the most powerful office-holder at the county level. Elected through a popular vote, which takes place on the same day as the general election, county governors are in charge of the overall management of county affairs. They enjoy a broad set of powers, which range from overseeing county development to heading the county executive committee. Stated plainly, the governor is the chief executive of the county. Given this important position, and as one respondent summarized, "the county governor [is now] the closest president that the people ... have."[26] Power that was once concentrated in the office of the president, in other words, has been devolved to county governors. From the perspective of voters, then, just as having a co-ethnic president was once understood to be crucial for securing the welfare of one's community, having a co-ethnic governor is now considered fundamental for accessing the Kenyan state.

While there has long been a pattern of ethnic voting in Kenya, albeit for defensive reasons, this research holds that the 2010 constitution has amplified the stakes around the ethnic identities of *local* political representatives, especially county governors.[27] This is not merely because clientelism continues to be a salient political force in Kenya – thereby generating expectations of ethnic patronage in many parts of the country – but even more so because of the considerable fiscal powers that governors now enjoy under the new constitutional dispensation. Put concretely, Article 16 of the new constitution established a body known as the Commission of Revenue Allocation (CRA), which was tasked with determining the distribution of "revenue raised by the national government [at two levels] – between the national and county governments [and] among the county governments."[28] As shown in Table 6.2, the CRA formula for revenue allocation provides all forty-seven counties with an equal share of 25 percent of the national revenue and splits another 2 percent based on counties' fiscal responsibilities. The remaining county-level allocations are determined on the basis of land area, population, and poverty. Consequently, there is considerable variation in the amount of money distributed to county governments, with larger, more populous, and poorer counties receiving more funds than their smaller and richer counterparts. In short, devolution has not

TABLE 6.2 CRA Formula for Revenue Allocation[29]

| Criterion | Weighting (%) |
|---|---|
| Population | 45 |
| Poverty Index | 20 |
| Land Area | 8 |
| Basic Equal Share | 25 |
| Fiscal Responsibility | 2 |

only increased competition over resources between counties but it has also heightened local rivalries to control these funds *within* counties.

Apart from determining county-level allocations, when devolution first came to pass, the CRA also had to establish how revenues would be shared between the national and county governments. Initially, it was decided that the county governments would receive 15 percent of the national revenue in the form of unconditional grants and that these grants would be used specifically for developmental purposes, such as building and maintaining local roads and providing health-care and pre-primary education.[30] However, county governors opposed this number for being too low and demanded that 45 percent of the national budget be reserved for them.[31] Eventually, the National Assembly (the lower house of Kenya's parliament) came to a compromise and for the last few years, county governments have received over 200 billion Shillings per annum, which is well over the 15 percent allocation that they were initially promised.[32] In 2015–2016, for instance, Kenya's forty-seven counties received 259 billion Shillings (approximately 2.44 billion dollars) in unconditional grants, which exceeded 30 percent of the national revenue for that fiscal year.[33] Given the significant amount of funding that is being channeled to county governments, voters, for their part, are keen to ensure that one of their "own" wins crucial county positions, such as the governorship.[34] Rather than eliminating the potential for electoral violence, then, by generating a new set of high-stakes elections around which citizens hope to access state resources, devolution has increased ethnic competition *within* counties. Stated concretely, the county system has done little to alter the *nature* of election violence in the country. Existing studies of election-related conflict have repeatedly shown that such violence takes place along ethnic and communal lines in Kenya.[35] Since its implementation, decentralization has failed to dampen the salience of ethnicity in the country. Instead, the heightened stakes of county-level elections have made pre-existing ethnic divisions electorally relevant in several parts of Kenya and as a result, new pockets of violence have emerged. Three such sites – Tana River, Marsabit, and Isiolo – where devolution produced conditions favorable to violence around the 2013 elections are analyzed below.

### Tana River: New Alliances, Pre-Election Clashes, and Changing Power Relations

In the run-up to the 2013 elections, the Coastal county of Tana River came to attract significant attention due to deadly communal clashes that broke out there. To many, the violence suggested that Kenya could be headed down the path to another conflict-ridden election.[36] These fears were not without foundation: with the exception of the 2002 presidential contest, every such election in Kenya had been accompanied by widespread violence, which had cost thousands of lives each time. However, Tana River's violence was unique for two key reasons. First, although the region had succumbed to communal clashes between its pastoral (Orma and Wardei) and agricultural (Pokomo) communities before, such violence had not been electoral per se. Indeed, in the two elections around which the Coast had fallen prey to violence – 1997 and 2007 – conflict had been concentrated in the districts of Likoni and Kwale, and in Mombasa district, respectively.[37] Second, located in a region that was predisposed to vote for the opposition alliance known as the Coalition for Reforms and Democracy (CORD), from an electoral incentives perspective, the outbreak of violence in Tana River made little sense. After all, because they do not offer much promise in terms of gaining swing votes, places that are electoral strongholds of one particular party or alliance are generally understood to be poor choices for instrumentalizing conflict.[38] In order to account for the violence in Tana River in 2012–2013, then, one has to look beyond these conventional explanations of electoral conflict.

This research holds that Tana River's violence should be understood as a consequence of new competitive dynamics introduced by the implementation of devolution. Over time, political power in this area had come to be concentrated in the hands of the agricultural Pokomos: both in 2002 and in 2007, for instance, two out of three parliamentary seats in the district had fallen to the Pokomo community. As such, and for some time, there had been a growing sense of marginalization among the Orma, which had only increased when a land adjudication program, through which Pokomo farmers began to obtain title deeds, was introduced in December 2000.[39] In this context, the creation of new county-level positions offered Orma elites a distinctive opportunity to reverse prevailing power relations. In addition, given the county's severe underdevelopment – the CRA had ranked Tana River as Kenya's fifth poorest county in 2011 – and the promise of funds from the national government, devolution generated a powerful set of incentives for Orma politicians to wield violence for electoral ends. Specifically, in 2013–2014, Kenya's national government allocated 200 billion Shillings to the counties, and Tana River's allocation for that year was 2.9 billion Shillings.[40] For a county that had long been left out of the central government's developmental projects, this was no small amount. In the run-up to the election, therefore, the prospect of a significant fiscal disbursement re-oriented the main axis of political competition in Tana River from the national to the local level. In short, decentralization set the stage for electoral conflict in the county: Orma elites were now keener than ever to prevent their rival Pokomos from ascending to political office. Furthermore, given the pre-existing divide between the two communities, instrumentalizing clashes was a viable strategy for Orma politicians to do so.

For violence to be effective, however – that is, for it to pay electoral dividends – the Orma could not act alone. Although precise proportions are not available, it is estimated that the Orma comprise approximately 28 percent of Tana River's population while the strength of the Pokomo lies at approximately 40 percent.[41] Thus, to secure prized county offices – such as that of the governor – and to build a winning coalition, the Orma needed an ally.[42] They found a natural fit in the pastoral Wardei community, whose members speak the same language (Orma) and follow the same religion (Islam). The Wardei were similar to the Orma in another important respect: successive Pokomo MPs had failed to effectively represent the interests of this community as well. Stated plainly, then, devolution in Tana River first and foremost created conditions that favored the organization of violence by rendering the long-standing fault-line between the region's agricultural and pastoral communities electorally salient. This attribute, in turn, encouraged the creation of a new alliance between the pastoral groups, who were keen to gain access to the state. With these crucial conditions in place, and with the aim of preventing the Pokomo from casting their votes, conflict was ignited by pastoral (largely Orma) politicians who drew on narratives and fears of marginalization to mobilize the Orma and Wardei against the Pokomo.

It was in this broader context that the first deadly clash in Tana River occurred in Kilelengwani village on August 14, 2012. The violence took the form of an attack by the Orma on the Pokomo. In subsequent days and weeks, similar clashes – sometimes Orma on Pokomo and sometimes the reverse – spread to other villages in Tana River including Kau, Riketa, Semikaro, Chamwanamuma, Darga, Laini, and Shirikisho. Event data reveals that the first wave of violence, which lasted until September 9, 2012 resulted in the loss of 123 lives and injured fifty-eight others.[43] On December 21, a second phase of violence shook Tana River, beginning in Kipao village, where over thirty-nine individuals were killed and another twenty were injured. Pokomo raiders were believed to be behind this attack. Not long after, communal clashes broke out in Nduru and Kibusu villages on January 9 and 10, 2013, respectively. It is estimated that this second wave of violence resulted in the deaths of sixty-two individuals and severely injured twenty-four others. Early on, then, the clashes in Tana River ensured that they would be a notable blot on Kenya's 2013 electoral record.

But did the violence work? Did the Orma and Wardei succeed in their efforts to overpower and prevent Pokomo elites from capturing political office? The results of the March 4 elections indicate that the answer to these questions is an affirmative one. As shown in Table 6.3, the Orma and Wardei communities succeeded in securing key county-level offices in Tana River, including the treasured governorship, which fell to Tuneya Hussein Dado (an Orma).

In addition, their co-ethnic candidates won the three MP seats from Garsen, Galole, and Bura constituencies. Beyond the election results, qualitative information gathered for this project also lends credence to the ideas that the violence in Tana River was (1) electorally motivated and (2) bore the desired results for the pastoral communities. Over the course of fieldwork, several interviewees noted the patently electoral nature of Tana River's violence. One respondent, for instance, accounted for the clashes as follows:

TABLE 6.3 2013 Tana River County Election Results

| Name | Position | Ethnic Group | Political Party | Coalition |
|------|----------|--------------|-----------------|-----------|
| Tuneya Hussein Dado | Governor | Orma | Wiper Democratic Movement-Kenya (WDM-K) | CORD |
| Ali Abdi Bule | Senator | Wardei | Federal Party of Kenya (FPK) | CORD |
| Halima Ware Duri | Women's Representative | Orma | Wiper Democratic Movement-Kenya (WDM-K) | CORD |
| Ibrahim Ahmed Sane | MP (Garsen Constituency) | Wardei | United Republican Party (URP) | Jubilee |
| Hassan Abdi Dukicha | MP (Galole Constituency) | Wardei | United Democratic Forum Party (UDF) | Amani |
| Ali Wario | MP (Bura Constituency) | Orma | The National Alliance (TNA) | Jubilee |

The violence was clearly linked to the election. No one can say that it was just a coincidence. You see, development programs in Kenya haven't really been designed to benefit nomadic communities like the Orma. So ... [the clashes were] all about making sure that the pastoral communities could come to power [at the county level].[44]

Another interviewee explained that the county system had made it paramount to ensure that co-ethnic politicians could be voted into *local* office:

There was politics behind it [the violence] ... especially, [with] the county governments, which were coming ... Also, the windfall economically that was expected [for the counties]. It [the violence] was political in the sense that even the former MPs were the ones even funding and organizing the militias to attack each other. So that "we disperse of these people out of this area so that my community when the elections come, we take the seats." That was the incentive [for violence that devolution created].[45]

Finally, a third interviewee held that the violence in Tana River had been deliberately instrumentalized to alter "who [i.e. which ethnic group(s) got to] take up governance in the county."[46]

These sentiments were not restricted to interview subjects alone and early on, President Kibaki's government also took a stand on the violence. Following the first wave of conflict, in September 2012, the MP from Galole constituency, Dhadho Godhana (a Pokomo), who was also serving as Assistant Minister of Livestock at the time, was charged with inciting the clashes in Tana River. Godhana was an aspirant for the governorship in Tana River.[47] Once the allegations against him emerged, Kibaki relieved Godhana of his ministerial position. For his part, however, Godhana held that his political rival, Internal Security Minister Yusuf Haji – who was backing Hussein Dado's bid for governor – had been behind the violence.[48] In the third week of January 2013, Godhana was cleared of the incitement charges against him.[49] Nonetheless, when combined with the interview data presented above, these allegations and counter-allegations strongly suggest that (1) the violence in Tana River was planned (and involved a handful of elites) and (2) the new county system – and the delegation of fiscal powers to county governments – had created powerful incentives to use violence as an electoral instrument.

In terms of who the beneficiaries of the violence were, respondents interviewed for this project repeatedly identified the Orma and Wardei as such. To put it in the words of one interlocutor for example, by creating "a ... sense of unity among the pastoralist groups," Orma elites were able to successfully deploy election-related conflict as a means to "remove the agricultural Pokomos from power."[50] Consequently, "the Pokomos were decimated ... The clashes ensured that they could not vote for their preferred candidate[s] because many of them were displaced from their homes."[51] Although concrete information on the distribution of funds in the county is not available, recent evidence also suggests that, as one might expect, pastoral elites have favored their own in composing the county government.[52]

Taken together, then, as is true of other episodes of pre-election conflict in Kenya – including the clashes witnessed around the 1992 and 1997 presidential contests – the 2012–2013 violence in Tana River proved to be effective as it depressed voter turnout among the targeted community (i.e. the Pokomos) and thereby helped those who wielded violence to ascend to political office. At the same time, however, it is important to note that what distinguishes Tana River from previous episodes of pre-election conflict in Kenya is that these clashes were actually spawned by devolution reforms. In other words, they took place in association with local, rather than national, elections. As such, the evidence reveals that while holding at bay elites' incentives for organizing election-related violence around the presidential election, devolution created new conditions – and generated attendant mechanisms – that resulted in two separate waves of conflict around the 2013 county elections in Tana River.

## Marsabit: Electoral Fault-Lines, Swing Votes, and Post-Election Violence

Another site that experienced electoral violence in association with its 2013 local elections was Marsabit. This county, which is located in the arid and semi-desert northeastern area of Kenya, has a long history of violent conflict. Indeed, due to its proximity to neighboring Somalia, Marsabit is understood to be a particularly unstable part of Kenya. This instability has repeatedly come to the fore through violent cattle raids, communal clashes, and banditry. In short, "violence is far from being something of the past in Marsabit."[53]

Beyond witnessing the kinds of conflicts identified above, Marsabit has also experienced electoral violence. In October 1997, for instance, two months before the presidential election, the Catholic Diocese of Marsabit reported that "200 people had been killed, 6000 displaced, [and] over 25000 heads of cattle, 21000 goats, 1000 camels, and 127 donkeys [had] been stolen" in the preceding month of September.[54] While resource-related conflict of this nature was not new to Marsabit at the time, its timing just ahead of the presidential election strongly suggested that the clashes had been electorally motivated. More recent scholarship has identified yet another reason – climate change – due to which Marsabit is at a high risk of experiencing violent conflict in the future.[55]

As is the case with Tana River, Marsabit is poor and largely underdeveloped. In fact, according to the CRA, the county is the fourth poorest in all of Kenya, and is only outranked by Wajir, Mandera, and Turkana counties. The majority of the local population here is comprised of pastoral communities, which include the Gabra, Borana, Rendille, Turkana, Ariaal, and Samburu. The main non-pastoral groups in the region are the Burji, who engage in agriculture and trade, and the Somalis, who are traders. Although reliable sub-national data on the size and proportion of these groups is not available, the Borana are known to be a powerful demographic force in Marsabit.[56]

Existing studies on inter-ethnic dynamics in this area have shown that since 2000, the relationship between two communities – namely, the Borana and the Gabra – has declined considerably.[57] Increased political competition has apparently contributed to this deterioration: of the four constituencies in Marsabit, one (Moyale) is dominated by the Borana, while another (North Horr) is dominated by the Gabra.[58] Prior to the implementation of devolution, there was a fairly consistent pattern of representation: since 1992, Moyale and Saku constituencies have only had Borana MPs while only Gabra politicians have risen to parliament from North Horr. The fourth constituency in Marsabit – Laisamis – was represented by Rendille politicians from 1992 onwards until Joseph Lekuton (a Maasai) won the seat in 2007, and subsequently retained it in 2013. At the constituency level, therefore, and for a considerable period of time, local patterns of power-holding in Marsabit were quite stable, and favored the Borana. Although several other communities were arguably disadvantaged by these conditions, election-related conflict in the region was fairly rare.[59] This is because, prior to the 2013 elections, political power was concentrated in the presidency, and none of the communities in Marsabit (including the Borana) had much to gain from the Kikuyu and Kalenjin presidents who controlled the national purse-strings.

The arrival of devolution, however, changed things quite drastically. First, the county system offered these marginalized groups a unique opportunity to take control of their own affairs. Put differently, as in Tana River, devolution created a set of high-stakes local elections in Marsabit. In 2013–2014, for instance, Marsabit received 3.6 billion Shillings as its county allocation from the national government.[60] Second, and within this context of increased fiscal capacity and decentralized elections, ethnic competition within Marsabit county intensified. As a result, the fault-line between the Borana and Gabra took on a whole new meaning. Rather than being limited to cattle raids and periodic communal clashes, the county elections provided these communities with a chance to defeat their rivals and capture political power for the long term. In other words, devolution heightened the stakes for ensuring that co-ethnic politicians ascended to political office. As one respondent explained:

> What is happening in Moyale [constituency] or in Marsabit for that matter, it's all that … "My people, my community is not in the county government. When the county government is coming, for example, let us arrange ourselves and align ourselves so that

we can go into leadership." Basically, that is what [it is]: when the community fears that "our people" are going to be out [of power], they are not going to be in the county government, they tend to align themselves differently.[61]

In the wake of these revised expectations, a new multi-ethnic alliance was born in Marsabit. This coalition pitted the Rendille, Gabra, and Burji (ReGaBu) against the Borana. Stated differently, while the fault-line between the Borana and Gabra did not disappear, its composition did change somewhat, as several ethnic groups in Marsabit came together *against* the Borana. It is also important to note that this alliance did not come about overnight. On the contrary, efforts to bring the ReGaBu together were documented as early as July 2012.[62]

The logic behind this coalition was rooted entirely in the effects of the new county system. Stated plainly, the ReGaBu alliance followed directly from the fact that with the creation of Marsabit county, "no one single community [was in a position to] garner enough votes on [its] own" to win the local elections.[63] Thus, for both the Borana and the Gabra, the support of smaller groups became pivotal. As it turned out, both communities settled on the agricultural Burji as their best bet, whose members were subsequently "vigorously courted."[64]

For their part, national-level politicians also understood that local elections in Marsabit were high stakes, and that these contests could have an impact on the presidential election. More concretely, presidential candidates quickly realized "that votes for a governor from their party [would] likely ... translate into votes for themselves."[65] Consequently, rather than the presidential election taking precedence over the county contest, the entire logic of election campaigning in Marsabit turned on prioritizing local needs and considerations. Within this context, some national elites even went so far as to "court key power brokers," including elders, who could help convince their communities to support particular candidates and parties in the county election.[66]

Ultimately, as in Tana River, the elections in Marsabit produced some unexpected results. For the most part, the ReGaBu alliance held together, and as shown in Table 6.4, although this coalition did not succeed in pulling off a clean sweep – because previous patterns around the parliamentary elections held up – it did manage to ensure that the governor's post did not fall to the Borana.

TABLE 6.4 2013 Marsabit County Election Results

| Name | Position | Ethnic Group | Political Party | Coalition |
|------|----------|--------------|-----------------|-----------|
| Ukur Yatani Kanancho | Governor | Gabra | Orange Democratic Movement (ODM) | CORD |
| Godana Hargura | Senator | Rendille | Orange Democratic Movement (ODM) | CORD |
| Nasra Ibrahim Ibren | Women's Representative | Somali | Orange Democratic Movement (ODM) | CORD |
| Roba Sharu Duba | MP (Moyale Constituency) | Borana | United Democratic Forum Party (UDFP) | Amani |
| Francis Chachu Ganya | MP (North Horr Constituency) | Gabra | Orange Democratic Movement (ODM) | CORD |
| Ali Rasso Dido | MP (Saku Constituency) | Borana | United Republican Party (URP) | Jubilee |
| Joseph Lekuton | MP (Laisamis Constituency) | Maasai | Orange Democratic Movement (ODM) | CORD |

These surprising results led to a spate of post-election clashes in Marsabit, as different communities' fears about the lack of ethnic inclusion in county government were mobilized for violent ends.[67] In other words, rather than violence being used to influence electoral outcomes (as was the case in Tana River), in Marsabit communal clashes broke out following, and as a reaction to, the election results. The first set of clashes occurred on September 14, 2013, and lasted for more than a week. Over 100 people perished in this round of violence. According to survivors' accounts, the clashes appeared to have been deliberately instrumentalized by Borana elites who were unwilling to accept the victory of the ReGaBu.[68] In early December, a second wave of violence broke out in the villages of Odha and Holale near Moyale town. This time, the clashes erupted after Borana militiamen attacked three vehicles traveling on the A2 highway. From Odha and Holale, conflict spread to Butiye and Sessi villages, where retaliatory attacks on Boranas took place. At the end of these clashes, another twenty people in Marsabit county had been killed. Not long afterwards, in mid-December 2013, charges for inciting violence were leveled against Borana elites Roba Sharu Duba, the MP from Moyale constituency, and Golicha Galgalo Guyo, the representative from Butiye ward (also in Moyale).[69] A second set of charges against the two men followed in April 2014.[70] Six months later, in October 2014, all charges were dropped.[71] Nonetheless, the fact that legal proceedings were initiated at all is noteworthy, because it suggests that as in Tana River, there was an understanding that the clashes in Marsabit were also politically motivated.

In the end, the violence in Marsabit did not change local electoral outcomes. Based on the timing of the clashes – which came several months after the election – the only way the results could have been altered through violence is if the ReGaBu had been forced to negotiate over their victory. However, this did not happen. Moreover, and after some internal challenges, the Marsabit council of elders once again endorsed Ukur Yatani Kanancho (the current governor and a Gabra) as their preferred candidate for the gubernatorial seat.[72] Based on a 2013 agreement, the elders were also expected to endorse a Rendille for the position of senator, a Burji as deputy governor, and a Garre as the women's representative.[73] Despite these efforts, which aimed at retaining key county-level positions in Marsabit among the ReGaBu, Mohamud Mohamed Ali (a Borana) emerged as the winning gubernatorial candidate in Marsabit in 2017. In short, this time, the fortunes from 2013 were reversed at the local level.

### Isiolo: Electoral Fault-Lines, Resource Competition, and Political Violence

The third and final case at the heart of this study is Isiolo, which is located in Kenya's former Eastern province. Like Tana River and Marsabit, Isiolo ranks among the country's poorest counties, holding the eighth position according to the CRA. Sub-national data suggests that anywhere between 63 and 76 percent of Isiolo's population lives below the poverty line.[74] As such, it is not surprising that for the 2013–2014 fiscal year, Isiolo's county allocation from the national government was a sizeable 2.4 billion Shillings.[75]

Most of the ethnic communities in Isiolo are pastoralists, including the Borana, Samburu, Turkana, and Somalis. However, the area is also home to a sizeable Meru minority, who are historical allies of the Kikuyus, and who work as farmers and traders. Like Marsabit, communal violence in Isiolo is not an altogether new phenomenon. In the 1990s, for instance, Isiolo witnessed clashes between the Borana and the Somalis, which were understood to have stemmed from competition over accessing grazing land. Violence was also reported in Isiolo in 1997 in association with the presidential election of that year.[76] A third major spate of conflict in the district (now county) broke out between January and March 2000, with a subsequent wave in May of that year. This time, the violence in Isiolo pitted the Borana and Samburu on one side against the Somalis on the other. The precise death toll from the conflicts of 2000 is still debated, but estimates put the numbers at 40 to 100 casualties.[77] On the face of it and like the violence of the 1990s, these clashes involved "fighting over pasture land [and] cattle rustling."[78] However, closer analysis has revealed that electoral machinations contributed to the violence. Specifically, scholars have held that the arrival and registration of Somalis as voters had influenced local voting patterns in Isiolo.[79] Furthermore, it has been argued that the reinstatement of multiparty competition had heightened ethnic rivalries in the region, as "local politicians want[ed] to expel the Merus who [were] associated with the opposition."[80]

Despite its brushes with election-related conflict in the late 1990s and early 2000s, Isiolo did not experience conflict during Kenya's 2007–2008 post-election violence. Since then, however, and especially since 2011, the county has become a site of escalating communal violence.[81] In fact, between November 2011 and February 2012, conflict in Isiolo, Marsabit, and Mandera counties claimed the lives of "at least 120 people" and displaced another 77,000 from their homes.[82] The clashes in Isiolo, in particular, took place between November 2011 and January 2012. This violence cost at least twenty people their lives and resulted in the displacement of 10,000 others.[83] As one influential report has noted, "the fighting pitted the Turkana community against the Somali[s] who had support from the Borana community."[84] Thus, at least on the face of it, the 2011–2012 violence in Isiolo resembled previous events of pastoral conflict in the region. The fighting apparently even started out "as a dispute over grazing land and cattle rustling."[85]

The November 2011 to February 2012 violence was followed by a second set of clashes, which began in late March and continued into April 2012. Over the course of this wave of violence, it is estimated that at least 500 Turkana families from Isiolo town were displaced from their homes.[86] Although initially attributed to clashes over land and cattle, over time, it became clear that "the fighting was about county politics [as well as] the coming general elections."[87]

Isiolo county is composed of two parliamentary constituencies: Isiolo North and Isiolo South. In both constituencies, but especially in Isiolo North, the Borana are the demographically dominant group.[88] As a result, they have held a major electoral advantage, as evidenced by the fact that Boranas have produced "nine out of the eleven MPs [who have been] elected" since the formation of the constituency in 1966.[89] Nonetheless, since the 2007 election, when the Borana MP candidate managed to secure a narrow victory over the second-place finisher (a Turkana), the community has become increasingly concerned about its political future in Isiolo.[90]

These anxieties only appear to have heightened since the introduction of devolution. At times, as in the clashes of November 2011 to January 2012, it has appeared that the Boranas have tried to support the Somalis, presumably in an attempt to garner Somali votes. At other times, however, Boranas and Somalis were pitted against one another and engaged in violent conflict. Around the 2013 election, for instance, when some of the clashes targeted Isiolo's Somalis, the violence was explained in terms of pre-planned attempts to "drive [Somalis] away from the county so that they could not register as voters."[91] To be sure, Borana versus Somali conflicts in Isiolo continued intermittently into 2017. Although the most recent incidents appeared to be related to a fight over resources, with the county elections quickly approaching, the Isiolo council of elders "warned locals to be wary of politicians" who could exploit them for electoral ends.[92] Altogether, then, there is a considerable body of evidence, which suggests that the new county system has contributed to increasing violence among pastoral communities (particularly between the Boranas and Somalis) in Isiolo.

Simultaneously, conflicts between local herder groups and the farming Meru community in Isiolo have been on the rise. To quote one report,

> In late October 2015 deadly clashes pitted Somali, Boran[a] and Samburu herders against Meru farmers along the ... county border resulting in six deaths. A few days later, riots erupted in Isiolo town following the death of a Meru *boda-boda* (motorbike-taxi) operator; [the] Boran[a], Somali and Turkana then looted Meru shops and blocked the Isiolo–Nanyuki highway.[93]

To account for these conflicts, some analysts have held that devolution has increased the legibility of minority communities (in

Isiolo's case, the Meru) who the other groups are keen to freeze out of power.[94]

The 2013 election results from Isiolo lend some credence to such claims. With the exception of the MP seat from Isiolo North, which fell to a Turkana candidate (Joseph Samal Lomwa), all of the main county positions (governor, senator, and women's representative) as well as the parliamentary seat for Isiolo South fell to Borana candidates, albeit from varied clans. These results are striking not only because they illustrate the fact that the Merus were kept out of power, but also because they show that the Borana failed to capture the MP seat from Isiolo North, a position that they had long dominated. Thus, although it cannot be conclusively established, the evidence from Isiolo strongly suggests that the new county system has served to reinforce pre-existing cleavage structures both within the pastoral community and between pastoralists and farmers. Moreover, these heightened divisions appear to have given rise to some important changes in electoral fortunes.

While the new electoral salience of old ethnic cleavages can help us to account for pre-vote conflicts in Isiolo, a complete explanation of these clashes as well as the more recent and escalating herder–farmer violence necessitates an acknowledgment of the crucial place that the county occupies within the Kenya Vision 2030 program. This initiative, launched by former President Kibaki in June 2008, aims to transform Kenya into an industrializing, middle-income country by the year 2030. At the heart of this program are several national and regional development projects, one of which is LAPSSET (Lamu Port, South Sudan, and Ethiopia Transport). LAPSSET seeks to create a "transport corridor between Kenya and Uganda and … better integrate Ethiopia and South Sudan into East Africa."[95] Isiolo will be a key node within this corridor, and it is one of the sites where construction for important infrastructure projects has already begun. So far, Isiolo's airstrip has been transformed into an international airport, which was officially opened by President Uhuru Kenyatta on January 20, 2017.[96] According to reported figures, the total estimated cost of LAPSSET is $23 billion (roughly 2 trillion Kenyan Shillings).[97] Within this context, then, the intensifying ethnic clashes in Isiolo are not only attributable to the new high-stakes elections created by devolution, but these patterns are also related to increasing competition between different sub-national groups to control the county's development projects. As such, it is not surprising that in a 2016 list of counties released by Kenya's National Cohesion and

Integration Commission (NCIC), Isiolo figured as one of thirty-three sites that was likely to experience violence around the 2017 elections.[98]

## Conclusion

Following the post-election crisis of 2007–2008, Kenya promulgated a new constitution in 2010, which ushered in a series of important institutional changes in the country. Central among these reforms was the introduction of devolution. At the time of its implementation, there was considerable optimism that by reducing the concentration of power in the presidency, devolution would serve to diminish elites' incentives for orchestrating electoral violence.

Through a controlled comparison of three Kenyan counties – Tana River, Marsabit, and Isiolo – all of which experienced violence in association with their 2013 local contests, this research has shown that at least in Kenya's first "post-conflict" elections, these hopes were not realized. To be sure, devolution is perceived to have brought many benefits to Kenyans including easier access to officials, increased public participation, and improved health services, roads, and local employment opportunities.[99] Furthermore, according to a 2016 survey, more than three-quarters of the Kenyan population supports devolution.[100] With regard to the potential for violence, however, while it is reasonable to expect that clashes on the scale of those seen in 2007–2008 are unlikely to repeat themselves, by increasing ethnic competition within counties, devolution has only provided a partial solution for curbing election-time conflict. Specifically, the chapter has illustrated that the country's county system has created a new set of high-stakes contests around which such violence is likely to occur. This is because by devolving political, administrative, and especially *fiscal* powers to the forty-seven newly created counties, decentralization reforms in Kenya have actually heightened the stakes of electoral competition at the local level. In particular, the fact that counties now receive unconditional grants for developmental purposes from the central government has had at least three crucial consequences for the dynamics of political competition.

First, and with reference to county elections in 2013, the availability of these funds rendered pre-existing ethnic divisions electorally relevant and manipulable in many parts of the country. In Tana River, for example, a long-standing divide between the pastoral Orma and agricultural Pokomo took on new electoral meaning in the run-up to the elections, and local politicians used this divide to organize violence in a bid to capture prized county-level positions. Similarly, in Isiolo, devolution and the associated promise of accessing devolved fiscal resources amplified divisions between different pastoral groups. Second, and within Isiolo county once again, competition over a large development and infrastructure project heightened rivalries between pastoral communities on the one hand and the agricultural Meru group on the other. Evidence from the ground suggests that some of the violence in this region was deployed in a concerted attempt to freeze Merus out of county offices. Third, devolution caused a shift in prevailing faultlines in some parts of Kenya. Subsequently, new electoral coalitions were cobbled together ahead of the elections in 2013, which threatened and sometimes succeeded in ousting long-time power-holders from their political positions. In Marsabit, for instance, the creation of the ReGaBu alliance prevented the Borana from capturing any of the county-level offices. This turn of events led to a spate of communal clashes in the aftermath of the local election there. Given the ethnic heterogeneity of many Kenyan counties, the challenge for the country going forward will be to streamline devolution so as to prevent unequal access to power and resources – problems that have typically accompanied national-level elections – from setting in more permanently around sub-national (i.e. county-level) contests.

In conclusion, this study has proposed an original theory, and offered new evidence from Kenya, on how devolution reforms can generate rather than stymie elites' incentives for organizing election-related conflict. With reference to the three Kenyan cases at the heart of this research, the study has shown that various causal mechanisms contributed to the culmination of such violence around the 2013 elections, with clashes occurring both before and after county-level contests. The timing of some of these conflicts is important, as they challenge the prevailing wisdom, which classifies violent events that occur six months before and three months after an election as being electoral in nature. As shown in the cases of Tana River and Isiolo, however, some communal clashes took place more than six months before local county elections were held and they still appeared to have served an electoral purpose. Similarly, some of the violence in Marsabit and Isiolo occurred after the closure of the three-month post-election window.

A vital implication that emerges from this research, then, is that institutional changes such as devolution can actually serve to widen the period over which elites face incentives to organize election-related conflict. For example, violent clashes that broke out in Baringo and Laikipia counties several months prior to local-level elections gave some analysts pause about whether the Rift Valley would descend into chaos yet again.[101] Furthermore, in 2017, as the election results started to trickle in, counties such as Garissa succumbed to conflict over the gubernatorial race.[102] Thus, unlike the presidential contest, even though procedural concerns were generally not raised in relation to Kenya's county-level elections in 2017, in several closely fought sites, election-related conflict did take place.[103] Paying closer attention to the dynamics of county-level competition will be an important task for advancing future research on the drivers of electoral violence in Kenya. From a policy perspective, furthermore, findings from Kenya could help to guide practitioners about how to structure and implement devolution in developing democracies so as to prevent not only national-level electoral violence but also more localized clashes from occurring in the future.

## Notes

1    Nelson Kasfir, "Agency across Changing Sites."

2    Kramon and Posner, "Kenya's New Constitution," 89.

3    Nyanjom, "Devolution in Kenya's New Constitution," 11.

4    Elder et al., "Elections and Violent Conflict in Kenya," 12; and anonymous interview (professor of political science), interview by author, Nairobi, Kenya, December 12, 2013.

5    Cornell and D'Arcy, "Plus ça Change?"; and D'Arcy and Cornell, "Devolution and Corruption in Kenya."

6    Abdille and Abdi, "Kenya"; International Crisis Group, "Kenya's Coast"; Mohamud and Mosley, "Insecurity in Northern Kenya"; and Sharamo, "The Politics of Pastoral Violence."

7    Kasfir, "Agency across Changing Sites"; Shilaho, "Third Time Lucky?"

8    Kasfir, "Agency across Changing Sites"; Branch et al., *Our Turn to Eat.*

9    Kasfir, "Agency across Changing Sites," 56.

10    Whitaker and Giersch, "Voting on a Constitution," 6.

11    Ibid., 6; Cornell and D'Arcy, "Plus ça Change?," 175; Kasfir, "Agency across Changing Sites," 56.

12    Whitaker and Giersch, "Voting on a Constitution," 1.

13    Mueller, "Dying to Win."

14    Kramon and Posner, "Kenya's New Constitution," 90.

15    Cornell and D'Arcy, "Plus ça Change?"; D'Arcy and Cornell, "Devolution and Corruption in Kenya"; Hassan, "Continuity Despite Change"; Mutiga, "Kenya"; and Long et al., "Choosing Peace over Democracy."

16    For a comprehensive discussion of these reasons, refer to Brancati, *Peace by Design.*

17    Ibid., 8.

18    Brancati, "Decentralization"; and Brancati, *Peace by Design.*

19    Brancati, "Decentralization," 652.

20    See, for example, Jinadu, "Federalism, the Consocional State, and Ethnic Conflict in Nigeria"; Kendhammer, "Talking Ethnic but Hearing Multi-Ethnic"; Deshpande, "Assembly Elections"; and Wilkinson, *Votes and Violence.*

21    van Klinken, *Communal Violence and Democratization in Indonesia.*

22    Straus and Taylor, "Democratization and Electoral Violence in Sub-Saharan Africa, 1990–2008," 19–20.

23    Human Rights Watch, "High Stakes," 1.

24    Republic of Kenya, Commission on Revenue Allocation (CRA), "Kenya County Fact Sheets."

25    Collier, *Breaking the Conflict Trap*; Fearon and Laitin, "Ethnicity, Insurgency, and Civil War"; and Cleven, "Elites, Youth and Informal Networks."

26    Anonymous interview (professor of political science), interview by author, Nairobi, Kenya, December 12, 2013.

27    Bratton and Kimenyi, "Voting in Kenya."

28    Republic of Kenya, *Constitution of Kenya*, Article 216, 2010.

29    Republic of Kenya, Commission on Revenue Allocation (CRA), "Revenue Allocation Formula." Also see Cheeseman et al., "Decentralization in Kenya," 15.

30    Kimenyi, "Devolution and Resource Sharing in Kenya."

31    Shilaho, "Third Time Lucky?," 162.

32    For details, see Cheeseman et al., "Decentralization in Kenya," 14–15.

33    Ongiri, "Counties to Get Sh48bn More in New Budget Deal."

34    Anonymous interview (Republican Congress, i.e. RC, politician), interview by author, Mombasa, Kenya, September 27, 2013.

35    Kahl, *States, Scarcity, and Civil Strife in the Developing World*; Klopp, "'Ethnic Clashes' and Winning Elections."

36    BBC, "Kenya Tana Delta Massacres Raise Election Violence Fear"; also see Africa Report, "Kenya's Tana Delta Burning."

37    Note that with the implementation of the new county system, the district is now a defunct administrative unit in Kenya.

38    Wilkinson, *Votes and Violence.*

39    Martin, "Conflicts between Pastoralists and Farmers in Tana River District," 174.

40    Republic of Kenya, Commission on Revenue Allocation (CRA), "County Budgets 2013–2014." On file with the author.

41    Author's calculations based on 2009 Kenya census data.

42    County elections in Kenya use a plurality threshold.

43    The author collected this event data for a related project. The dataset will be publicly available once all projects whose research it supports have been submitted for peer review. For more details on the dataset, see Malik, "Constitutional Reform and New Patterns of Electoral Violence," 346–347.

44    Anonymous interview (religious leader), interview by author, Mombasa, Kenya, October 4, 2013.

45    Anonymous interview (RC politician), interview by author, Mombasa, Kenya, September 27, 2013.

46    Anonymous interview (professor of history), interview by author, Nairobi, Kenya, January 29, 2013.

47    Human Rights Watch, "Kenya."

48    Ibid. Also see Ndonga, "Dhadho Godhana Sacked over Tana Killings."

49    Mung'ahu, "MP Godhana Cleared of Incitement Charges."

50    Anonymous interview (TNA politician), interview by author, Nairobi, Kenya, October 17, 2013.

51    Anonymous interview (civil society leader), interview by author, Mombasa, Kenya, September 25, 2013.

52    Mwawasi, "Tana River Governor Accused of Hiring Relatives in Plum County Jobs."

53    Witsenburg and Adano, "Of Rain and Raids," 519.

54    Kagwanja, "Politics of Marionettes," 88.

55    Witsenburg and Adano, "Of Rain and Raids."

56   Scott-Villiers et al., "Roots and Routes of Political Violence in Kenya's Civil and Political Society"; Obuya, "Politics a Key Factor in the Perennial Marsabit Conflict."

57   Witsenburg, "Ethnic Tensions in Harsh Environments"; and Carrier and Kochore, "Navigating Ethnicity and Electoral Politics in Northern Kenya."

58   Carrier and Kochore, "Navigating Ethnicity and Electoral Politics in Northern Kenya," 141.

59   In fact, in the event dataset employed by this research, the only cases of violence in the region that can be classified as electoral are the aforementioned raids of September 1997.

60   Republic of Kenya, Commission on Revenue Allocation (CRA), "County Budgets 2013–2014." On file with the author.

61   Anonymous interview (RC politician), interview by author, Mombasa, Kenya, September 27, 2013.

62   Nzioka, "High Stakes in Contest for Governor Seat."

63   Carrier and Kochore, "Navigating Ethnicity and Electoral Politics in Northern Kenya," 143.

64   Ibid.

65   Ibid., 144.

66   Ibid.

67   Nyabira and Ayele, "The State of Political Inclusion of Ethnic Communities under Kenya's Devolved System."

68   Obuya, "Politics a Key Factor in the Perennial Marsabit Conflict."

69   Daily Nation, "MP Charged over Marsabit Clashes."

70   Agoya, "Moyale MP Roba Duba Charged Afresh over Incitement."

71   Mungiti, "Court Acquits Moyale MP Roba Duba of Incitement Charge."

72   Barasa and Bett, "Elders to Choose between Ukur Yatani and US-based Adano for Marsabit Governor's Seat"; Barasa, "Ukur Yatani Finally Gets Elders' Blessings to Seek Re-Elections as Marsabit Governor."

73   Barasa and Bett, "Elders to Choose between Ukur Yatani and US-based Adano for Marsabit Governor's Seat."

74   Abdille and Abdi, "Kenya"; Sharamo, "The Politics of Pastoral Violence."

75   Republic of Kenya, Commission on Revenue Allocation (CRA), "County Budgets 2013–2014." On file with the author.

76   Kagwanja, "Politics of Marionettes."

77   Kimenyi and Ndung'u, "Sporadic Ethnic Violence"; Hornsby, Kenya, 657.

78   Kimenyi and Ndung'u, "Sporadic Ethnic Violence," 137.

79   Ibid.

80   Ibid.

81   Boye and Kaarhus. "Competing Claims and Contested Boundaries."

82   Human Rights Watch, "High Stakes," 4.

83   Ibid., 38.

84   Ibid.

85   Ibid.

86   IRIN, "Several Thousand Displaced after Fresh Clashes in Isiolo."

87   Human Rights Watch, "High Stakes," 38.

88   Sharamo, "The Politics of Pastoral Violence," 6.

89   Carrier and Kochore, "Navigating Ethnicity and Electoral Politics in Northern Kenya," 140.

90   Sharamo, "The Politics of Pastoral Violence," 6.

91   Carrier and Kochore, "Navigating Ethnicity and Electoral Politics in Northern Kenya," 140.

92   Jebet, "Borana and Somali Herders in Isiolo Told to End Conflict"; Jebet, "Isiolo Elders Caution Politicians on Divisive Talk in Campaigns."

93   Abdille and Abdi, "Kenya."

94   Ibid.

95   Ibid.

96   Muchui, "Uhuru to Officially Open Isiolo International Airport."

97   Leftie, "Kenya Poised to Roll Out Ambitious Sh2 Trillion Transport Corridor Project."

98   NTV, "NCIC Has Marked 33 Counties as Potential Poll Violence Hotspots."

99   United Nations Development Program, "Making Devolution Work," 1.

100  Ibid.

101  Human Rights Watch, "Kenya."

102  News 24, "Kenya Reports Vote Violence in Garissa County."

103  One major exception to this trend was in Kirinyaga county where Martha Karua disputed Anne Waiguru's victory and held that the gubernatorial elections had not been free and fair. For more details, see Muchira, "Karua."

## References

Abdille, Abdullahi, and Rashid Abdi. "Kenya: Development, County Governments and the Risk of 2017 Election Violence." *International Crisis Group* (blog), April 7, 2016. www.crisisgroup.org/africa/horn-africa/kenya/kenya-development-county-governments-and-risk-2017-election-violence (accessed March 10, 2017).

Africa Report. "Kenya's Tana Delta Burning." *The Africa Report*, December 11, 2012. www.theafricareport.com/News-Analysis/kenyas-tana-delta-burning.html (accessed February 2, 2017).

Agoya, Vincent. "Moyale MP Roba Duba Charged Afresh over Incitement." *The Daily Nation*, April 4, 2013. www.nation.co.ke/news/politics/Moyale-MP-Roba-Duba-charged-afresh-over-incitement/1064-2267176-kiqadu/index.html (accessed December 12, 2016).

Barasa, Lucas. "Ukur Yatani Finally Gets Elders' Blessings to Seek Re-Elections as Marsabit Governor." *The Daily Nation*, December 7, 2016. www.nation.co.ke/counties/marsabit/Elders-finally-endorse-Yatani/3444778-3478668-huhp2t/ (accessed December 20, 2016).

Barasa, Lucas, and Ken Bett. "Elders to Choose between Ukur Yatani and US-based Adano for Marsabit Governor's Seat." *The Daily Nation*,

December 7, 2016. www.nation.co.ke/counties/marsabit/Gabra-final-choice-Marsabit-governor/3444778-3477862-format-xhtml-unhqxqz/index.html (accessed January 15, 2017).

Boye, Saafo, and Randi Kaarhus. "Competing Claims and Contested Boundaries: Legitimating Land Rights in Isiolo District, Northern Kenya." *Africa Spectrum* 46, no. 2 (2011): 99–124.

Brancati, Dawn. "Decentralization: Fueling the Fire or Dampening the Flames of Ethnic Conflict and Secessionism?" *International Organization* 60, no. 3 (2006): 651–685.

Brancati, Dawn. *Peace by Design: Managing Intrastate Conflict through Decentralization*. New York: Oxford University Press, 2009.

Branch, Daniel, Nic Cheeseman, and Leigh Gardner, eds. *Our Turn to Eat: Politics in Kenya since 1950*. Münster, Germany: LIT Verlag, 2010.

Bratton, Michael, and Mwangi S. Kimenyi. "Voting in Kenya: Putting Ethnicity in Perspective." *Journal of Eastern African Studies* 2, no. 2 (2008): 272–289.

British Broadcasting Corporation (BBC). "Kenya Tana Delta Massacres Raise Election Violence Fear." *BBC News*, September 17, 2012. www.bbc.com/news/world-africa-19621246 (accessed February 14, 2014).

Carrier, Neil, and Hassan Kochore. "Navigating Ethnicity and Electoral Politics in Northern Kenya: The Case of the 2013 Election." *Journal of Eastern African Studies* 8, no. 1 (2014): 135–152.

Cheeseman, Nic, Gabrielle Lynch, and Justin Willis. "Decentralization in Kenya: The Governance of Governors." *Journal of Modern African Studies* 54, no. 1 (2016): 1–35.

Cleven, Erik. "Elites, Youth and Informal Networks: Explaining Ethnic Violence in Kenya and Kosovo." PhD Dissertation, Department of Political Science, Purdue University, 2013.

Collier, Paul. *Breaking the Conflict Trap: Civil War and Development Policy.* Washington, DC: The World Bank Group, 2003.

Cornell, Agnes, and Michelle D'Arcy. "Plus ça Change? County-level Politics in Kenya after Devolution." *Journal of Eastern African Studies* 8, no. 1 (2014): 173–191.

Daily Nation. "MP Charged over Marsabit Clashes." *The Daily Nation*, December 13, 2013. www.nation. co.ke/news/MP-charged-over-Marsabit-clashes/-/1056/2114490/-/f4gd4bz/-/index.html (accessed January 15, 2017).

D'Arcy, Michelle, and Agnes Cornell. "Devolution and Corruption in Kenya: Everyone's Turn to Eat?" *African Affairs* 115, no. 459 (2016): 246–273.

Deshpande, J.V. "Assembly Elections: Winnability Is All." *Economic and Political Weekly* 28, no. 46/47 (1993): 2505.

Elder, Claire, Susan Stigant, and Jonas Claes. "Elections and Violent Conflict in Kenya: Making Prevention Stick." United States Institute of Peace, November 9, 2014. www. usip.org/sites/default/files/PW101-Elections-and-Violent-Conflict-in-Kenya-Making-Prevention-Stick.pdf (accessed January 10, 2015).

Fearon, James, and David Laitin. "Ethnicity, Insurgency, and Civil War." *American Political Science Review* 97, no. 1 (2003): 75–90.

Hassan, Mai. "Continuity Despite Change: Kenya's New Constitution and Executive Power." *Democratization* 22, no. 4 (2015): 587–609.

Hornsby, Charles. *Kenya: A History since Independence.* New York: I.B. Tauris, 2013.

Human Rights Watch. "Kenya: Investigate All Politicians in Tana River Violence." September 13, 2012. www.hrw.org/news/2012/09/13/kenya-investigate-all-politicianstana-river-violence (accessed January 14, 2013).

Human Rights Watch. "High Stakes: Political Violence and the 2013 Elections in Kenya." February 7, 2013. www.hrw.org/sites/default/files/reports/kenya0213webcover.pdf (accessed January 26, 2014).

International Crisis Group. "Kenya's Coast: Devolution Disappointed." July 13, 2016. www.crisisgroup.org/africa/horn-africa/kenya/kenya-s-coast-devolution-disappointed (accessed August 1, 2016).

IRIN. "Several Thousand Displaced after Fresh Clashes in Isiolo." April 2, 2012. www.irinnews.org/report/95219/kenya-several-thousand-displaced-after-fresh-clashes-isiolo (accessed February 15, 2013).

Jebet, Vivian. "Isiolo Elders Caution Politicians on Divisive Talk in Campaigns." *The Daily Nation*, February 1, 2017. www.nation.co.ke/counties/Isiolo/Isiolo-elders-caution-politicians/1183266-3795548-format-xhtml-3a5gxg/index.html (accessed April 14, 2017).

Jebet, Vivian. "Borana and Somali Herders in Isiolo Told to End Conflict." *The*

*Daily Nation*, March 13, 2017. www.
nation.co.ke/counties/Isiolo/
Herders-Isiolo-end-conflict/1183266-
3848050-5gsmf5/ (accessed April 14,
2017).

Jinadu, Adele L. "Federalism, the
Consociational State, and Ethnic
Conflict in Nigeria." *Publius* 15, no. 2
(1985): 71–100.

Kagwanja, Peter. "Politics of Marionettes:
Extra-Legal Violence and the 1997
Elections in Kenya," pp. 72–101,
in *Out for the Count: The 1997
General Elections and Prospects
for Democracy in Kenya*, edited
by Marinus M.E.M. Rutten, Alamin
M. Mazrui, and François Grignon.
Kampala: Fountain Publishers, 2001.

Kahl, Colin. *States, Scarcity, and Civil
Strife in the Developing World*.
Princeton, NJ: Princeton University
Press, 2006.

Kasfir, Nelson. "Agency across Changing
Sites: The Path to Kenya's 2010
Constitution," pp. 52–71, in *The
Politics of Governance: Actors and
Articulations in Africa and Beyond*,
edited by Lucy Koechlin and Till
Förster. Abingdon: Routledge, 2015.

Kendhammer, Brandon. "Talking Ethnic
but Hearing Multi-Ethnic: The
Peoples' Democratic Party (PDP) in
Nigeria and Durable Multi-Ethnic
Parties in the Midst of Violence."
*Commonwealth & Comparative
Politics* 48, no. 1 (2010): 48–71.

Kimenyi, Mwangi. "Devolution and
Resource Sharing in Kenya." The
Brookings Institution, October 22,
2013. www.brookings.edu/opinions/
devolution-and-resource-sharing-in-
kenya/ (accessed March 12, 2017).

Kimenyi, Mwangi, and Njuguna Ndung'u.
"Sporadic Ethnic Violence: Why
Has Kenya Not Experienced a Full-
Blown Civil War?," pp. 123–156, in
*Understanding Civil War: Africa*,
edited by Paul Collier and Nicholas

Sambanis. Washington, DC: The
World Bank Group, 2005.

Klopp, Jacqueline. "'Ethnic Clashes'
and Winning Elections: The Case
of Kenya's Electoral Despotism."
*Canadian Journal of African Studies*
35, no. 3 (2001): 473–517.

Kramon, Eric, and Daniel Posner. "Kenya's
New Constitution." *Journal of
Democracy* 22, no. 2 (2011): 89–103.

Leftie, Peter. "Kenya Poised to Roll Out
Ambitious Sh2 Trillion Transport
Corridor Project." *The Daily Nation*,
July 22, 2011. www.nation.co.ke/
news/1056-1206042-15f45p4z/index.
html (accessed March 25, 2017).

Long, James, Karuti Kanyinga, Karen
Ferree, and Clark Gibson. "Choosing
Peace over Democracy." *Journal of
Democracy* 24, no. 3 (2013): 140–155.

Malik, Aditi. "Constitutional Reform
and New Patterns of Electoral
Violence: Evidence from Kenya's
2013 Elections." *Commonwealth &
Comparative Politics* 56, no. 3 (2018):
340–359.

Martin, Pilly. "Conflicts between
Pastoralists and Farmers in Tana
River District," pp. 167–193, in
*Spaces of Insecurity: Human
Agency in Violent Conflicts in
Kenya*, edited by Karen Witsenburg
and Fred Zaal. Leiden: African
Studies Centre, 2012.

Mohamud, Nuur, and Jason Mosley.
"Insecurity in Northern Kenya:
Is the Government Losing
Its Grip?" *African Arguments*
(blog), January 6, 2014. http://
africanarguments.org/2014/01/06/
insecurity-in-northern-kenya-is-the-
government-losing-its-grip-by-nuur-
mohamud-sheekh-and-jason-mosley/
(accessed March 15, 2017).

Muchira, Christine. "Karua: Kirinyaga
Gubernatoral Elections Were Not
Free, Fair." *KBC*, April 18, 2018. www.
kbc.co.ke/kirinyaga-gubernatorial-

elections-not-free-fair-karua (accessed July 10, 2018).

Muchui, David. "Uhuru to Officially Open Isiolo International Airport." *The Daily Nation*, January 20, 2017. www.nation.co.ke/counties/Isiolo/ Uhuru-open-Isiolo-airport/1183266-3266-3681090-6vhm0e/ (accessed March 20, 2017).

Mueller, Susanne. "Dying to Win: Elections, Political Violence, and Institutional Decay in Kenya." *Journal of Contemporary African Studies* 29, no. 1 (2011): 99–117.

Mung'ahu, Alphonse. "MP Godhana Cleared of Incitement Charges." *The Star*, January 17, 2013. www.the-star.co.ke/news/2013/01/17/mp-godhana-cleared-of-incitement-charges_c727129 (accessed March 15, 2017).

Mungiti, Richard. "Court Acquits Moyale MP Roba Duba of Incitement Charge." *The Daily Nation*, October 9, 2014. www.nation.co.ke/counties/Roba-Duba-acquitted/1107872/2447722/-/view/printVersion/-/7wntkj/-/index.html (accessed October 14, 2016).

Mutiga, Murithi. "Kenya: Avoiding Another Electoral Crisis." International Crisis Group, March 3, 2017. www.crisisgroup.org/africa/horn-africa/kenya/kenya-avoiding-anotherelectoral-crisis (accessed March 10, 2017).

Mwawasi, Mkamburi. "Tana River Governor Accused of Hiring Relatives in Plum County Jobs." *The Star*, August 3, 2016. www.the-star.co.ke/news/2016/08/03/tana-river-governor-accused-of-hiring-relatives-in-plum-county-jobs_c1397678 (accessed December 15, 2016).

Ndonga, Simon. "Dhadho Godhana Sacked over Tana Killings." *Capital News*, September 13, 2013. www.capitalfm.co.ke/news/2012/09/

dhadho-godana-sacked-over-tanakillings/ (accessed February 22, 2015).

News 24. "Kenya Reports Vote Violence in Garissa County." *News 24*, August 10, 2017. www.news24.com/Africa/News/the-latest-kenya-reports-vote-violence-in-garissa-county-20170810 (accessed September 15, 2017).

NTV. "NCIC Has Marked 33 Counties as Potential Poll Violence Hotspots." *NTV*, November 26, 2016. http://ntv.nation.co.ke/news/national/2725528-3466176-format-xhtml-10q02cy/index.html (accessed January 12, 2017).

Nyabira, Ben, and Zemelak Ayele. "The State of Political Inclusion of Ethnic Communities under Kenya's Devolved System." *Law, Democracy, and Development* 2 (2016): 131–153.

Nyanjom, Othieno. "Devolution in Kenya's New Constitution." Constitution Working Paper No. 4, Society for International Development, 2011. http://sidint.net/docs/WP4.pdf (accessed September 20, 2013).

Nzioka, Patrick. "High Stakes in Contest for Governor Seat." *The Daily Nation*, July 20, 2012. www.nation.co.ke/news/politics/High-stakes-in-contest-for-governor-seat-/1064-1458624-i8ysshz/index.html (accessed October 10, 2013).

Obuya, Peter. "Politics a Key Factor in the Perennial Marsabit Conflict." *The Daily Nation*, January 18, 2014. http://mobile.nation.co.ke/news/Politics-a-key-factor-in-the-perennial-Marsabit-conflict/1950946-2151040-format-xhtml-10xm9t4z/index.html (accessed March 16, 2016).

Ongiri, Isaac. "Counties to Get Sh48bn More in New Budget Deal." *The Daily Nation*, January 30, 2015. www.nation.co.ke/counties/Counties-National-Treasury-Budget-

Proposals/1107872-2608126-2vg20dz/
index.html (accessed April 20, 2016).

Republic of Kenya. *Constitution of Kenya.*
2010. Article 216.

Republic of Kenya. Commission on
Revenue Allocation (CRA). "Kenya
County Fact Sheets." 2013. http://
crakenya.org/wp-content/
uploads/2013/10/Kenya-County-
Fact-Sheets_Dec-2011.pdf (accessed
January 12, 2013).

Republic of Kenya. Commission on
Revenue Allocation (CRA). "Revenue
Allocation Formula." 2014. www.
crakenya.org/information/revenue-
allocation-formula/ (accessed
March 15, 2014).

Republic of Kenya. Commission on
Revenue Allocation (CRA). "County
Budgets 2013–2014." 2017. (accessed
June 21, 2017). On file with the
author.

Scott-Villiers, Patta, Tom Ondicho, Grace
Lubaale, Diana Ndung'u, Nathaniel
Kabala, and Marjoke Oosterom.
"Roots and Routes of Political
Violence in Kenya's Civil and Political
Society: A Case Study of Marsabit
County." Institute of Development
Studies, June 1, 2015. www.ids.ac.uk/
publications/roots-and-routes-of-
political-violence-in-kenyas-civil-
and-political-society-a-case-study-
of-marsabit-county (accessed March
21, 2017).

Sharamo, Roba. "The Politics of
Pastoral Violence: A Case Study of
Isiolo County, Northern Kenya."
Future Agricultures Working
Paper No. 095. June 2014. https://
assets.publishing.service.gov.uk/
media/57a089c4ed915d3cfd000408/
FAC_Working_Paper_095.pdf
(accessed August 15, 2015).

Shilaho, Westen. "Third Time Lucky?
Devolution and State Restructure
under Kenya's 2010 Constitutional

Dispensation," pp. 147–177, in *African
State Governance: Subnational
Politics and National Power,* edited
by A. Carl LeVan, Joseph Fashagba,
and Edward McMahon. New York:
Palgrave Macmillan, 2015.

Straus, Scott, and Charlie Taylor.
"Democratization and Electoral
Violence in Sub-Saharan Africa,
1990–2008," pp. 15–38, in *Voting
in Fear: Electoral Violence in Sub-
Saharan Africa,* edited by Dorina
Bekoe. Washington, DC: United
States Institute of Peace, 2012.

United Nations Development Program.
"Making Devolution Work." United
Nations Development Program,
December 21, 2016. www.ke.undp.
org/content/kenya/en/home/library/
democratic_governance/making-
devolution-work.html (accessed
August 21, 2017).

van Klinken, Gerry. *Communal Violence
and Democratization in Indonesia:
Small Town Wars.* Abingdon:
Routledge, 2007.

Whitaker, Beth Elise, and Jason
Giersch. "Voting on a Constitution:
Implications for Democracy in
Kenya." *Journal of Contemporary
African Studies* 27, no. 1 (2009): 1–20.

Wilkinson, Steven. *Votes and Violence:
Electoral Incentives and Ethnic
Riots in India.* New York: Cambridge
University Press, 2004.

Witsenburg, Karen. "Ethnic Tensions in
Harsh Environments: The Gabra
Pastoralists and Their Neighbors in
Northern Kenya," pp. 120–140, in
*Spaces of Insecurity: Human Agency
in Violent Conflicts in Kenya,* edited
by Karen Witsenburg and Fred Zaal.
Leiden: African Studies Centre, 2012.

Witsenburg, Karen, and Wario Adano. "Of
Rain and Raids: Violent Livestock
Raiding in Northern Kenya." *Civil
Wars* 11, no. 4 (2009): 514–538.

# 7 | INSTITUTIONAL DESIGN, DEMOCRACY, AND PEACEBUILDING IN AFRICA

*Abu Bakarr Bah and Fredrick Ogenga*

## Introduction

Increasingly, democracy in Africa is challenged by growing disconnections between the notion of representation embedded in the doctrine of democracy and the electoral rules and processes that often produced winner-takes-all electoral outcomes. At its roots, democracy is about equal representation of the people in the institutions of the state. Such representation has often been understood in terms of individual citizens. Under the individualistic notion of representation, one-person-one-vote is an adequate way to ensure democratic representations.[1] However, this is only true to the extent that voting is based largely on individual interests and considerations. While many voters do make (rational) individual decisions on whom to vote for, it is equally true that voting is heavily influenced by group identity and interests. In many African countries, ethnic identity has been central to the way people vote, which is evident in the regional and ethnic voting patterns in many African countries. Ethnic and other forms of group interests and voting patterns raise fundamental questions about democratic representation, namely: Who is to be represented in the institutions of the state? What happens when individualistic representation does not produce group (e.g. ethnic, regional, religious) representation? This is the conundrum of orthodox multiparty democracy in Africa. These kinds of problems have led to violent conflicts in countries such as Nigeria, Liberia, Kenya, Côte d'Ivoire, Guinea, Central African Republic, South Sudan, and Ethiopia. We should note that Ethiopia's nascent ethnic federalism is an interesting experiment that can provide valuable long-term lessons despite some of the initial problems of its ethnic federalism.[2] A critical issue for scholars and practitioners is how to reduce the chances of war in post-conflict countries. As we note, post-conflict countries need to redesign their political institutions in ways that take into account the causes of conflict and provide the appropriate institutional solutions.

We raise this issue of ethnic representation, especially in post-conflict countries, to stimulate debate about the way African democracies are designed. While there are significant variations among African electoral systems, too often they have very limited opportunities to promote more solid ethnic and regional representation in the state. It is true that many African heads of state appoint a diverse group of people into their government, including ethnic minorities. However, such appointments are at the discretion of the president who may remove them at any time. Because such persons do not have a guaranteed place in the government, nor does their ethnic or regional group, they are often not able to meaningfully represent their ethnic or regional interests. In worst cases, the diversity is superficial because people in those positions tend to become puppets of a regime that is practically controlled by a certain ethnic group, thereby creating a false sense of representation. Our argument is that countries characterized by significant levels of ethnic or regional diversity need to think of democratic representation not just at the level of the individual, but also at the level of the groups (e.g. ethnic, religious, regional). As such, they need to design their political institutions in ways that promote group representation and reduce the risk of violent political conflicts tied to ethnicity and regionalism. Interestingly, there are many democracies that have features intended to promote group representation and moderate the potential for tyranny of the majority or tyranny of the most powerful group.[3] Such features are derived from deliberate institutional design to moderate the potential individualistic excesses of liberal democracy.

The overarching question in this chapter is how to make African states become peaceful democracies given the inherent conditions of (a) ethnic, religious, and regional diversity, (b) economic poverty, and (c) poor social services, such as education and healthcare, which often lead to political violence and war. Peace would require that African countries create decent economic and social conditions for people to be able to help themselves and also eliminate excessive forms of political and economic marginalization based on ascribed characteristics such as ethnicity, religion, or region or gender. To achieve these elements of peace, African countries must creatively design their institutions of governance so that they remain democratic and refrain from creating grievances rooted in marginalization. Indeed, institutions alone would not be enough – we need good leadership.[4] However, good leadership alone is not enough either. Good institutions are needed because even the best of leaders can get old, sick, and eventually pass away. Good institutions can reduce political chaos, even in situations of poor leadership. Arguably, proper institutional design can enhance peace and democratic consolidation in African countries and thereby reduce the chances for political violence and civil wars.

## Institutional Design: Democracy and Peacebuilding

In this chapter, we engage two key bodies of literature that examine African political problems from adjacent angles, but fail to address their inherent interconnections to institutional design. Broadly speaking, these are the democracy and peacebuilding literatures. The works on democracy provide rich analysis of the authoritarian and poor governance roots of political conflicts in Africa, while the peacebuilding studies examine the nature of conflicts and the efforts to resolve violent conflicts. While the former points to the threats to peace, the later examines the challenges of restoring peace and overcoming the causes of conflict. We find the peace nexus between these two bodies of work to be very intriguing. More importantly, we note the common deficit of these two bodies of work to address the issue of peace through an institutional design lens. For us, the notion of institutional design is a useful bridge between these two bodies of works and a critical element for achieving and consolidating peace and democracy. Institutional design is particularly essential in post-conflict settings where the risks of reverting back to war are very real.[5]

Institutional design refers to the deliberate and creative choice of political arrangements to foster a peaceful and democratic system of governance. Such choices are made through selective, informed, strategic, and well-intentioned adoption of existing rules and procedures for democratic governance that have worked in other countries.[6] Also, such choices must entail appropriate customization to adequately meet the historical, social, economic, and cultural realities of each African country. By institutional design, we do not mean a total recopying of the procedures and practices of other countries to be instantly transplanted into African countries. Institutional design is actually the opposite of blind and wholesome copying of Western political institutions or those of any country for that matter.

Post-conflict countries refers to African countries that have experienced major political violence, such as a civil war, mass elections-related violence, frequent and major inter-communal violence, etc. Moreover, post-conflict implies that the main protagonists in these kinds of countries have reached some form of reconciliation and agreement to resolve their disagreements through non-violent means. They would have stopped the major fighting that erupted and are working toward building democracy. Such countries would have achieved what Johannas Galtung called negative peace and should be working on what the Institute for Economics and Peace calls positive peace – working to create conditions to sustain peace and reduce the conditions that lead to violence.[7] Post-conflict countries in Africa include Kenya, South Africa, Angola, Ethiopia, Mozambique, Sierra Leone, Nigeria, and Liberia.

As we already indicated, studies of democracy and peacebuilding in Africa often raise two major questions: (1) What are the underlying causes of violent conflicts? (2) How can African countries design institutions that create conditions for peace and democracy? Collectively, these two questions point to the importance and challenges of consolidating peace and democracy. As we argue in this chapter, consolidating peace and democracy will require creative institutional design to deal with the core drivers of conflicts, such as ethnic and regional marginalization. However, studies of democracy and peacebuilding in Africa have not adequately addressed the issue of institutional design.

Most of the studies of democracy are focused on the transition from dictatorship to multiparty democracy. In particular, neoliberal approaches see the absence of liberal democracy as the main cause of conflicts in Africa.[8] As such, the remedy to conflict is simply to hold regular free and fair multiparty elections. As African countries moved toward democracy during the 1990s, the emphasis shifted toward structural impediments to the consolidation of democracy.[9] However, institutional design remains the weakest aspect in studies of African democracies. Efforts to study institutional design in Africa are limited to works on federalism, consociationalism, and minority rights, most notably in South Africa, Nigeria, and Ethiopia.[10]

Similarly, the literature on peace and conflict has not adequately addressed issues of institutional design. Instead, such works typically focus on the causes and forms of conflict or the mechanics of peacekeeping. A key part of those works advance the greed versus grievance thesis.[11] Another set of studies deals with the brutal nature of the civil wars and peacekeeping.[12] Overall, African peace and conflict studies too fail to explore the links between institutional design and the structural conditions for peace. Instead, structural factors are mostly framed within the political economy of war discourse.[13]

There is also another body of work on postwar issues, most notably transitional justice, postwar reconstruction, and regional intervention. However, these works are more concerned with human rights and postwar human development than addressing structural challenges to democracy and institutional options. Transitional justice studies typically deal with war crimes and reconciliation.[14] Some of the other studies focus on security sector reform.[15] There are also studies on the regional mechanisms for dealing with human security issues arising from civil wars and the poor governance issues that lead to civil war. A notable part of the regional human security discourse focuses on the African Peace and Security Architecture (APSA), with a particular focus on the African Standby Force and high-level mediation through the Panel of Eminent Persons.[16] Another strand of the regional discourse centers on democracy promotion and good governance, especially in relation to the African Charter on Democracy, Elections, and Governance (ACDEG) and the New Partnership for African Development (NEPAD).[17] Despite the richness of these bodies of work, the study of institutional reforms in the postwar reconstruction literature is limited to questions of implementation and enhancing the effectiveness of extant institutions.[18] The studies focus on human security, good governance, and regional norms without addressing the core question of institutional choices to address core drivers of conflicts.

Despite the failure to properly explore institutional choices to consolidate peace and democracy, the extant scholarship on democracy and peacebuilding in Africa raises many intriguing questions about the relation between institutional design on the one hand and democracy and peacebuilding on the other hand. Some of the questions that we find to be pressing are: What is the nature of institutional design in post-conflict African countries? How do institutional reforms address the underlying causes of conflict? How does the institutional design enhance the conditions for peace and democracy? What are the gaps and shortcomings in the reform processes?

## African Institutional Design: A Historical Lens

This chapter does not necessarily seek to provide definitive answers to any of the questions above. Rather, it hopes to provoke a bold intellectual and policy discourse around the problematic relation between institutional design and the consolidation of peace and democracy in post-conflict African countries. To stimulate this discussion, we point to some general observations about institutional design in Africa.

Our first observation goes back to the immediate postcolonial era. A notable feature of African states at the time of independence was the stark similarity between their political institutions and those of the former colonial powers – British multiparty parliamentary system, French republicanism, etc. – though this was mostly in form rather than practice. At independence, African countries became "democracies," with rules and produces similar to those of the former colonial powers. Of course the problem was not the idea of representation and accountability – a democracy so to speak – but how those ideas were institutionalized and practiced. The immediate postcolonial institutions virtually ignored the precolonial and colonial legacies of ethnic identities and regional political blocs.[19] The independence constitutions assumed that people will vote as individuals with no burden of ethnic, regional, or religious loyalties – be they natural or politically manufactured. As we learned, virtually all those imported democracies collapsed into one-party or military regimes. In some cases ethnically and regionally motivated political violence and civil wars erupted soon after independence.

The second observation relates to African one-party-cum-socialist and military regimes. The argument for one-party and military regimes in Africa was that multiparty elections promote ethnic divisions. As such, the solution was to eliminate multiparty politics and make every person belong to one party, which would promote national unity.[20] We must confess that this was an institutional design effort. However, there were some problems with this institutional choice. The first problem was that one-party systems did not have a proven record of promoting free societies. Even in the best cases of the Soviet Union and East European countries, the economic gains from socialism were limited, while the political costs were excessive.[21] Second, the borrowing failed to take into account that the socialist systems in Europe were meant to address class inequality, not ethnic or religious differences. In fact most European countries tried to address the ethnicity issue by creating national states (e.g. Poland for Poles, Hungary for Hungarians, Bulgaria for Bulgarians, etc.). The European countries that emerged from the First and Second World Wars, and more recently the fall of the Soviet Union and Yugoslavia, were mostly ethnic majority countries with few and small minority groups. The situation in Africa was significantly different. Instead of class differences, the key problem in Africa at the time of independence was ethnic-cum-regional differences, which were exacerbated during colonial rule. As such, the class-based ideology of one-party-cum-socialism promoted by African leaders was a fundamentally improper institutional design for the problem of ethnic political competition for power in most African countries. The adoption of one-party systems could have simply been an error in judgment or a deliberate effort to use the one-party system as a way to further marginalize political competitors from other ethnic groups and regions. In short, African one-party-cum-socialist systems and military regimes were the wrong institutional choices for promoting peaceful multiethnic democracies in Africa. Those choices were made either naively or maliciously. The net result was that by the early 1990s, most African countries had failed and became civilian or military dictatorships on the verge of civil war, if not already in war.[22]

The third observation is about the rebirth of multiparty democracy during the 1990s, which has been a lost opportunity to creatively design institutions based on the lessons of democracy during the immediate post-independence period and the failed one-party regimes that followed. The democratic transitions of the 1990s were characterized by several things. In particular, there were national conferences and dialogues to ensure the formation of transitional governments and free and fair multiparty elections.[23] However, most of the transitions were manipulated by ruling parties to retain power, mostly as pseudo-democracies.[24] In some countries disagreement over the transitional election or the subsequent election led to violence resulting in civil wars or low-intensity conflicts, such as in the Democratic Republic of the Congo, Côte d'Ivoire, Sierra Leone, and Kenya. It is also important to note that most of the countries have been undermining multiparty democracy by rigging elections or extending presidential term limits.

Our fourth observation is about the new rules that have been introduced to African democracies after major upheavals or violence, especially since the 1990s. These new rules are indeed notable efforts at designing state institutions so that they can promote more peaceful democracies. One major pan-African rule was the ban on coups and unconstitutional change of government or extension of term limits.[25] The African Union (AU) instituted the rule to automatically expel member states that have had an unconstitutional change of government. The rule has been generally applied in some form, but not to Egypt. In a similar way, presidential term limits have been introduced in the constitutions of many African countries. While we consider this to be a creative institutional arrangement to ensure democratic transfer of power, it misses the problem of rotating power among ethnic groups or regions. Under the presidential term limits model, one person cannot stay in power forever, but members of a particular ethnic group or region can stay in power indefinitely as long as they maintain their ethnic coalition and voting base.[26] The issue of rotating power – not just among individuals but among groups – is one that can be addressed through more creative institutional design.

### Institutional Design: Lessons and Missed Opportunities

Despite the problematic neoliberal form of most African democracies, there are a few cases of institutional design in some countries, most notably Nigeria. Other countries, notably Côte d'Ivoire, missed opportunities to transform their creative transitional conflict resolution measures into durable institutional arrangements. In this chapter, we focus on Nigeria and Côte d'Ivoire to highlight elements of institutional design that can be useful. More importantly, the cases illustrate the notion of institutional design.

Despite all the violence and democracy pitfalls experienced in Nigeria, the country provides an invaluable lesson for institutional design as a way to make democracy more representative of the country's ethnic and regional diversity. Nigerian democracy and federalism have been extensively studied – albeit not often framed in terms of institutional design.[27] Some of the notable institutional design features in Nigeria include the federal arrangement, creation of new states and local government areas, the Federal Character principle, the electoral rules for the presidency, the derivation principle for revenue allocation, and the informal rotation of presidential candidates by the major political parties.[28]

With respect to federalism and the creation of new states, Nigeria moved from three regions at the time of independence to thirty-six states in the present day. Many of the states have clear ethnic majority groups. This is an important step toward ethic representation, but there is still too much fiscal centralization. If Nigeria can move toward a system whereby each state is capable of generating its own operating revenue, the issue of unfair distribution of resources will be significantly reduced. Under such a model, revenues from natural resources can be placed in a national fund, which can be used only for development projects – equitably across the country. This would require an approach that sees the state largely through the prism of local and state revenue generation instead of national revenue distribution.

The 1979 Constitution introduced the Federal Character principle. Since then, it has been enshrined in all Nigerian constitutions. The principle is that in every state entity or program all efforts must be made to ensure that people from different parts of the country are included. While the application of the principle has been less than optimal, it remains a central reference point for political representation and equity in Nigeria.[29]

Since 1979, all Nigerian constitutions and election laws require that a candidate for the presidency must win at least 25 percent of the votes in at least two-thirds of the states.[30] This means that a person must have significant support in nearly all parts of the country in order to become president. This requirement has repeatedly led to the formation of fairly broad ethnic coalitions that are more inclusive than what would have happened under the simple majority approach to multiparty elections.

The 1999 Constitution of Nigeria gives every state the right to retain 13 percent of all revenues from its minerals. This was to address long-standing grievances of economic marginalization from minority groups, especially in oil-producing states. Though this does not solve all the social and economic injustices, it is an improvement on prior arrangements that allowed majority groups that control the federal government to have total control over oil revenues.

Another important point is that Nigeria's main political parties have a very strong norm of rotating their presidential candidates between the north and the south. Since the reintroduction of democracy in 1999, two of the presidents are from the north, while the other two are from the south. This outcome is in large part a direct result of the rotational system that has been adopted and respected by the main political parties. Although the north–south representation system falls short of full ethnic political representation, it is a significant improvement on Nigeria's democracy during the 1960s.

While Nigeria represents an important effort at adopting creative institutional design, Côte d'Ivoire is a notable example of a missed opportunity to create durable institutional arrangements that would promote ethnic and regional inclusion. Côte d'Ivoire experienced massive political violence and eventually a civil war. The political violence in Côte d'Ivoire began in 1999, when Alassane Ouattara was disqualified from running for the presidency by southern politicians on the grounds that he was not a natural-born citizen. The political violence escalated into a civil war in 2002 and lasted until the 2007 Ouagadougou Peace Accord, which included a power-sharing agreement. After the peace accord, the country was peaceful until the results of the 2010 presidential elections were announced. Violence erupted when the two main presidential candidates both installed themselves as president. Laurent Gbagbo refused to accept the election results certified by the United Nations, which declared Ouattara winner of the 2010 presidential election. The stalemate was ended with the military defeat and capture of Gbagbo by rebel forces loyal to Ouattara and backed by UN and French peacekeepers. Throughout the conflict, Gbagbo represented the southern interest, while Ouattara and the rebel forces represented northerners.

The Côte d'Ivoire civil war was rooted in two problems: (1) a power struggle between northern and southern elites after the death of founding president Félix Houphouët-Boigny and (2) the attempt by southern politicians to deny citizenship to mainly people from the north. As far back as 1995, southern politicians introduced the doctrine of *Ivoirite*, which was enshrined in the 2000 Constitution. In essence, Ivoirite rules stated that for one to be a natural-born citizen, the person's parents must be natural-born citizens. Under the rules, one has to provide documentation of ancestry going back to the colonial period. Under the 2000 Constitution, only people who met this restrictive definition of natural-born citizen could be president, own land, and even get government jobs.[31] The problem with this exclusionary notion of citizenship is that Côte d'Ivoire has had huge immigrant populations going back to the late colonial period. Moreover, there are significant numbers of people who simply do not have documented proof of the place of birth of their parents, let alone their grandparents. The rules affected mostly northerners. In fact, Ouattara was prevented from contesting the 2000 presidential election on the grounds that his parents were not natural-born citizens of Côte d'Ivoire – an allegation he denied. So, the war was both about asserting the citizenship rights of Ouattara and his fellow northerners, and a struggle for power between southern and northern elite.

What is interesting about Côte d'Ivoire is the ways the conflict was revolved, notably the 1996 Ouagadougou Peace Accord. Both the citizenship issue and the power struggle between northerners and southerners were resolved through temporary institutional arrangements to facilitate ethnic and regional inclusion.[32] With respect to the citizenship issue, the Ouagadougou Peace Accord established temporary mobile courts which would issue citizenship papers to anyone who could provide two witnesses attesting that at least one of the person's parents is an Ivoirian. The agreement also called for the establishment of a national identification system based on biometric technology. This arrangement was a creative way of upholding Ivoirian citizenship laws, which were primarily based on ancestry. At the same time, it makes accommodation for the basic reality that many people born in Côte d'Ivoire, especially the poor and illiterate, never had a birth certificate in the first place.

In terms of the power issue, the Ouagadougou Peace Accord was complemented with a power-sharing arrangement that gave Gbagbo the presidency and the rebel forces got the office of prime minister.[33] The two parties also held equal ministerial position. No party had the power to remove the other side from the power-sharing government. This arrangement maintained peace from 2007 to 2010. Unfortunately, Côte d'Ivoire missed the opportunity to institutionalize this consociational governance arrangement into its constitution. Instead it took the path of conducting multiparty elections as usual, which resulted in renewed war. A critical question that should be considered is what would have happened if Côte d'Ivoire had enacted the power-sharing arrangement into law or made it a permanent feature of its constitution – possibly with a sunset clause. Arguably, the power-sharing arrangement was more representative of Côte d'Ivoire's diversity than what has been established by simple multiparty election. Gbagbo and many southerners refused to accept the election results because they knew that they would be marginalized by northerners – just as they did to northerners in the past. Southern fears of being marginalized by northerners have largely become a reality as we see from the selective application of justice and the entrenchment of northern elite into key security and administrative positions of the state.

## Conclusion

The case for institutional design rests on the simple fact that African countries have multiparty democracy mechanisms and political institutions that were designed mainly for European countries that were national states.[34] European national states were fundamentally different from the multiethnic states that were carved out of colonial rule. African ethnic diversity is a reality that cannot be eliminated. This diversity has to be embraced with a creative lens to democracy and governance. Africa's diversity requires a consociational approach to democracy as has been the case in other heterogeneous countries (e.g. United States of America, Belgium, Lebanon, Malaysia, Bosnia-Herzegovina).[35] Unfortunately, very few African countries have engaged in institutional design and thought of the state outside of the Westphalian-colonial-state box.

African countries can benefit from some form of consociational governance arrangement that does not make elections a winner-takes-all ethnic political outcome. It is true that many able African leaders do maintain inclusive governments. However, the problem is that they manipulate the process in order to reduce members of other ethnic groups to mere tokens who can be pacified and replaced at any time.

Consociationalism can increase the chance of people following electoral rules and accepting results. One key problem of African elections is that members of minority or certain ethnic groups know that they will not win elections because of ethnic voting. In such situations, it is more likely that people will not follow electoral rules or even accept the results because they know they would never win. Democracy cannot work when there are permanent winners and permanent losers. If groups know that they will be part of the government and get a meaningful say in the state, they are more likely to follow the rules and accept the results, which would promote peace.

Consociationalism can help institutionalize inclusion so that more ethnic groups and regions have a real chance at meaningful representation within the state. Interestingly, there are cases from which African countries can draw some lessons. Bosnia-Herzegovina has such an arrangement of collective presidency and federalism among Serbs, Croats, and Muslims. Lebanon also has a consociational parliamentary arrangement among Christians, Sunni Muslims, and Shiite Muslims. Malaysia also has a very complex consociational political, economic, and cultural arrangement among the native Muslim majority and the Chinese minority.[36] The system of checks and balances, the Senate, and more importantly the Electoral College in the United States are all elements of consociationalism. Consociational arrangements do run the risk of becoming excessively rigid or even outdated. However, consociational arrangements can be revisited, especially when they have sunset clauses, and be phased out when they are no longer useful. The central point in this chapter is not really the specific arrangements that any country has or would adopt. Our argument is that democracies must be creatively designed so that political institutions reflect the diversity of the state and produce meaningful representation for individuals and groups, and thereby avoid tyranny of the minority or tyranny of the majority.

## Notes

1   Bah, "Changing World Order and the Future of Democracy in Sub-Saharan Africa"; Dahl, *Polyarchy*; Linz and Stepan, *Problems of Democratic Transition and Consolidation*.

2   Abbink, "Ethnic-based Federalism and Ethnicity in Ethiopia"; Keller, "Ethnic Federalism, Fiscal Reform, Development and Democracy in Ethiopia"; Mengisteab, "New Approaches to State Building in Africa."

3   De Tocqueville, *Democracy in America*.

4   Obadare and Adebanwi, *Governance and the Crisis of Rule in Contemporary Africa.*

5   Barnett et al., "Peacebuilding"; Call and Cousens, "Ending Wars and Building Peace."

6   Dahl, *Polyarchy*; Linz, *Problems of Democratic Transition and Consolidation*; Elster et al., *Institutional Design in Post-Communist Societies*; Bah, *Breakdown and Reconstruction.*

7   Galtung, "Violence, Peace, and Peace Research"; Galtung, *Peace by Peaceful Means*; Institute for Economics and Peace, "Positive Peace Report."

8   Bratton and Van de Walle, *Democratic Experiments in Africa*; Van de Walle, "Africa's Range of Regimes"; Randall and Svåsand, "Political Parties and Democratic Consolidation in Africa"; Resnick and Van de Walle, *Democratic Trajectories in Africa.*

9   Bratton and Mattes, "Support for Democracy in Africa"; Ball and Ramachandran, *Beyond Structural Adjustment*; Bratton, *Voting and Democratic Citizenship in Africa*; Bratton and Mattes, *Public Opinion, Democracy, and Market Reform in Africa.*

10   Diamond, *Class, Ethnicity, and Democracy in Nigeria*; Horowitz, *A Democratic South Africa?*; Suberu, *Federalism and Ethnic Conflict in Nigeria*; Bah, *Breakdown and Reconstruction*; Sisk, *Democratization in South Africa*; Keller, "Ethnic Federalism, Fiscal Reform, Development and Democracy in Ethiopia"; Abbink, "Ethnic-Based Federalism and Ethnicity in Ethiopia."

11   Collier and Hoeffler, "Greed and Grievance in Civil War"; Reno,

Corruption and State Politics in Sierra Leone; Jackson and Rosberg, Personal Rule in Black Africa; Bayart, The State in Africa; Bratton and Van de Walle, "Neopatrimonial Regimes and Political Transitions in Africa"; Kpundeh and Johnston, Politics and Corruption in Africa; Chabal and Daloz, Africa Works; Bah, "State Decay and Civil War"; Bah, "State Decay."

12 Straus, The Order of Genocide; Autesserre, The Trouble with the Congo; Bah, "Civil Non-State Actors in Peacekeeping and Peacebuilding in West Africa"; Bah, "Democracy and Civil War"; Bah, "The Contours of New Humanitarianism"; Bah, International Security and Peacebuilding; Utas and Jörgel, "The West Side Boys"; Peters, War and the Crisis of Youth in Sierra Leone; Hoffman, "The Civilian Target in Sierra Leone and Liberia"; Hoffman, "The Meaning of a Militia"; Bøås, "Liberia and Sierra Leone – Dead Ringers?"; Adebajo, Building Peace in West Africa; Ellis, The Mask of Anarchy.

13 Zack-Williams, "Sierra Leone"; Ross, "How Do Natural Resources Influence Civil War?"; Ross, "What Do We Know about Natural Resources and Civil War?"

14 Linton, "Cambodia, East Timor and Sierra Leone"; Wilson, The Politics of Truth and Reconciliation in South Africa; Evenson, "Truth and Justice in Sierra Leone"; Corey and Joireman, "Retributive Justice"; Shaw, "Memory Frictions"; Jalloh, "The Contribution of the Special Court for Sierra Leone to the Development of International Law."

15 Gbla, "Security Sector Reform under International Tutelage in Sierra Leone"; Ebo, "The Challenges and Lessons of Security Sector Reform in Post-conflict Sierra Leone"; Sawyer, "Remove or Reform?"; Bah, "People-Centered Liberalism."

16 Bah, "African Agency in New Humanitarianism and Responsible Governance"; Darkwa and Attuquayefio, "Analysis of Norm Diffusion in the African Union and the Economic Community of West African States"; Onditi et al., "The Quest for a Multidimensional African Standby Force."

17 Obi, "The African Union and the Prevention of Democratic Reversal in Africa"; Chabal, "The Quest for Good Government and Development in Africa"; Bah, "People-Centered Liberalism."

18 Anderson, Do No Harm; Thomas, "Global Governance, Development and Human Security"; Duffield, Global Governance and the New Wars; Schümer, New Humanitarianism; Denney, "Reducing Poverty with Teargas and Batons"; Bah, "The Contours of New Humanitarianism"; Bah, "People-Centered Liberalism."

19 Bah, Breakdown and Reconstruction; Mamdani, Citizen and Subject.

20 Nyerere, Ujamaa; Nkrumah, Neo-Colonialism; Ake, Democracy and Development in Africa.  ˙

21 Cohen and Arato, Civil Society and Political Theory; Linz and Stepan, Problems of Democratic Transition and Consolidation.

22 Bah, "Changing World Order and the Future of Democracy in Sub-Saharan Africa"; Bratton and Van de Walle, Democratic Experiments in Africa.

23 Bah, "Changing World Order and the Future of Democracy in Sub-Saharan Africa"; Bratton and Van de Walle, Democratic Experiments in Africa.

24 Bah, "Changing World Order and the Future of Democracy in Sub-Saharan Africa"; Bratton and Van de Walle, Democratic Experiments in Africa.

25 OAU/AU, Declaration on the Principles of Governing Democratic Elections in Africa.

26 Malik, "Mobilizing a Defensive Kikuyu–Kalenjin Alliance."

27  Bah, *Breakdown and Reconstitution*; Suberu, *Federalism and Ethnic Conflict in Nigeria*; Diamond, *Class, Ethnicity, and Democracy in Nigeria*.

28  Bah, *Breakdown and Reconstitution*; Suberu, *Federalism and Ethnic Conflict in Nigeria*; Diamond, *Class, Ethnicity, and Democracy in Nigeria*.

29  Bah, *Breakdown and Reconstitution*; Suberu, *Federalism and Ethnic Conflict in Nigeria*.

30  Bah, *Breakdown and Reconstitution*.

31  Bah, "Democracy and Civil War"; Geschiere, *The Perils of Belonging*.

32  Bah, "Democracy and Civil War"; Geschiere, *The Perils of Belonging*.

33  Bah, "Democracy and Civil War," 597-615; Geschiere, *The Perils of Belonging*.

34  Tilly and Ardant, *The Formation of National States in Western Europe*; Mamdani, *Citizen and Subject*; Bah, *Breakdown and Reconstitution*.

35  Horowitz, *Ethnic Groups in Conflict*; Salamey and Payne, "Parliamentary Consociationalism in Lebanon"; Kuroda, *The Origins of the Twelfth Amendment*.

36  Belloni, "Peacebuilding and Consociational Electoral Engineering in Bosnia and Herzegovina"; Tzifakis, "The Bosnian Peace Process"; Sigri et al., "Managerial Capacity in Peacekeeping Operations"; Salamey and Payne, "Parliamentary Consociationalism in Lebanon"; Siddique and Suryadinata, "Bumiputra and Pribumi"; Suryadinata, *Chinese and Nation-building in Southeast Asia*.

## References

Abbink, Jon. "Ethnic-based Federalism and Ethnicity in Ethiopia: Reassessing the Experiment after 20 years." *Journal of Eastern African Studies* 5, no. 4 (2011): 596–618.

Adebajo, Adekeye. *Building Peace in West Africa: Liberia, Sierra Leone, and Guinea-Bissau*. Boulder, CO: Lynne Rienner Publishers, 2002.

Ake, Claude. *Democracy and Development in Africa*. Washington, DC: Brookings Institution Press, 2001.

Anderson, Mary B. *Do No Harm: How Aid Can Support Peace – or War*. Boulder, CO: Lynne Rienner Publishers, 1999.

Autesserre, Séverine. *The Trouble with the Congo: Local Violence and the Failure of International Peacebuilding*. New York: Cambridge University Press, 2010.

Bah, Abu Bakarr. "Changing World Order and the Future of Democracy in Sub-Saharan Africa." *PROTEUS: A Journal of Ideas* 21, no. 1 (2004): 3–12.

Bah, Abu Bakarr. *Breakdown and Reconstitution: Democracy, the Nation-State, and Ethnicity in Nigeria*. Lanham, MD: Lexington Books, 2005.

Bah, Abu Bakarr. "Democracy and Civil War: Citizenship and Peacemaking in Côte d'Ivoire." *African Affairs* 109, no. 437 (2010): 597–615.

Bah, Abu Bakarr. "State Decay and Civil War: A Discourse on Power in Sierra Leone." *Critical Sociology* 37, no. 2 (2011): 199–216.

Bah, Abu Bakarr. "State Decay: A Conceptual Frame for Failing and Failed States in West Africa." *International Journal of Politics, Culture, and Society* 25, no. 1–3 (2012): 71–89.

Bah, Abu Bakarr. "Civil Non-State Actors in Peacekeeping and Peacebuilding in West Africa." *Journal of International Peacekeeping* 17, no. 3–4 (2013): 313–336.

Bah, Abu Bakarr. "The Contours of New Humanitarianism: War and Peacebuilding in Sierra Leone." *Africa Today* 60 (2013): 3–26.

Bah, Abu Bakarr. "African Agency in New Humanitarianism and Responsible Governance," pp. 148–169, in *International Security and Peacebuilding: Africa, the Middle East, and Europe*, edited by Abu Bakarr Bah. Bloomington, IN: Indiana University Press, 2017.

Bah, Abu Bakarr, ed. *International Security and Peacebuilding: Africa, the Middle East, and Europe.* Bloomington, IN: Indiana University Press, 2017.

Bah, Abu Bakarr. "People-Centered Liberalism: An Alternative Approach to International State-Building in Sierra Leone and Liberia." *Critical Sociology* 43, no. 7–8 (2017): 989–1007.

Ball, Nicole, and Vijaya Ramachandran, eds. *Beyond Structural Adjustment: The Institutional Context of African Development.* New York: Palgrave Macmillan, 2006.

Barnett, Michael, Hunjoon Kim, Madalene O'Donnell, and Laura Sitea. "Peacebuilding: What Is in a Name?." *Global Governance: A Review of Multilateralism and International Organizations* 13, no. 1 (2007): 35–58.

Bayart, Jean-François. *The State in Africa: The Politics of the Belly.* New York: Polity Press, 2009.

Belloni, Roberto. "Peacebuilding and Consociational Electoral Engineering in Bosnia and Herzegovina." *International Peacekeeping* 11, no. 2 (2004): 334–353.

Bøås, Morten. "Liberia and Sierra Leone – Dead Ringers? The Logic of Neopatrimonial Rule." *Third World Quarterly* 22, no. 5 (2001): 697–723.

Bratton, Michael, ed. *Voting and Democratic Citizenship in Africa.* Boulder, CO: Lynne Rienner Publishers, 2013.

Bratton, Michael, and Robert Mattes. "Support for Democracy in Africa: Intrinsic or Instrumental?" *British Journal of Political Science* 31 (2001): 447–474.

Bratton, Michael, Robert Mattes, and Emmanuel Gyimah-Boadi. *Public Opinion, Democracy, and Market Reform in Africa.* New York: Cambridge University Press, 2005.

Bratton, Michael, and Nicholas Van de Walle. *Democratic Experiments in Africa: Regime Transitions in Comparative Perspective.* New York: Cambridge University Press, 1997.

Bratton, Michael, and Nicolas Van de Walle. "Neopatrimonial Regimes and Political Transitions in Africa." *World Politics* 46, no. 4 (1994): 453–489.

Call, Charles T., and Elizabeth M. Cousens. "Ending Wars and Building Peace: International Responses to War-torn Societies." *International Studies Perspectives* 9, no. 1 (2008): 1–21.

Chabal, Patrick. "The Quest for Good Government and Development in Africa: Is NEPAD the Answer?" *International Affairs* 78, no. 3 (2002): 447–462.

Chabal, Patrick, and Jean-Pascal Daloz. *Africa Works: Disorder as Political Instrument.* Bloomington, IN: Indiana University Press, 1999.

Cohen, Jean L., and Andrew Arato. *Civil Society and Political Theory.* Cambridge, MA: MIT Press, 1994.

Collier, Paul, and Anke Hoeffler. "Greed and Grievance in Civil War." *Oxford Economic Papers* 56, no. 4 (2004): 563–595.

Corey, Allison, and Sandra F. Joireman. "Retributive Justice: The Gacaca

Courts in Rwanda." *African Affairs* 103, no. 410 (2004): 73–89.

Dahl, Robert Alan. *Polyarchy: Participation and Opposition*. New Haven, CT: Yale University Press, 1973.

Darkwa, Linda, and Philip Attuquayefio. "Analysis of Norm Diffusion in the African Union and the Economic Community of West African States." *African Conflict and Peacebuilding Review* 4, no. 2 (2014): 11–37.

De Tocqueville, Alexis. *Democracy in America*. Washington, DC: Regnery Publishing, 2003.

Denney, Lisa. "Reducing Poverty with Teargas and Batons: The Security-Development Nexus in Sierra Leone." *African Affairs* 110, no. 439 (2011): 275–294.

Diamond, Larry, J. *Class, Ethnicity, and Democracy in Nigeria: The Failure of the First Republic*. Syracuse, NY: Syracuse University Press, 1988.

Duffield, Mark. *Global Governance and the New Wars: The Merging of Development and Security*. London: Zed Books, 2001.

Ebo, Adedeji. "The Challenges and Lessons of Security Sector Reform in Post-conflict Sierra Leone: Analysis." *Conflict, Security & Development* 6, no. 4 (2006): 481–501.

Ellis, Stephen. *The Mask of Anarchy: The Destruction of Liberia and the Religious Dimension of an African Civil War*. New York: NYU Press, 2001.

Elster, Jon, Claus Offe, and Ulrich K. Preuss. *Institutional Design in Post-Communist Societies: Rebuilding the Ship at Sea*. New York: Cambridge University Press, 1998.

Evenson, Elizabeth M. "Truth and Justice in Sierra Leone: Coordination between Commission and Court." *Columbia Law Review* (2004): 730–767.

Galtung, Johan. "Violence, Peace, and Peace Research." *Journal of Peace Research* 6, no. 3 (1969): 167–191.

Galtung, Johan. *Peace by Peaceful Means: Peace and Conflict, Development and Civilization*. Thousand Oaks, CA: Sage, 1996.

Gbla, Osman. "Security Sector Reform under International Tutelage in Sierra Leone." *International Peacekeeping* 13, no. 1 (2006): 78–93.

Geschiere, Peter. *The Perils of Belonging: Autochthony, Citizenship, and Exclusion in Africa and Europe*. Chicago, IL: University of Chicago Press, 2009.

Hoffman, Danny. "The Civilian Target in Sierra Leone and Liberia: Political Power, Military Strategy, and Humanitarian Intervention." *African Affairs* 103, no. 411 (2004): 211–226.

Hoffman, Danny. "The Meaning of a Militia: Understanding the Civil Defense Forces of Sierra Leone." *African Affairs* 106, no. 425 (2007): 639–662.

Horowitz, Donald L. *Ethnic Groups in Conflict*. Berkeley, CA: University of California Press, 1985.

Horowitz, Donald L. *A Democratic South Africa? Constitutional Engineering in a Divided Society*. Berkeley, CA: University of California Press, 1991.

Institute for Economics and Peace. "Positive Peace Report: Conceptualizing and Measuring the Attitudes, Institutions and Structures that Build a More Peaceful Society." 2015. available at http://economicsandpeace. org/wp-content/uploads/2015/10/ Positive-Peace-Report-2015.pdf.

Jackson, Robert H., and Carl Gustav Rosberg. *Personal Rule in Black Africa: Prince, Autocrat, Prophet, Tyrant*. Berkeley, CA: University of California Press, 1982.

Jalloh, Charles Chernor. "The Contribution of the Special Court for Sierra Leone to the Development of International Law." *African Journal of International and Comparative Law* 15, no. 2 (2007): 165–207.

Keller, Edmond J. "Ethnic Federalism, Fiscal Reform, Development and Democracy in Ethiopia." *African Journal of Political Science* 7, no. 1 (2002): 21–50.

Kpundeh, Sahr John, and Michael Johnston. *Politics and Corruption in Africa: A Case Study of Sierra Leone.* Lanham, MD: University Press of America, 1995.

Kuroda, Tadahisa. *The Origins of the Twelfth Amendment: The Electoral College in the Early Republic, 1787–1804.* Westport, CT: Greenwood Publishing, 1994.

Linton, Suzannah. "Cambodia, East Timor and Sierra Leone: Experiments in International Justice." *Criminal Law Forum* 12 (2001): 185–246.

Linz, Juan J., and Alfred Stepan. *Problems of Democratic Transition and Consolidation: Southern Europe, South America, and Post-communist Europe.* Baltimore, MD: Johns Hopkins University Press, 1996.

Malik, Aditi. "Mobilizing a Defensive Kikuyu–Kalenjin Alliance: The Politicization of the International Criminal Court in Kenya's 2013 Presidential Election." *African Conflict & Peacebuilding Review* 6, no. 2 (2016): 48–73.

Mamdani, Mahmood. *Citizen and Subject: Contemporary Africa and the Legacy of Late Colonialism.* Princeton, NJ: Princeton University Press, 1996.

Mengisteab, Kidane. "New Approaches to State Building in Africa: The Case of Ethiopia's Ethnic-based Federalism." *African Studies Review* 40, no. 3 (1997): 111–132.

Nkrumah, Kwame. *Neo-Colonialism: The Last Stage of Imperialism.* Edinburgh: Thomas Nelson and Sons, 1966.

Nyerere, Julius. *Ujamaa: Essays on Socialism.* New York: Oxford University Press, 1968.

OAU/AU. *Declaration on the Principles of Governing Democratic Elections in Africa.* AHG/Decl. 1 (XXXVIII). Heads of State and Government of the Organization of African Unity. 38th Ordinary Session of the Assembly of the OAU. Durban, 2002.

Obadare, Ebenezer, and Wale Adebanwi, eds. *Governance and the Crisis of Rule in Contemporary Africa: Leadership in Transformation.* New York: Palgrave Macmillan, 2016.

Obi, Cyril. "The African Union and the Prevention of Democratic Reversal in Africa: Navigating the Gaps." *African Conflict and Peacebuilding Review* 4, no. 2 (2014): 60–85.

Onditi, Francis, Pontian Godfrey Okoth, and Frank K. Matanga. "The Quest for a Multidimensional African Standby Force." *African Conflict & Peacebuilding Review* 6, no. 1 (2016): 69–88.

Peters, Krijn. *War and the Crisis of Youth in Sierra Leone.* New York: Cambridge University Press, 2011.

Randall, Vicky, and Lars Svåsand. "Political Parties and Democratic Consolidation in Africa." *Democratization* 9, no. 3 (2002): 30–52.

Reno, William. *Corruption and State Politics in Sierra Leone.* New York: Cambridge University Press, 1995.

Resnick, Danielle, and Nicolas Van de Walle, eds. *Democratic Trajectories in Africa: Unravelling the Impact of Foreign Aid.* New York: Oxford University Press, 2013.

Ross, Michael. "How Do Natural Resources Influence Civil War? Evidence from Thirteen Cases."

*International Organization* 58, no. 1 (2004): 35–68.

Ross, Michael L. "What Do We Know about Natural Resources and Civil War?" *Journal of Peace Research* 41 (2004): 337–356.

Salamey, Imad, and Rhys Payne. "Parliamentary Consociationalism in Lebanon: Equal Citizenry vs. Quotated Confessionalism." *The Journal of Legislative Studies* 14, no. 4 (2008): 451–473.

Sawyer, Edward. "Remove or Reform? A Case for (Restructuring) Chiefdom Governance in Post-conflict Sierra Leone." *African Affairs* 107, no. 428 (2008): 387–403.

Schümer, Tanja. *New Humanitarianism: Britain and Sierra Leone, 1997–2003.* New York: Palgrave Macmillan, 2008.

Shaw, Rosalind. "Memory Frictions: Localizing the Truth and Reconciliation Commission in Sierra Leone." *International Journal of Transitional Justice* 1, no. 2 (2007): 183–207.

Siddique, Sharon, and Leo Suryadinata. "Bumiputra and Pribumi: Economic Nationalism (Indiginism) in Malaysia and Indonesia." *Pacific Affairs* 54, no. 4 (1981): 662–687.

Sigri, Unsal, M. Abdulkadir Varoglu, and Ufuk Basar. "Managerial Capacity in Peacekeeping Operations," pp. 99–119, in *International Security and Peacebuilding: Africa, the Middle East, and Europe*, edited by Abu Bakarr Bah. Bloomington, IN: Indiana University Press, 2017.

Sisk, Timothy D. *Democratization in South Africa: The Elusive Social Contract.* Princeton, NJ: Princeton University Press, 1995.

Straus, Scott. *The Order of Genocide: Race, Power, and War in Rwanda.* Ithaca, NY: Cornell University Press, 2013.

Suberu, Rotimi T. *Federalism and Ethnic Conflict in Nigeria.* Washington, DC: United States Institute of Peace Press, 2001.

Suryadinata, Leo. *Chinese and Nation-building in Southeast Asia.* Singapore: Marshall Cavendish, 2004.

Thomas, Caroline. "Global Governance, Development and Human Security: Exploring the Links." *Third World Quarterly* 22, no. 2 (2001): 159–175.

Tilly, Charles, and Gabriel Ardant. *The Formation of National States in Western Europe.* Princeton, NJ: Princeton University Press, 1975.

Tzifakis, Nikolaos. "The Bosnian Peace Process: The Power-sharing Approach Revisited." *Perspectives* (2007): 85–101.

Utas, Mats, and Magnus Jörgel. "The West Side Boys: Military Navigation in the Sierra Leone Civil War." *Journal of Modern African Studies* 46, no. 3 (2008): 487–511.

Van de Walle, Nicolas. "Africa's Range of Regimes." *Journal of Democracy* 13, no. 2 (2002): 66–80.

Wilson, Richard. *The Politics of Truth and Reconciliation in South Africa: Legitimizing the Post-Apartheid State.* New York: Cambridge University Press, 2001.

Zack-Williams, Alfred B. "Sierra Leone: The Political Economy of Civil War, 1991–98." *Third World Quarterly* 20 (1999): 143–162.

# INDEX

www.ingramcontent.com/pod-product-compliance
Lightning Source LLC
Chambersburg PA
CBHW050427280326
41932CB00013BA/2018